SINCE LACAN

SINCE LACAN
Papers of the Freudian
School of Melbourne
Volume 25

Edited by
Linda Clifton

Routledge
Taylor & Francis Group

LONDON AND NEW YORK

First published 2016 by
Karnac Books Ltd.

Published 2018 by Routledge
2 Park Square, Milton Park, Abingdon, Oxon OX14 4RN
711 Third Avenue, New York, NY 10017, USA

Routledge is an imprint of the Taylor & Francis Group, an informa business

British Library Cataloguing in Publication Data

A C.I.P. for this book is available from the British Library

ISBN-13: 9781782202028 (pbk)

Typeset by V Publishing Solutions Pvt Ltd., Chennai, India

CONTENTS

ACKNOWLEDGEMENTS

Chapter Two: This chapter by Oscar Zentner was previously published in Spanish in *Me cayo el veinte Revista de psicoanalisis* as "Lacan, estacion Caracas" in 2012, and is reprinted here in English by permission of the journal editor.

Chapter Four: *Father outside*, by Nick Flynn. Poem quoted by permission of the author.

Chapter Nineteen: This chapter by Oscar Zentner was previously published in Spanish in *Me cayo el veinte Revista de psicoanalisis* as "De la iniciación erótica a la muerte" in 2012, and is reprinted here in English by permission of the journal editor.

Madeline Andrews is a member of the Freudian School of Melbourne: School of Lacanian Psychoanalysis. She practices psychoanalysis privately and in specialist state-wide consultancy and treatment work in the public sector. She is the editor of the Freudian School of Melbourne web-based journal, *Écritique*.

Linda Clifton is a psychoanalyst in private practice. She is an analyst of the school, a former director of the Freudian School of Melbourne and current editor of its *Papers*, having edited the two preceding volumes, *Writing the Symptom* and *Invention in the Real*. Her psychoanalytic papers are published in the *Papers of the Freudian School of Melbourne* and in *Écritique*, the Newsletter of the School.

Michael Currie is a psychoanalyst practicing privately in Melbourne and is an analyst member of the Freudian School of Melbourne. He also consults part time to child and adult public mental health services. From 2002 until 2010 he founded and worked in a public outpatient psychoanalysis clinic at the Centre for Psychotherapy in New South Wales. He has written two books on the treatment of aggression in children and adolescents, published by Melbourne University Press.

Helen Dell is a member of the Freudian School of Melbourne. She is a singer and a singing teacher. She also works as a research fellow in

English and Theatre Studies at the University of Melbourne, studying medieval music and literature, especially when joined together as song. Her Ph.D. thesis has been published as a book: *Desire by Gender and Genre in Trouvère Song*, published with Boydell & Brewer (2008). She has recently completed a second book: *Music and the Medievalism of Nostalgia* for Cambria Press. Her current project is the publication of a collection of essays to be entitled *Singing Death*, on the ways in which music expresses and responds to the profound disturbance that death presents to the living. She has also published a number of essays and book chapters in medieval and medievalism studies.

Alicia Evans is a psychoanalyst and analyst member of The Freudian School of Melbourne. She has published psychoanalytic papers in the journals *Nursing Inquiry* and *Nursing Philosophy*, and her doctoral thesis was titled "Discourses of anxiety in nursing practice: a psychoanalytic case study". Alicia regularly presents her work at The Freudian School of Melbourne's seminars and has a particular interest in the interrogation of psychoanalytic theory via the work of Michel Foucault. She has a psychoanalytic practice in inner-city Melbourne.

Sarah Jones Ferguson is a psychoanalyst. She is an analyst member of the Freudian School of Melbourne, School of Lacanian Psychoanalysis. She works in private practice in Melbourne. Sarah has also worked in public practice and in education and professional development in psychoanalysis, analytic psychotherapy, and counselling. She has published psychoanalytic papers in a number of books and journals. Sarah convenes the seminar, Freud's later works.

Guy Le Gaufey is a French psychoanalyst who has practised psychoanalysis since 1975. He was a Member of the École Freudienne de Paris from 1973 until its dissolution in 1980. The next year he created, with four friends and colleagues, the revue of psychoanalysis *Littoral* (31 issues until 1989). He was the co-founder of the École Lacanienne de psychanalyse in 1985, and successively secretary of this school (1985–1989), and director (1992–1996 and 2000–2004).

The author of numerous papers since 1973 he has published in different revues, in France and abroad, writing in French, Spanish, and English.

Books: *L'incomplétude du symbolique* (epel, Paris, 1991); *L'éviction de l'origine* (epel, Paris, 1994); *Le lasso spéculaire. Une étude traversière de l'unité imaginaire* (epel, Paris, 1997); *Anatomie de la troisième personne* (epel, Paris, 1999); *Le pas tout de Lacan. Consistance logique, conséquences cliniques* (epel, Paris, 2006); *El caso inexistente. Una compilación clínica* (epeele, Mexico, 2006); *C'est à quel sujet ?* (epel, Paris, 2009); *L'objet* a. *Approches de l'invention de Lacan* (epel, Paris, 2012); *Hiatus sexualis. Le non-rapport sexuel selon Lacan,* (epel, Paris, 2013).

Translations from English to French: Philip Larkin, *Church going,* sixty-four poems in a bilingual translation (Solin, Paris, 1991); Ian Dowbiggin, *La folie héréditaire* (epel, Paris, 1993); Leo Bersani, *Le rectum est-il une tombe ?* (L'unebévue, Paris, 1999); Georges Bauer, *Tu m', ou l'hérétique érotique de Marcel Duchamp* (L'unebévue, Paris, 1999); John Rajchman, *Constructions,* (L'unebévue, Paris, 2000); Vernon Rosario, *L'irrésistible ascension du pervers entre littérature et psychiatrie* (epel, Paris, 2000); Judith Butler, *Antigone. La parenté entre vie et mort* (epel, Paris, 2003); Elisabeth Ladenson, *Proust lesbien* (epel, Paris, 2004); Mark Jordan, *L'invention de la sodomie dans la théologie médiévale* (epel, Paris, 2006); Philip Larkin, *La vie avec un trou dedans* (Éditions Thierry Marchaisse, Paris, 2011); Philip Larkin, *Une fille en hiver,* (Éditions Thierry Marchaisse, Paris, 2011); Robin George Collingwood, *Toute histoire est histoire d'une pensée,* (epel, Paris, 2010); Lee Edelman, *L'Impossible homosexuel,* (epel, Paris, 2013).

Peter Gunn is a psychoanalyst in private practice in Melbourne. He is an analyst member of The Freudian School of Melbourne. He has published numerous psychoanalytic papers, including in *Papers of The Freudian School of Melbourne* and *Écritique: Letters of The Freudian School of Melbourne*, and he presents regularly within the School and elsewhere. He comes from a background in pure mathematics and social work, and he has a continuing interest in keeping the field of psychoanalysis open to interrogation from other modes of production. As part of a larger project which he is calling "The body of madness", he has recently written on the late work of Antonin Artaud.

Jon Kettle is a member of the Freudian School of Melbourne, School of Lacanian Psychoanalysis. He works as a senior psychologist in public mental health services, a psychology institute, and also in private practice. He works with people of all ages and a wide range of problems, particularly psychosis.

Rodney Kleiman is a psychoanalyst. He is an analyst of the school and co-director of the Freudian School of Melbourne. Originally trained as a psychiatrist, he now works predominantly in private practice with an ongoing appointment as consultant with mental health services. He has published numerous articles in the *Papers of the Freudian School of Melbourne* and is a regular presenter at seminars and psychoanalytic conferences. He has a particular interest in the questions posed by psychosis and its potential treatment.

Malcolm Morgan works as a psychoanalyst in private practice. He is an analyst member of the Freudian School of Melbourne, and has worked for many years in organisational settings that provide support and therapy to people who have received psychiatric diagnoses.

Tine Nørregaard is a psychoanalyst working in private and public practice, and is an analyst member of the Freudian School of Melbourne. In the past she has been an associate lecturer at the University of Copenhagen, and since 2007 has co-convened the monthly seminar Psychoanalysis and the child with Michael Gerard Plastow. She has published numerous articles in English and in Danish, as well as translations from French and Portuguese to English. Some of her psychoanalytic papers appear in *Papers of the Freudian School of Melbourne* and in *Ecritique, the Newsletter of the School*, of which she was also a co-editor from 2000 to 2003.

David Pereira is a psychoanalyst in private practice in Melbourne, Australia, where he is an analyst of the school and is currently a director of the Freudian School of Melbourne. He has written numerous articles on theoretical and clinical psychoanalysis published in both the *Papers of the Freudian School of Melbourne* and elsewhere and was formerly consultant psychoanalyst with the Alfred Hospital Child and Adolescent Mental Health Service, and Senior Clinician with the Department of Child Psychotherapy, Royal Children's Hospital, Melbourne.

Michael Gerard Plastow is a psychoanalyst working in private practice in Melbourne. He is an analyst of the school, The Freudian School of Melbourne, School of Lacanian Psychoanalysis. He also practises in the public sector as a child psychiatrist at the *Alfred Child and Youth Mental Health Service* where he leads a multi-disciplinary team. He has convened a seminar on "Psychoanalysis and the Child" over a number of years, with Tine Nørregaard, also a psychoanalyst in The Freudian School of Melbourne. In 2014 he published through Karnac the book: *What is a Child?: Childhood, Psychoanalysis, and Discourse*.

Michael has published extensively in the psychoanalytic, psychiatric, and academic literature. He frequently presents his work at colloquia and conferences in Australia, Europe, and Latin America. He has a particular interest in the question of translation in psychoanalysis and has translated a number of papers into English, from French, Spanish, and Portuguese. His translation into English of Jacques Lacan's seminar

The Knowledge of the Psychoanalyst was published in 2013 in a bilingual non-commercial edition by the Association Lacanienne Internationale.

Megan Williams is a psychoanalyst practising in Melbourne. She is an analyst member of the Freudian School of Melbourne. She has participated in and presented at psychoanalytic seminars over many years and previously lectured in psychoanalysis at Victoria University. She has published numerous articles in a variety of psychoanalytic journals. Her PhD thesis examined Freud's and Lacan's work on anxiety and she is currently working on the question of the father in psychoanalysis.

Oscar Zentner is a Lacanian psychoanalyst in private practice in Melbourne who trained in Buenos Aires, Argentina. He introduced Lacan's psychoanalytic ideas in Australia in 1977, when he co-founded the first School of Lacanian Psychoanalysis in the English-speaking world. He co-founded and was editor for several years of the *Papers of The Freudian School of Melbourne*, the first psychoanalytic publication in Australia. He held The Lacanian psychoanalytic seminar for many years at Prince Henry's Hospital, Department of Psychological Medicine, Monash University. A Senior Fellow (Hon) at the School of Social and Political Sciences at the University of Melbourne, he has held The Lacanian psychoanalytic seminar since 2001. He is co-editor of the book *Lacan Love—Melbourne seminars and other works* by Jean Allouch, published by *Lituraterre,* Melbourne, 2007; co-author of the book *El problema económico en Freud,* Buenos Aires, Argentina, 1980; and author of the book *A Escuta Psicanalítica—Efeitos de uma Etica,* Recife, Brasil 1995. He has published numerous psychoanalytic articles in English, French, Portuguese, and Spanish.

Previous editors of the Papers of the Freudian School of Melbourne: David Pereira and Oscar Zentner.

LOGOS

… I was isolated from the rest of the world … and thus I was forced to become original.

—*Joseph Haydn*[1]

In the following brief excerpt from his seminar in Paris on June 10th 1980, Lacan gave his reasons for travelling at the age of eighty to Venezuela.

Those Latin-Americans, as they are called, unlike those who are here, have neither seen me nor heard me live—well—that does not prevent them from being *Lacanos*.

Moreover it seems that it helps. I am transmitted over there through writing and it is said that I have put down roots. In any case this is what they believe.

For sure it is the future and for that reason, going to see interests me.

I am interested to see what happens when my person does not act as a screen for what I teach. It is quite possible that they can make good use of my mathemes. (1981, pp. 97–98)

As one might speak of *The Four Last Songs* of Richard Strauss, Lacan's subsequent words in Caracas in July that same year were heard with the weight of last words. At the same time as these last words were being heard in Caracas, the first published Lacanian writings in English, the *Papers of the Freudian School of Melbourne*, were appearing in bookshops in Melbourne and elsewhere.

The Freudian School of Melbourne, founded in 1977, was never impeded by the possible effect of the person of Lacan acting as a screen for what he taught. Neither was the School blessed nor impeded by the assertion that it constituted the future. Blessing or impediment? Could it be that a certain isolation fosters originality, necessitates inventiveness? Lacan was interested to see what would happen when his person did not act as a screen. "It is quite possible that they can make good use of my mathemes."

Since Lacan is the latest production of the work of the School. It is the work of analysts and members of the School, including as well a paper "Lacan, Caracas station" by Oscar Zentner, co-founder of the School, and a special first instalment, several chapters translated from the French of a book *C'est à quel sujet?* by French psychoanalyst, Guy Le Gaufey, who visited the School to speak and teach in 2011.

In the opening paper "Incest, identity and difference" David Pereira addresses the significance of the time since Lacan, the more than three decades since Lacan's death. He raises the question of what difference the teaching of Lacan has made in the field of psychoanalysis. What has been made of Lacan's teaching? These are questions that both he and Oscar Zentner take up explicitly in this volume, producing a critique of the "mis"-directions taken in the past thirty years. This critique explicates and takes further Lacan's own assertion of being "traumatised by misunderstanding" which he tired of "dissolving" (1981, p. 98).

An answer to the question of the difference introduced by Lacan, can in fact be sought in each of the papers in this volume. Although many paths of enquiry are taken, each paper is marked, albeit differently, by its origin in Lacanian discourse and at the same time, paradoxically perhaps, by a certain originality. Thus while there is no guarantee that isolation produces originality, this volume attests to an originality that continues to spring forth in the work of the school.

To highlight just a few such moments of originality: David Pereira's proposition that the function of the analyst is to be a "truly aesthetic listener"; Oscar Zentner's idea of a possible "non-canonical" reading of a mistake made by Lacan; Megan Williams's honing of the idea of the father in a psychoanalysis as "the father only I could have had"; Peter Gunn's refusal to recede from the complexity of the question of how to listen to the outliers of society, now subsumed within the contemporary nomenclature of homelessness; the new "raw" voice of Michael Currie's child, surely an attempt at a truly aesthetic listening; Michael Gerard Plastow's invention of a new signifier, the *kangaroo rat man*, a cross fertilisation of time, discourse, and culture.

Since Lacan indicates that "good use" has indeed been made of Lacan's mathemes … and more.

Linda Clifton

Note

1. Quoted in Sisman, E. R. (Ed.) *Haydn and his World* Princeton University Press 1997, p. 1.

PART I

LACANIAN DISCOURSE

CHAPTER ONE

Incest, identity, and difference

David Pereira

The passing of now more than thirty years since the death of Jacques Lacan affords us a premise to pose questions, both of what difference Lacan made in the field of psychoanalysis, together with what has been made of his teaching. Lacan himself was not hopeful in this regard when in a Seminar on 15th March 1972 he rather ungraciously contended that: "When I die one can expect, in the same field, a veritable torrent of filth, which is already showing itself ..." (1971–1972). If Lacan was someone who was able to maintain a flux or flow within the field of psychoanalysis by marking a difference, then whether this has lapsed into a closed circuit of the familiar and well-worn or whether we are still able to use Lacan's teaching to continue to make and mark a difference ought to remain a question for us.

Let us begin with difference as suffered, producing the anguished cries which resound off the walls of our consulting rooms. On one of the walls of my consulting room hangs a painting which was given to me when I first started to practice psychoanalysis. It is a painting by an Australian artist—Robyn Metcalf, and incorporates the following text whose source is unknown to me.

I will never cheat you said Leandro
Fervently as she thought that he
Had not understood her and
That the difficulties of
Language would always
Be between
Them
Always words
And language were
Trifling if only she could
Be always sure of the always
The always and always with Leandro

It is of course tempting, is it not, to associate the text in this painting with what has been postulated by Lacan who declared that it is through this very impossibility of saying it all that the truth holds on to the real. In any case you already see that I have found the temptation too hard to resist. Even without the Lacanian imprimatur, the text immediately places us within the anguished undercurrent of our day to day work. We read here the desperate wish for a relation, and its failure; where any words of consolation reek with the stench of a derisive irony.

This painting and the text imposed upon it allows me, not to draw any conclusions, but to pose the following question. What words become possible, even necessary, in the face of this impasse, this impossibility? What words, what kind of words, would make a real difference? This, I want to stress, is not an abstract or philosophical pondering. It is for me a very real question. In regard to the words appearing in this painting imposed upon the backdrop of a turbulent and violent Heraclitean sky, this is what we could say that every analyst knows and says—always words and plenty of them.

What however do all analysts know and not say publicly? This is a question posed and answered by D. H. Lawrence in his 1920 work *Psychoanalysis and the Unconscious* where we already find a critique of the way in which the Freudian unconscious is drifting from what Lawrence regards as the "true nature of the unconscious" (2005, p. 10). Wanting to oppose psychoanalysis to a moral system, he poses the following:

> Here is an issue which every analysis is perfectly willing to face. Among themselves the analysts are bound to accept the incest-craving as part of the normal sexuality of man [...]. Once, however,

you accept the incest-craving as part of the normal sexuality of man, you must remove all repression of incest itself. In fact, you must admit incest as you now admit sexual marriage, as a duty even […].

Psychoanalysis will never openly state this conclusion. But it is to this conclusion that every analyst must, willy-nilly, consciously or unconsciously, bring his patient. (2005, p. 7)

By the time he writes *Fantasia of the Unconscious* published the following year, 1921, Lawrence has begun to despair further of the possibilities of psychoanalysis.

And I ask you, what good will psychoanalysis do you in this state of affairs? Introduce an extra sex-motive to excite you for a bit and make you feel how thrillingly immoral things really are. And then—it all goes flat again. Father complex, mother complex, incest dreams: pah, when we have had the little excitement out of them we shall forget them as we have forgotten so many other catch-words. And we shall be just where we were before: unless we are worse, with *more* sex in the head, and more introversion, only more brazen. (Ibid., p. 161)

Whilst I will disagree with Lawrence about the "willy-nilliness" of the question of how one brings the analysis and the concept of difference which prevails there to the point of incest, we must nonetheless agree that the use of dried up and ossified concepts which preserve an ortho-doxy will not pave the way to the precision we require in respect of this question of what words make a real difference.

In Lawrence's view it appears that psychoanalysis doesn't offer very much once we have turned away from the horror of incest; perhaps this same horror which Lacan contends that the analyst encounters in consequence of his act. Lawrence allows us to pose the question of what we know but do not, or cannot, find a way to say outside of an insistent duality whose limited concept of difference is inaugurated by the pro-hibition of incest. The manner in which Lawrence poses the problem of incest, therefore, allows us a means to take further the question of how difference might be thought and voiced.

The prohibition of incest, the so called universal sexual law, car-ried and dramatised by the Oedipus complex, produces and thereby guarantees the distinctly human mode of sexuality. This is to say that it differentiates us from animals. Herein lays the first of a series of differentiations founded upon a duality—animal/human—which the prohibition of incest installs.

Now what constitutes this difference between the human and the animal, effected and supported by the prohibition of incest, such as to allow us to speak of distinctly "human relations" or human sexuality? In choosing an animal to consult on this question it was difficult to go past that shapely boxer bitch—"Justine"—to give her her name—to whom Lacan pays considerable tribute in his seminar of 29th November 1961, the year he devoted his seminar to the subject of "Identification". "My dog", Lacan tells us in a quite charming passage, "has without any doubt the gift of speech …" However, "it does not mean she possesses language totally" (1961–1962). The difference between Lacan and his dog is that she never takes him for another. In this resides the principle difference between the animal and the pure speaking subject for whom is afforded this possibility of signifying substitution which gives him access to "human relations".

Now the curious thing about these "human relations" is that, Lacan tells us quite clearly, he was free to enjoy them with Justine, in whose face he could at times, just every now and then, discern a certain look of a woman of the world! At this point then, what defines "human relations", human sexual relations, is this capacity for differentiation and signifying substitution; to take one for another, to attribute to the dog a certain look of a woman of the world. Through this, Oedipus understood as the dramatisation of the prohibition of incest, installs a very particular concept of difference; a particular form of differentiation and representation which essentially underwrites our familiar place within language, as well as the mode of human sexuality. This will have some consequences for the way in which difference might be thought.

Incestus, from the Latin, refers us to that which is polluted, defiled or unclean and speaks of a certain problem of contamination or unchecked flow. The checking of this contaminating flow installs and rigidly maintains a structure deployed as contradictions and oppositions. The horror of incest, therefore, is associated with a collapsing of borders and blurring of identities; a collapse of the familiar way in which difference is thought and identity ascribed in such a way as to maintain a duality within the sexual domain.

Georges Bataille, in his consideration of the question of incest in *Volume II of The Accursed Share,* notes that because the object of human sexual desire cannot be defined or grasped in a precise way, "Only the rule of incest, universal but with variable modalities, can make it sufficiently familiar" (1991b, p. 32). The irony here is found in the fact that the prohibition of incest as structuring of the modes of human sexuality, in installing the operation of signifying substitution, renders any new object familiar, of the family. Something is posed as different in order to be rendered the same. It thus establishes a closed circuit of sorts, what Lawrence called "a dirty little family secret", remaining within the family and making its mark on the concept of difference which ensues from this. In place of the torrent of filth we have a stagnating cesspool.

With this "sufficiently familiar" human relations are tied to family relations. The closed circuit maintains language and the sexual on a bedrock of duality, taking difference at the Symbolic level of mutual exclusion and contradiction and consigning truth to the operation of the dialectic. This is the Symbolic consequence of the prohibition of incest, which paradoxically and ironically makes incest possible precisely through the fact of signifying substitution afforded to humans and not animals.

The "true unconscious", so called by Lawrence, and useful for our purposes, is not however to be found whilst it remains possible to continue to establish yet another signifying substitution guaranteed by the auspices of Oedipus. Is this the catch-cry of a return to animal sexuality, to renounce the prohibition which installs us within the realm of human relations? Not at all. It is not as simple as denouncing or transgressing the prohibition. Rather, a question of how we situate its effects—as Symbolic or as Real.

Thus far the prohibition of incest has been situated as Symbolic, affording the possibility of symbolically committing incest through a signifying substitution which allows us to construct the irony of familiarity. One makes it different in order to declare it the same. The Symbolic guarantees human relations in anchoring things so as to check the flow of the "formless mass" to which Saussure referred (1966, p. 94). The question is whether this impedes an encounter with the Real or impossible of human relations through which difference may be thought "otherly"? In this perspective, from the side of the prohibition of incest as Symbolic, truth is symbolised but not realised. We fall short therefore of the subject realised as an effect of truth in the Real, as Lacan will pose it in *L'Etourdit* (1973, p. 16) after having already indicated it in the *Identification* seminar in referring to the subject as that which is charged to bring truth into the real.

Let us turn now to how we might situate this prohibition of incest as Real impossibility; how it is realised in effect in psychoanalysis where the subject is produced as a response made in the face of an encounter with impossibility, rather than forever caught within a series of substitutions, representations, and oppositions, premised on a comfortable duality funded by Oedipus.

A thoroughgoing critique of the Oedipalising of psychoanalysis and its familiarising of the unconscious and sexuality forms the basis of Deleuze and Guattari's controversial work *Anti-Oedipus: Capitalism and Schizophrenia*, first published in 1972. Their offensive took aim at the tendency to a reductive duality in sexuality and the atrophied notion of difference which this then bred into the field of thought.

In responding to criticisms about this work Deleuze wrote the following:

> And if psychoanalysts, ranging from the most stupid to the most intelligent ones, have as a whole greeted the book with hostility, but defensively rather than aggressively, that's obviously not just because of its content but because of this growing current of people getting fed up listening to themselves saying "daddy, mommy, Oedipus, castration, regression" and seeing themselves presented with a really inane image of sexuality in general and of their own sexuality in particular. (1995, p. 8)

The account which is given of the way in which this work was written, and what they were attempting to do there, is inseparable from the thesis which it advances.

> One thing is rather shocking about books of psychiatry or even psychoanalysis, and that is the pervasive duality between what an alleged mental patient says and what the doctor reports—between the "case" and the commentary on the case. It's logos against pathos: the mental patient is supposed to say something, and the doctor says what it means in terms of symptoms or sense. This allows what the patient says to be crushed [...].

> Now, we didn't think for a minute of writing a madman's book, but we did write a book in which you no longer know who is speaking […] a doctor, a patient, or some present, past or future madman speaking […].
>
> Strangely enough, if we tried to get beyond this traditional duality, it's because there were two of us writing. Neither of us was the madman and neither the doctor …
>
> This process is what we call "a flow" […] it surpasses all duality. (2004, p. 218)

In this incestuous form of writing we are reminded of the so-called "problem" of contamination and unchecked flow which belong to the polluting effects of "incestus". Whilst the Symbolic signifying structure of substitution is premised on difference as duality, contradiction, and opposition, difference is here realised as "flow". In the end, the unconscious for Deleuze and Guattari is not a theatre of representation but a factory of production.

> It is no more structural than personal, it does not symbolise anymore than it imagines or represents; it engineers, it is machinic. Neither imaginary nor symbolic, it is the Real itself, the "impossible real" and its production. (1972. p. 53)

So, human relations find their limit, not in the animal, from whom the prohibition of incest separates us, but in the "machinic", as that which always overflows the problem of difference between two sexes. For Deleuze, to reduce the question of sex to the banality of difference between the sexes was the best way to misunderstand sexuality. We find Lacan also drawing our attention to something quite problematical concerning Freud's formulation of Oedipus. It concerned for him something quite different from the phenomenon of maternal incest, opening rather onto an impossible sexual situated as a surplus to sexual jouissance—a non-human jouissance—to which the sexual—human sexual relations—nonetheless plays host (1969–1970).

What do we mean by "non-human"? Having, in the nicest possible way, dismissed her do we now have to summon Justine again?

Within the pages of *Anti-Oedipus* we find a reference to Marx from his "Critique of Hegel's 'Philosophy of Right'", where Marx asserts that "the true difference is not the difference between the two sexes, but the difference between the human sex and the 'nonhuman sex'" (1972, p. 294). This is clearly not a question of animals, nor of animal sexuality.

Indeed, it becomes clear that not only is something quite different involved, a different concept of difference begins to evolve, to mutate from these strange affirmative, non-restrictive, and inclusive but disjunctive syntheses which populate the pages of *Anti-Oedipus*. As Deleuze writes in *Difference and Repetition*, the work which he claimed all other future works to be an elaboration of, it was important to not confuse the concept of difference itself with merely conceptual difference (1994, p. 27).

The non-human appears in the work of Lacan as the object *a*, that specific form of the partial object which also resists being taken one for another; that is resists the formula of signifying substitution. It becomes "the index of what is nonhuman in sex" (1972, p. 355). Importantly, in putting a limit to the endless series of representations and substitutions, it allows us to isolate a crucial function of the signifier, not as disqualified, as the authors of *Anti-Oedipus* would have us do, but *de-qualified*. What would this mean? That it appears as difference itself without reference to oppositions, contradictions or substitutions. Now what is quite peculiar about this difference itself is that it is possessed of a certain kind of unity which Lacan has recourse to Kant to identify. In the seminar of 28th February 1962, concerning this function of unity, he contends that it is not the unifying unity of the *Einheit* but the distinctive unity of the *Einzigkeit*. The distinction is between unifying unity as a norm and a distinctive unity which becomes the premise of difference itself. "This absolute singularity of the subject is a reflection of the expression of what cannot be matched from the dual opposition of one sex to the other sex" (1964–1965).

The confines of a differentiation given by the prohibition of incest as Symbolic, as it consolidates a duality of sex, falls short of difference itself as a realisation of difference. A distinction affords itself here between the symbolisation of difference and the realisation of difference, a distinction which Lacan's object *a* lends weight to. Not a case of the prohibition of incest operating symbolically and separating us from animals by affording us the possibility of signifying substitution, but of what incest implies of real impossibility and therefore real production.

I began with the question of the words that may be possible in response to the impossible demand apparent in the text incorporated into a painting I referred to at the outset. I will stop at the point of these de-qualified words whose singularity rather than substitutability becomes marked; to stop in order to conclude with something I heard from an analysand which perhaps speaks more eloquently of this question.

My analysand, a woman, reported that she had telephoned her husband in a state of distress, for reasons that are not important at present. He had, some two or three days before, flown to the United States on business. In her distress she said to him "I want you home in half an hour". An impossible demand. How does the husband respond? A ordinary man will curse and swear and say that he will conclude his business and return as soon as he can, given the constraints of time and space. A reasonable man will say that he will arrange for a new flight and because of time and space will be there within forty-eight hours. These are all well qualified words, they have not yet been able to respond to an impossible demand from the side of an absolute singularity. What has stayed with me about my analysand's report of this man, is that he spoke without qualification, responding to an impossible demand with an impossible proposition—pure polluting filth. He said, "I will be there."

CHAPTER TWO

Lacan, Caracas station*

Oscar Zentner

The erudite commentator Horapolo (C. Leemans) wrote: but this story of the vulture was eagerly taken up by the fathers of the Church, in order to refute by means of a proof drawn from the natural order, those who denied the virgin birth …

—*Sigmund Freud*[1]

The relation of the Madonna is more complex than what is thought. This worries me. But it remains that I situate myself with her better than Freud in the real …

—*Jacques Lacan*[2]

O blessed Virgin … made mother without co-operation of man. For here the ear was the wife, and the angelic word the husband.

—*St. Eleutherius*[3]

---

*This essay was published in *Me cayó el Veinte,* No 24, Revista de Psicoanálisis, *L'ecole lacanienne de psychanalyse,* Mexico, 2012, p. 27.

One repays a teacher badly if one remains only a pupil. And why, then, should you not pluck at my laurels? You respect me; but how if one day your respect should tumble? Take care that a falling statue does not strike you dead! You had not yet sought yourself when you found me. Thus do all believers—Now I bid you lose me and find yourselves; and only when you have all denied me will I return to you.

—*Friedrich Nietzsche*[4]

W e can read that, exactly thirty-eight years ago during the presentation of the seminar *L'insu que sait de l'une-bévue s'aille à mourre* (Lacan, 1976–1977), Lacan once again wrote the formula of the psychoanalytic discourse on the blackboard. A first reading of this session of the seminar could give weight to the assumption that what is being read, is actually what took place. However, if we challenge and interrogate this *received truth* with a second reading as well as the added advantage of elapsed time, we must come to a different conclusion.

I have some reasons for revisiting this session of the seminar. Among them, I would like to suggest to you a kind of pseudo-oxymoron, that is *that what took place* thirty-eight years ago, simply *did not happen, it did not come to pass;*[5] that, in other words, Lacan's teaching at a given moment had been about to forge an unforeseeable path, with the possibility of passing on something new but, as I will prove, this path was pitifully cut short.

Indisputably, what *did not come to pass, took place*; so much so that the *sequelae* still concern us today.

The *sequelae* in question could be read in and after the session of March 8th 1977 (1976–1977),[6] when Lacan, while writing on the blackboard, attempted once more to distinguish the truth from the real: that is to say, the object *a*, the real, as not coinciding with the truth. He therefore began to propose:

I reminded you that the place of the semblance, where I situated the object *a*, is not the place which I have articulated for the truth, […].

$$\frac{a}{\cancel{S}} \quad \frac{S_1}{S_2}$$

After writing this non-canonical formula, he questioned himself aloud, saying:

> How could a subject sustain with all his limitations, his weakness, the place of the truth, and even so to arrive in this way at verifiable results, to know that a knowledge …

At which point, Miller interrupted and corrected Lacan by reminding him:

> That is not the way you wrote it previously.

To which Lacan retorted:

> Could you see how one can get tangled up?

He then began to erase[7] the formula from the blackboard and wrote instead, the *exact* canonical formulae, and furthermore, adding aloud:

$$\frac{a}{S_2} \quad \frac{S}{S_1}$$

> "This is indisputably better; however, the failure between the two lower places is yet more problematic S_1 is not more than the beginning of knowledge, *a knowledge that is always content to begin, and so reaches nothing …*". (1976–1977, emphasis ours)

At this time, Lacan, finding little—at variance with Picasso's dictum: I do not seek, I find—was actively seeking and in that quest, he sometimes tangled himself up. On this occasion, however, he had neither had nor was he given the opportunity to get lost[8] in order to discover by himself the best way out.[9] Given the atypical written formula of the psychoanalytic discourse, before Miller's interruption, the written formula most certainly would have taken Lacan, and consequently us, into uncharted waters of the psychoanalytic discourse. Instead, what could have taken place, did not come to pass.

Had he been given that opportunity, he would have then perhaps found the way out by himself, and he could have developed the necessary modification, which that unusual formula required. The interruption had the consequences of an injunction. This impediment provoked, at the very least, a wasted teaching: firstly, we will never know what Lacan was aiming at by writing *the psychoanalytic discourse* with that formula, articulating the truth of the underscored weakness of the subject; and, secondly, how that formula could have modified what was increasingly becoming, against Lacan, *the Lacanian Gospel of the psychoanalytic discourse*.

Once he had corrected the formula, *what took place did not happen*: it did not pass on to us. A teaching, even if debatable or *worse*[10] incorrect, was lost forever; and let's face it, the audience, his students, did not voice a single concern, as if weighed down with the *vado retro* of the injunction.

Therefore, today, at the present hour, confronted with *what took place, but did not come to pass*, what should we do? Should we act prudently and do nothing, as has been certainly the case until now? Here, I am not posing a rhetorical question. Furthermore I am proposing that prudence is not always the best path to follow.

I therefore maintain, *a minima*, that Lacan, *finding* himself outside the canonical way, would have been able to make an attempt at a solution with unheard of propositions.

The interruption and correction were far from erroneous; on the contrary, Lacan was according to his own positions wrong, and Miller was rightly *exact* and absolutely *precise* (Zentner, 1982, p.188). However, let us pause and consider for a moment: what if that which Lacan was trying to *pass on*, with the *anomalous formula*, was an *heretical*[11] proposition, as if by contradicting himself he was going to battle against the *rigor mortis* of the canonical marble?

At this point I would like to call the reader's attention to the fact that Lacan was giving the seminar *L'insu que sait de l'une-bévue s'aille à mourre* at this time: that is, not long before the last three years prior to his dissolution of *L'ecole freudienne de Paris*. His school had become marmoreal, canonical, or, in his own harsh words, *had turned towards sense, thus becoming a Church*.[12]

> [...] You are not ignorant of the problem which I had with my school in Paris. I resolved it as it should be: taking it by the root; that is, uprooting it—my pseudo—school [...]. (1980, p. 103)

This is eloquently expressed by identifying *l' ecole freudienne de Paris* to ... Carthage through his borrowing of Cato's words: *Carthago delenda est!* But quoting is very different from reading and reading is very different from interrogating, therefore we ask what as far as we know was never asked before, who represented Rome (silent, yet present) and who represented Carthage? It is not a secret that Freud identified himself with Hannibal, of Carthage.[13] From this point, without forcing anything, was not Lacan finally saying that his approach was not Freud's? Thereafter any illusion of continuity between Freud and himself, that is Freudo-Lacanism, was exactly the Carthage—as had become embodied in his school—that needed to be destroyed?

So let us now read again the heretical formula, in which the attributes of the (S)[14] occupied the place of truth, and when Lacan interrogated himself aloud:

> [...] How could a subject sustain, with all his limitations, his weakness, the place of the truth, and even so to arrive in this way at verifiable results, to know that a knowledge [...]. (1976–1977)

The whole structure of the sentence readily indicates that Lacan was forewarning his audience to pay attention, as if he was veering towards completely unexpected terrain, as if he was opening new ground with the unprecedented formula.

Therefore, a re-reading of the transcription of the seminar shows how the interruption and correction irremediably aborted what would necessarily have been a new proposition.

My argument is based upon the fact that Lacan did not take the interruption lightly. The proof is that he alluded in this context to his *discourse to the Belgians* (2005), speaking of how psychoanalysis could veer off into swindling, while at the same time emphasising the difference between a *gross mistake and lapsus linguae*. Because ... *elementary, my dear Watson* ... it is never a question of a *lapsus linguae* when we are dealing with writing!

The devotion shown in the correction is exact;[15] however, this does not prevent Lacan from making ironic remarks, speaking of those who *meant* and *wished him well*, indicating how good wishes, like good intentions, paved all the way ... to hell. This is how he conveys it:

[...] There are people who mean well towards me ... (obviously) ...
they do not know me, inasmuch as I myself am not full of good
intentions[16] ... Some well-meaning people wrote letters to me saying
that my babbling the other day, concerning the psychoanalytic
discourse, was a lapsus.

What differentiates the lapsus from a gross error? I am more
inclined to classify as an error what here is intended to be classified
as lapsus ... What annoys me is that they think that I had committed a lapsus in a question, if I may say so, of writing ... [...] ... In
the moment in which I am, *I do not find as much as I seek* (emphasis
ours). In other words, I am going in circles, spinning around ...
And this is what happened: the letters written on the blackboard
were spinning and tangling me up ... I was insisting on this by
turning my letters and telling you about the S_1 that appeared to
assure a S_2 (knowledge). (1977b, p. 7)

If we concur with Lacan that S_1 *is always the beginning of knowledge*,
canonical knowledge, I add—a knowledge that always conforms itself
to begin (1976–1977, p. 16), it is not difficult to see why it is easy to find
oneself sliding. As a result, the possible solution that Lacan could have
worked out to resolve *the tangling up* will never be known. In fact, the
undesirable result of that interruption was to deprive us, his readers as
much as his audience of an urgently needed revision of so-called psychoanalytic discourse.

The dimension of the aborted attempt at a solution was not unim-
portant: so much so, that it still concerns us to the extent that some elements of the aborted solution of the session of that seminar re-emerged,
unnoticed, fortuitously,[17] some years later.

This re-emergence took place almost three years after the seminar
L'insu que sait de l'une-bévue s'aille à mourre. The occasion to which we
are referring was without recourse to any second chance; it was definitive, final.

It took place in the context of "The reunion on the teaching of Lacan
and psychoanalysis in Latin America in Caracas", 1980. It was here, that
I heard during his seminar, Lacan bluntly marking his many differences
with Freud.

As far as I am aware, no serious study and analysis of the Caracas
seminar, has been published so far, so let us have a closer re-reading of
that seminar:

I come here (Caracas) before casting away my Freudian Cause[18]. As you can see, I appreciate the adjective. If you want, it is your turn to be Lacanians.[19] I am Freudian. This is why it is pertinent to tell you … about the debate I have with Freud. And not from now. I am going to give you a resumé … Here it is: my three are not those of Freud: my three are the real, the symbolic, and the imaginary … It should be said that what Freud drew in his so-called second topic is not without clumsiness … (1980, p. 104)

As we have already written the seminar *L'insu* was given three years prior to the *dis—solution of l'ecole freudienne de Paris*,[20] and the dissolution took place almost simultaneously with the Caracas seminar.

In Caracas, Lacan read and addressed the question of the Virgin through the painting of *The Madonna* by Bramantino. I would like to underscore once more, that what I attempt in this essay, was until now, never questioned before, as if the repetition by rote gave place both to a sacred Lacan and to an osmosis of sacred knowledge.

We witnessed in Caracas his description of the most salient and enigmatic aspects of the painting, however it was very strange indeed that he did not mention that this painting was at odds with the established canon, as it contains, *a minima,* an anomaly. Bramantino represents the Virgin offering a palm[21] to someone who is not a martyr.[22]

At the time of Caracas, and in contrast with the written formula of the seminar *L'insu,* examined previously, Lacan not only disregarded this anomaly, but also contributed to it either by design or by making a *lapsus linguae* that transformed the foreground of the painting by referring to a frog; whereas in fact, in the painting there is no frog, but a toad.

It is *le crapaud* (the toad) and not *la grenouille* (the frog). It is the *toad* that represents the Devil in the iconography of the painting and not the *frog,* which Lacan chooses by *design* or *lapsus* as *the nostalgia that* (the woman!) *is not a frog.*

To cut down the *prevailing debility* (Lacan dixit), and to be clear, for animals that are not *affected* by the *cancer* of language, the sexual relation *does exist.* However if this is not clarified as has been the case so far, then what is the reason to introduce the notion of nostalgia? If not, for that previous mythical moment, so to say, before Eve (the mother of all mortals) took the forbidden fruit, when she as yet did not know, in the strict Biblical sense, about carnal knowledge.

According to this, we can pose an apparently forbidden question, that of the origin of language. It is my proposition, that "forbidden" or not, nonetheless, Lacan alluded to this through making of the subject, at once sexual and a speaking subject, as if the Original Sin, had been displaced into the impossibility of the sexual relation for the speaking being. Pay heed, not for the individual for whom the sexual relation exists. Our good luck was that either way, by design or by *lapsus linguae,* Lacan at Caracas was not corrected.

Lacan, as we know, received a Roman Catholic education and he was beyond doubt very well versed in the Old and New Testaments. Accordingly, it is not difficult to conclude that he knew the following words very well:

> Jesus said that whoever seeks, should not stop seeking until he finds and, when he finds, he will be thrown into confusion.[23] (Dan 7:27, Leviticus 1:29, Ap 1:6, 3:21, 5:10, 20:4)[24]

Then, I wonder whether Lacan's *seeking,* before being interrupted, would have taken him as far as finding, therefore as far as sharing with us the *confusion,* thus redoubling the anomaly of the formulae with another one regarding the painting.[25] Is it tenable to propose that, three years previously, a similar, *non-canonical* seeking and confusion, with the formula of the psychoanalytic discourse of *L'insu,* had been aborted, but that this time he succeeded in passing it on to us? This is exactly what I assert. But, then why was he not corrected in Caracas?

Supplanting *ex-professo or by lapsus* the toad with the frog[26] was another way of alluding to the *lack of sexual relation* (proportion), another pivotal difference with Freud's theories of genital maturation and consequent *existence of sexual relations.*

The seminar of Caracas in its content and its audience was like a large Fresco[27] painted and signed by *haste.*[28] And who else could have signed it, when death was drawing hither and thither?

> [...] I must take courage; encouraged myself with the memory that Freud, at my age, was not dead. (1980, p. 105)

At Caracas, Lacan made his differences with Freud explicit on diverse fronts. Yet these are the differences that remain, for the majority of Lacanians, a *noli me tangere.*[29]

Let us begin with the Virgin to appreciate the dimension opened by Lacan's stance:

> [...] But it remains that with her (The Madonna) I locate myself better than Freud (my emphasis) in the real, interested in what there is of the unconscious, because the jouissance of the body leans against the unconscious [...]. (1980)

The Lacanians took up this affirmation with alacrity and repeated it *ad nauseum* without, however, interrogating its provenance. Let us recall Lacan's words from Caracas in regard to his pseudo-school: a pseudo-school has pseudo pupils and pseudo pupils never interrogate.

Here, we should clarify once more, the Caracas seminar was problematic as much as for those of us who were there, as for those who were not there.

Here, reader I will ask you some degree of patience, otherwise I will find myself hurried up, where I should clarify many problematic things.

The Caracas seminar took place, of all places in a neutral psychoanalytic desert, not in Paris, or Buenos Aires with its enormous psychoanalytic, but not neutral community where Lacanian psychoanalysis took root before any other place in the Americas, in the late sixties, thanks to the work of Oscar Massota, who received the first seminars of Lacan from the hands of Enrique Pichon-Riviere.

In Caracas, the number of French analysts accompanying Lacan, probably did not exceed more than thirty. The number of Latin-Americans, was probably in the order of at most three hundred, and the vast majority of them was from Argentina, and a lesser number from Brazil, Uruguay, and Australia. However the question for the French colleagues was vastly different from that of the other analysts present. There were those, probably a minority, who were there but were not altogether convinced of the necessity of the dissolution of L'ecole freudienne de Paris, and many who were together in Caracas were later on a different path. The same in due time occurred to the Latin-Americans. However it is not within my purpose to describe in more detail this here.

For the English reader my recommendation is to read Elizabeth Roudisnesco's *The History of Psychoanalysis in France* (1990). This history, despite some inaccuracies and debatable appraisal of Lacan, remains indispensable to begin with for any serious attempt to study and understand things which although belonging to the past, are still with us. To dispel some confusion is also important to know that from Australia, there were only two analysts invited, María-Inés Rotmiler de Zentner, and myself.

This very brief recounting was also a way of letting you know that this essay has not been born out of any secondary text, slogan repetitions, or *flatus voces* and why I positioned myself with the following words that by quoting I make mine:

> We therefore find ourselves at the antipodes of "Jacques said" … In the sense that according to Wittgenstein, the pupil is the one who asks questions. This formula implies a 180 degree turn around in relation to Socrates, as it was Socrates, not his pupil, who asked questions (this is exemplified in the Meno, where the position of pupil is held by someone who was not and had no chance of ever becoming a pupil—a slave). (Allouch, 2007, p. viii)

For us the proof of the above resides in the fact that it never occurred to them (the Lacanians) to question the source of Lacan's statement regarding the Madonna, as if it came *ex-nihilo* and not *ex-religio*. To overcome this religious appraisal of Lacan, it is necessary above all else, first to engage ourselves in a verifiable interrogation of his affirmations and secondly to end the scandal which it is at play here.

To put it plainly, the scandal to which we referred is no secret. It is the *noli me tangere* of the Freudo-Lacanians, their refusal *to know what is at play:* that is, the non-continuity from Freud to Lacan, plus Freud's atheism, and also, as he always maintained, his being part of the Jewish people.[30]

On similar grounds, Lacan often referred to Roman Catholicism as the *true religion,*[31] in accordance with the French colloquial expression. Nonetheless, even when this is a colloquialism, it would be a serious mistake, if not a disservice, to underestimate his Roman Catholic education. On this point, I am not alone:

> *Ton "Lacan, Caracas" m'a beaucoup intéressé. Il ne fait aucun doute en te lisant que l'idée de rapprocher l'erreur corrigée par Miller et le lapsus de Caracas rana/sapo* [Allouch uses the Spanish words for frog/toad, respectively in the email] *est heuristique, même si je n'ai pas bien su saisir ce qui s'est passé entre ces deux metidas de pata* [Allouch uses the

Spanish words for blunder]: *un redoublement d'une même question non élaborée? Une avancée de l'une à l'autre? Une correction de l'une par l'autre? Toujours est-il que la question du christianisme de Lacan est plus que jamais présente, tu en témoignes aussi. Et c'est donc à elle que je vais consacrer mon prochain séminaire. Un abrazo,(sic) Jean*[32]

Anticipating possible objections, I would like to emphasise that I am not suggesting that Lacan was a practising Roman Catholic, or that he believed in God and attended Mass. He was in effect far less constrained than Freud to examine the question of the Trinity, as well as that of the Madonna.

One more proof of the above is Lacan's characterisation of the *Moses-isation* of psychoanalysis, whereby Freud, making of *the Father the dead Father*[33] paradoxically protected him and made him unconscious.[34] One of the sources for such an affirmation is also the source for the examination of the Madonna: the works of Ernest Jones.

Ernest Jones characterised Jewish religion by the pre-eminence of the Father, distinguishing it from both the Trinitarian concept of the Roman Catholic Church, where the Father and the Son (*the filioque*) generate the Holy Ghost, and the Orthodox Church, where both the Holy Ghost and the Son are generated from the Father, they are *ex-Patris*.

Lacan, in contrast with Jones,[35] put forward his heretical position not to give an account of the infantile sexual theories but rather to emphasise that, with the exception of *Roman Catholicism*, no-one except himself in the field of psychoanalysis, put forward the lack of sexual relation (proportion). This lack had already been addressed by *the true religion (la Vera Religio)*[36] with the impregnation of the Virgin by the logos. Once again proving what we stated above it is the logos, contrary to many held ideas, that is the infrastructure on which the lack, the impossibility of sexual relations dwells.

Let us re-read his ultra-condensed seminar in Caracas, where he stated:

> *Je me contente de noter que le silence attribué au Ça comme tel, suppose la parlote. La parlote à quoi s'attend l'oreille, celle du "désir indestructible" s'en traduire.*
>
> [I am content to note that the silence attributed to the It as such presupposes chit chat. The chit chat which the ear expects is that of the indestructible desire when translated …]. (Lacan, 1980)

To be compared with what Jones wrote:

> A belief, often forgotten nowadays, but preserved in the legends
> and traditions of the Catholic Church, is that the conception of Jesus
> in the Virgin Mary was brought about by the introduction into her
> ear of the breath of the Holy Ghost … There are many versions of
> this current in the Middle Ages; Langlois quotes the following one
> from the XVII Century: *Rejouyssez-vous, Vièrge, et Mère bienheureuse,
> Qui dans vos chastes flancs conçeutes par L'ouyr, L'Esprit-Sainct oper-
> ant d'un très-ardent désir, est L'Ange l'annonçant d'une voix amoureuse.*
> (1964, pp. 268–269)
>
> Rejoice Blessed Virgin and Mother that your chaste belly will
> conceive by listening to the ardent desire of the Holy Spirit; it is the
> amorous voice of the Angel annunciating it.

While Jones[37] referred to the highly exquisite and stylised painting
of the Annunciation by Simone Martini, Lacan referred to the hermetic
painting by Bramantino of the Madonna with Child, Saint Ambrose
and Saint Michael (Il Trittico di San Michelle): this painting represents
an almost masculine Virgin who presides and triumphs over both the
Devil, represented by a dead toad, and a dead Arius.[38]

While the subject matter of the painting—the vanquishing and
equating of the Devil to Arius—is a clear re-affirmation of the tenets
of the Church, the painting, like Lacan's *"lapsus linguae"*—frog instead
of toad—contains an enigmatic anomaly: the Virgin,—against canon—
gives a palm to someone who is not a martyr, Saint Ambrose,[39] yet
someone who, as the name indicates, is testimony to eternity which, for
the true religion (*la Vera Religio*), is the resurrection of the flesh—from
whence it extracts its triumph.[40]

All the above was outside Freud's tradition, outside his education
and interest. We can say without any exaggeration that he was completely indifferent to Jones's work.

But, as we know, matters are usually much more complex than they
seem to be. In this case, they can be exemplified because they can be
read, since for some, Lacan among them, matters were, if I may say so:
gnostic, that is *Scilicet*.[41]

We cannot know for certain if Lacan implicitly referred to the
(heretical) Gnostic Gospel of Saint Thomas, yet given the malice of
which Lacan was capable I would rather tilt the scales; to affirm if

this would not have been *his* "beautiful" way of spoiling, under the *organising Committee* nose and beforehand, any *Kata- Holon* attempt in Caracas.

> Jesus said: Perhaps people think that I have come to cast peace upon the world. They do not know that I have come to cast conflicts upon the earth: fire, sword, and war. For there will be five in a house: there'll be three against two and two against three, father against son and son against father, and they will stand alone.[42]

Here, Jesus resembles Yahweh, the jealous, cruel and vengeful God of the Old Testament.

But could Lacan have said all this at the end of his life, without leaving as a *sequelae* the question of some, ah!, ah,! … anti-Semitism?

To take up again our hypothesis: three years before Caracas, Lacan was, differently from Cato's Carthage fighting a lost battle against the Lacanians, who made gospel of so-called psychoanalytic discourse. Then, when not expected and contrary to appearances, Caracas[43] gave him the opportunity, despite his *pseudo-students,* to not deliver the hoped-for result, perhaps by then Lacan was no longer listened to or read. Consequently, this gave him the possibility, despite all odds, of passing on his singular heresy: *Kata- Holon* Lacanian theory, that simply does not exist.

Or as Pierre Boulez says:

> Why compose works that have to be recreated every time there are performed? Because definite (composition) seems no longer appropriate to musical thought as it is today [...] which is increasingly concerned with the investigation of a relative world. A permanent "discovering". (1984, p. 163)

Postscriptum

Some questions from a non—hypothetical reader posing a *non sequitur*:

It is hard to see precisely where this paper is leading.

It is hard to see that Lacan did not make an error in writing up the psychoanalytic discourse in 1977.

If you were to suggest what the outcome of this "error" might be then it would add more substance to your paper.

Consequently, why is it of relevance (this paper) to the practice of psychoanalysis?

It would be essential to clarify the above if your paper is to have substance.

It is also not clear what your position is on what you feel to be Lacan's attempt for his work not to become a church-like dogmatism. Although you say that he differentiated his position from Freud, he also stated that he was a Freudian.

My non-hypothetical answers to my non-hypothetical reader, are that *there is* "*sequitur*"[44] to the non-hypothetical reader:

Lacan quite clearly and explicitly dissolved his *école* because according to him it was turning into a Church, with which as it happens I agreed and still agree.

Certainly Lacan stated that he was Freudian, and it was up to us if we wanted to be Lacanians. This is true. However the meaning has to be qualified. Lacan's statement implies: *I am Freudian*, that is to say I work in the field that is Freudian, but the unconscious is not of Freud … but of Lacan, as he explicitly named it (*une bévue*).

Of course Lacan made an "error" in 1977, which was confused as "*lapsus linguae*". The correction by Miller impeded Lacan's own possible solution (e.g., to see how he would have resolved it (unravelled it)).

Instead in front of Miller's correction he went back to the "known ways": and wrote the canonical formula. However in Caracas he made a *lapsus linguae*, since this time he was reading aloud, yet he was not corrected.

Why was he not corrected at Caracas? I gave my hypothesis in this essay, as well as implicitly pointing out, that his *lapsus linguae* (by design or *gaffe*) was connected to the non-existence of the sexual relation. This itself suffices for a patent difference with Freud.

But above and beyond, my essay is also about the "fallacy" of the Freudo-Lacanians, who insist in a kind of continuation from Freud to Lacan, where my position, to answer your question, rather than one of continuity is of an almost epistemological cut.

And last but not least, the essay states that what Lacan told us in Caracas implied that so-called Lacanian theory does not exist. This was referred to in his remark that Freud produced a most delusional thought more than any he himself produced. Which one? To try to make out of a particular method a science. A particular method is neither a science nor is it a theory. It is a method. But above and beyond, what is at play is the problem of the transmission of psychoanalysis. This was heard and seen in act, by the premature correction of Lacan's "mistaken" formula of the psychoanalytic discourse. In this direction my essay cannot say where Lacan could have taken us because neither you nor I is blessed with the capacity of reading thoughts. However one thing is certain, the non-canonical formula he wrote on the blackboard as the formula of the psychoanalytic discourse, would have taken him, and as a consequence us to uncharted waters. It is this forced abortion, which shows the struggle Lacan was carrying out within his school against the attempt to convert his teaching into a religious one. Having lost the battle he resorted shortly before dying to uprooting his school, but the struggle which is far from over still goes on.

Now reader, I would like to thank you for not having left me alone, for having been with me as I was going backwards and forward in my thesis. At this junction however, we have to farewell each other until another propitious occasion might bring us to meet once more.

Notes

1. Freud, S, quoting a C. Leemans, Editor & commentator of Horapolo in *Horapollonis Niloï Hieroglyphica*, Amsterdam, 1835, pp. 83–84. SE Vol XI, p. 90, footnote.
2. Lacan, J. Caracas seminar, July 12 de 1980, translated from the French by Oscar Zentner and María—Inés Rotmiler de Zentner, *Papers of The Freudian School of Melbourne*, vol. II, Melbourne, 1980, p. 105.
3. Ernest Jones, "A Psychoanalytic Study of the Holy Ghost Concept", (read in the Seventh International Psycho-Analytical Congress, el 27 de September de 1922), *Essays in Applied Psycho-Analysis*, vol. II: *Essays in Folklore, Anthropology and Religion*, The Hogarth Press and The Institute of Psycho-Analysis, London, 1951, cap. XIV, p. 362.
4. Zentner, O. From Nietzsche's *Thus spoke Zarathustra*, quoted in *Fucking with death—preceded by cure or life*, unpublished.
5. In both senses as a *lost* teaching, as what was not passed on, as much as what Lacan established for his school as *the pass.*
6. Jacques Lacan, Seminar *L'insu que sait de l'une-bévue s'aile à mourre* (1976–1977), and session 8 March 1977, Edited by Jacques-Alain Miller published in *Ornicar?* N° 12/13, December 1977, p. 4 to 16; N° 14, Easter 1978, p. 4 to 9; N° 15 Summer 1978, p. 5 to 9; N° 16, Autumn 1978, p. 7 a 13, (the correction I am referring to can be found in this number p. 13);

N° 17/18, Spring 1979, p. 7 to 23, (the "annoyance" is to be found in p. 7). Emphasis mine.

7. Like Friday's footprint on the sand, which by being erased becomes a sign. That is *what represents something for someone else.*

8. "Nothing better than getting oneself lost in order to learn how to orient yourself in the terrain." (Creole proverb).

9. Traveller there is no path, the path is made as one travels (*Caminante no hay camino, se hace el camino al andar*).

10. In fact, one of the seminars of Lacan was called: ... *Ou pire,* that is: ... Or worse!

11. Heresy, Lacan dixit, is to choose.

12. Lacan, J. "[...] we know the price Freud had to pay, allowing the psychoanalytic group to dominate the discourse and as a consequence to become a Church." Papers of The Freudian School of Melbourne, Vol. 2, p. 106, Letter 5 January, Paris. (Our translation).

13. I thank Michael Currie for asking me in my seminar "On the Judaism of Freud and the Roman Catholicism of Lacan", at Melbourne University who represented whom.

14. Freud in a letter to Fliess distinguished *the judgment of attribution* from *the judgement of existence,* the first typical of paranoia, while the second of paraphrenia. This is the rationale for Lacan's characterisation of an analysis as a *controlled paranoia.*

15. See Lacan's "Purloined letter", where he demonstrates the difference between exactitude and rigour, the former belonging to the Prefect of police whilst the second to Dupin.

16. Lacan, J. "[...] Freud already called for our attention regarding the mandate *Love your neighbour as you love yourself."* Seminar *The ethics of psychoanalysis, 1960–1961.*

17. A similar situation was the injunction of Lacan's teaching, by the International Psychoanalytic Association; he interrupted his seminar On the Names of the Father, withholding from the IPA the logical steps necessary to conceive an end of an analysis, among others that if the Father is protected all analyses arrived to the *cul de sac,* of the Oedipal situation.

18. I underscore the fact that Lacan defined the cause as follows: there is cause, when something does not work.

19. Anyone, who has read Lacan, can recognise the fine irony he employs, he, was Lacan, therefore he was prevented from being Lacanian!, Or in his own words, even Napoleon did not believe he was Napoleon.

20. Lacan's dissolution of L'ecole freudienne de Paris, pitifully, was followed by a foundation of a new school, based in love, as he wrote, convoking: To those who love me!

21. Palms were only given to martyrs.
22. "Martyr" means witness. See: The Universal English Dictionary, Edited by Henry Cecil Wyld, p. 709: *Marter (Latin) =Martyr, Martur (From late Greek) = a witness.*
23. Clement of Alexandria quotes this, but without giving the source.
24. The Coptic text of St. Thomas, together with a translation line by line in English, French, German and Dutch, was firstly published in: The Gospel according to Thomas (Edited byAntoine Guillaumont, Henri-Charles Puech, Gilles Quispel, Walter Till & Yassah 'Abd al-Masih), Leiden, Holland: E. J. Brill; New York: Harper & Brothers; London: Collins, 1959.
25. Bramantino's painting shows in the foreground a toad, and not a frog.
26. In French, as in Spanish, toad is preceded by a masculine article whilst frog by a feminine one. In animals not affected by "the cancer of language", there are sexual relations. Whence the *nostalgia that a woman is not a frog,* as he says in Caracas.
27. Not dissimilar to Signorelli's Frescoes of "The Four Last Things" in the Orvieto Cathedral.
28. See the Function of Haste in Lacan's logical problem of the three prisoners.
29. This majority reminds me of the pertinent words of Borges: saying: *For Argentineans, history has the status of the Gospel.*
30. To put it bluntly and without niceties, this was not a light question for Freud; it is enough to remember that he wished Sabina Spielrein, at the time, to break off her love for Jung and get married to a Jewish man, *to have a Jewish son!*
31. It is also the canonical way of differentiating the Roman Catholic Church from the Orthodox Church.
32. Allouch, Jean. The following is a literal transcription of Jean Allouch's email to me on 25th April 2014: *I have found your "Lacan, Caracas" very interesting. Reading you, there is no doubt that the idea of bringing together the error corrected by Miller and the rana/sapo (frog/toad) lapsus in Caracas is heuristic, even though I have not been able to quite understand what happened between those two metidas de pata* (blunders): *an intensification of the same un-elaborated question? A progression from one to the other? A correction of one by the other? Whatever the answer, the question of Lacan's Christianity is more than ever present, as you also show. And it is therefore this question that I will address in my next seminar. Un abrazo,* (Best regards), *Jean.* Translated from the French by Nicole Chavannes.
33. Lacan dixit.

34. The impasses of Freudian psychoanalysis, above and beyond those which could be confirmed in the "unending" of the analysis are based on this Mosesisation of the analysis. This is what Lacan withheld from the psychoanalytic community when on being expelled from the International Psychoanalytic Association, he suspended at the same time his seminar *On the names of the Father,* depriving them from knowing what was the same obstacle which they never failed to meet.

35. Jones was not named in Caracas; he was named and highly recommended twelve years before in the seminar *On Angst,* in which Lacan speaks of *The Madonna's conception through the ear, remarking upon the protestant malice of Jones in the satisfaction with which this Welshman dedicates this article of 1914 ...*

36. Do not fear, I meant colloquially!

37. Lacan's dexterity as I showed it in the way he was able to separate grain from chaff, in Jones' proposition on the *Aphanisis of desire.* Zentner, O. (1979) *Aphanisis.* Papers of the Freudian School of Melbourne, voI, I.

38. The Trinitarian historian Socrates of Constantinople reports that Arius first became controversial under the bishop Achillas of Alexandria, when he made the following syllogism: he said, "If the Father begat the Son, he that was begotten had a beginning of existence: and from this it is evident that there was a time when the Son was not. It therefore necessarily follows, that he had his substance from nothing".

39. It might not have been alien to Bramantino's intention, by introducing this anomaly, to equate immortality with being a martyr, since "martyr" is "witness" and Ambrose means immortal. These are things that I insist, given Lacan's education, he must have known.

40. Either *ex-professo* or by *lapsus,* Lacan's added anomaly would not be alien to either heresy (Lacanian theory does not exist) or to *RSI (Real, Imaginary and Symbolic,* pronounced in French as *heresy!*), using in this way Bramantino's ambiguous painting, a painting that unites the lack of sexual relation, immortality and martyrdom. These are things that, due to his education, Lacan was well equipped to know.

41. *Scilicet tu peux savoir ce qu'en pense L'Ecole freudienne de Paris,* was the name of the official journal of L'ecole freudienne de Paris. This *you can know,* however, was easier *written* than *done.* This is known, and yet is it really known? Mishima makes Isao, the character of *Runaway horses,* say: "to know and not to act upon is yet not to know", as it was taught by the Neo-Confucian school. Then, I repeat: *You can know*—that is to say, a singular 'you": that is, each one among those who decided for a *yes* or a *no.*

42. The Gnostic Society Library, The Nag Hammadi Library, Point 16 del Gospel.

43. I was in Caracas where I heard Lacan reading this seminar. There, I was also impacted by his immense solitude; the only way to convey it by alluding to Oedipus in Colonna—when everyone wants his death to take place in their domains (*religio*) because that will bring them good fortune. Let us recognise that the Marquis de Sade took far better precautions, bequeathing his ashes to be dispersed by the wind in the thick of the woods, so as to be erased from the memory of men. The fact that he did not succeed does not alter our argument.

44. *Non Sequitur:* it does not follow, is correct Latin, and *Sequitur* by itself cannot be used as "it follows", but I allowed myself to make an exception, and for a very valid reason: psychoanalysis per se is exception.

CHAPTER THREE

C'est à quel sujet?*

Guy Le Gaufey

Caveat

In the process of writing *C'est à quel sujet?*, I frequently thought that some chapters would be difficult (or even impossible) to translate into English because they rely on very specific properties of the French language. For example, the fundamental difference in Lacan's teaching between "I" ("*je*") and "me" ("*moi*"), basic in French grammatical forms such as "*je me lève*", "*je m'évanouis*" or "*je m'ennuie*", a key point in this book, disappears in English (I stand up, I faint, I am bored). Other chapters would be difficult to understand for English speaking readers as they lean on philosophical studies not translated into English. So a translation of the whole book turned out to be very problematic. That was, at first, the reason for a partial translation.

But what if we serialised it? Why not split up what has already been truncated? After all, isn't it the fate of the Lacanian subject to be torn apart by the unremitting functioning of the signifier? Let that part-book

---

*Translators: "Foreword"—Phillip Anderson, Nicole Chavannes and Francoise Muller Robbie; "The making of the subject" and "The signifier as such": Nicole Chavannes and Francoise Muller Robbie.

be published in slices! So the present issue contains the "Foreword", "The making of the subject" and "The 'signifier as such'", and the next one will offer "The emergence of the new subject", "To exist" and "The vanishing subject".

Furthermore, and in spite of usual grammatical English customs in the matter of conjugation, the French present narrative has been kept most of the time when I speak, not so much about what Jacques Marie Lacan did when he wrote this and that, but about what his text is presently telling us.

Foreword

It is amusing to note that the word "subject" that seems to draw together the most important elements of what makes man a rational animal is also used to designate "a dead body used for the study of anatomy, dissection, vivisection" (Le Grand Robert, 2001, p. 820).[1] From liberty to servitude, the shades of meaning of this term are so broad that it borders on homonymy. Law, politics, medicine, literature, the arts cannot do without it. It has had a highly significant role in philosophy. It figures in the everyday vocabulary of the French "man in the street", down to the proverbial *concierge* with the famous question: "*C'est à quel sujet?*" ("What do you want?" and literally "What is the subject of your presence and implicit request?"). And then, to thicken the plot, psychoanalysis took hold of it.

Such was Jacques Lacan's wager. Even though the term turns out to be almost non-existent in Freud's works (yet German uses it as much as French), Lacan never ceased using it as one of the pivotal points of his construction. It is true that his "specular self", from the very first developments of the mirror stage, hardly overlapped the Freudian ego and left vacant the place of the subject that the pair of nominalised pronouns "*moi-je*" already built into French (as opposed to German, English or Spanish). However, it took a few seminars for Lacan, around the beginning of the 1960s, to launch into working out a particular meaning of the term "subject" outside the philosophical sphere in which Descartes, Hegel, and Heidegger had until then mapped it out in valuable and contradictory ways. From May 1959, coming out of his long commentary on *Hamlet*, towards the end of the seminar *Desire and its Interpretation*, the urgency of a new definition of the subject and the object at play in the analytic cure becomes evident, and Lacan launches into it, taking different tentative pathways, before arriving, more than two years later, over the first lessons of the seminar *Identification*, at a particularly concise formulation in which subject and signifier define each other: "The signifier represents the subject for another signifier." Strange turn of phrase, the apparent universality of which accentuates even more its immediately incomprehensible nature, as if one were confronted with a smooth, rounded and impenetrable stone, centred on an enigmatic repetition.

Modifications and additions, constant as the seminars went on, do not seem to have prevented the formulation from remaining active until the end.[2] It was, however, so often repeated, by Lacan first of all, then by his followers, that it has become a refrain that, given the axiomatic status it has acquired, it would be improper to question openly: who would dare ask what a point is or a straight line in the face of the difficulties of a problem of geometry? Except that, to appreciate at their true value the shifts that Lacan—perhaps—made its definition undergo, it is indispensable to explore what was at stake in its constitution, to study closely the to-ing and fro-ing that preceded the emergence of the canonical expression.

This sort of textual research is nevertheless but an initial rough survey. To remain stuck on the site of the discovery alone, never leaving its labyrinth, is to risk giving oneself over quickly to hero worship, bowing down before he who was able to come to a decision at a point where his predecessors were still babbling on. The discoverer, on the other hand, following up all the many options that lead to his own solution, stood in a vast setting only partially known to him. No need here to assume that he read all the authors who contributed to the field in which he was working, or to imagine some kind of osmosis which could have affected him through more or less porous cultural membranes. The reader's library, his desk on which the seminars sit next to completely different texts, that is the work space in which such a discovery finds, or does not find, its rationality in at times expected and at times unexpected encounters, all of which, however, contribute to giving a differential value to that which, at first sight, can seem self-evident or belonging to the realm of pure insight.[3]

Such is the process by which Lacan distances the subject yet to come from knowledge, then from identity, and even from the fundamental attribute of reflexivity, before finally arriving at anchoring it to a signifier that, by this very fact, is no longer the signifier of linguistics.

This procedure, very twentieth century in style, becomes clearer when related to what the Latin Averroists invented towards the end of the thirteenth century, calling it "possible intellect." They had the nerve at the time to assert, at the risk of being burnt at the stake, that the proposition "man thinks" was "false or improper"; that a subject that was no-one had to be conceived of, alone in having the agency of thinking the thoughts located in the soul of everyone. The revival of medieval studies means that these difficult texts can be approached today with a gaze freed of inhibition, despite the sharp differences between epistemes. When their audacity (flayed by Aquinas who transmitted them by dint of condemning them with the full force of his rhetoric) is simply registered, strange affinities quite quickly become apparent.

To call Lacan an Averroist would not make much sense, but the positions that he takes over the two years of a sustained working-through of the theme of the subject, put him face to face with choices that, in a very different context, were at times the same as those of the Averroists. Putting the two together better allows one to grasp the extent to which Lacan's theoretical decisions are not imposed on him solely by the subject matter he intends addressing—the Freudian unconscious, the analytic cure—but also by the formal constraints that are imposed on anyone who ventures into such theoretical areas.

Alain de Libera, who will serve as our guide here in approaching these distant texts, did a lot to give substance to what he calls, following the English historian and philosopher R. G. Collingwood, "QAC", "question-answer complexes" {"CQR"} (2002, pp. 31–43).[4] This slightly off-putting term designates networks of statements that are actually upheld in contexts and eras that may have little in common, but that, each in its own way, delineate some of the ways of thinking around formally close issues. This methodological standpoint has as its foundation the conviction that it is not possible to properly appreciate a new element of knowledge without establishing the network of questions and issues to which the element in question seeks to bring a solution. It follows that the first duty of any reader of a QAC is to constitute, at his own risk, at least some of the questions that have given rise to one answer rather than another.

Bringing to light other modes of working in the face of other formally related difficulties allows one to read not a "genealogy", direct or indirect, but indeed an "archaeology", a stratification of knowledges which reveals the fact that a construction that seems to be completely new has only been able to develop along certain planes, across different fault lines, down tracks that other lines of enquiry, often inaccessible to the discoverer, found themselves forced to take. By giving his support to Freud's modernity, by seeking to found an unconscious "subject" (when "subject" is most often synonymous with "consciousness"), Lacan can be seen as revisiting ground already trodden and responding to the demands of coherence that had their hours of glory between Paris and Oxford some seven centuries before.

A large part of what stands to be gained in the operation would be lost if its focus were on predecessors. To be first is not enough, and QAC do not improve with age in the barrels of history; they stagnate there. However much a contemporary of Lacan, Foucault has nonetheless his place here, just like the Latin Averroists: that of sharing in some QAC. It is well known that their paths crossed. Nothing confirms they read one another much over the period of their later work (the opposite tends to be true), but it is beyond doubt that during the 1950s and 1960s they bathed in the same zeitgeist that the term "structuralism" expresses poorly. They both read Heidegger and Beckett, Canguilhem and Genet, Merleau-Ponty and Blanchot, and many others. It may be true that the notion of "discourse" launched by Foucault propelled Lacan (who was already using the term widely) towards the complex elaboration of his "four discourses". There is, however, no reason to think that the "enunciative function" constructed by Foucault in his *Archaeology of Knowledge* owes anything at all to the "phallic function" that Lacan was starting to develop at the same time. Both will nevertheless be explored inasmuch as they each set up a subject that comes forward in a fundamental absence of reflexivity. Each the variable of a function, these subjects are stripped of the two properties that, classically, go together: reflexivity and consciousness. The first of these properties being above all grammatical, care will be taken to investigate the different voices—passive, active, reflexive—that determine the relation of subject to verb, so as to get a glimpse of the extent to which the snares of grammar inform, in the silence of habitual usage, the ways in which this theme is thought through.

Many other question-answer complexes could have been invoked, so protean the subject can reveal itself to be. That would have involved the risk of burying Lacan's fragile invention under layer upon layer of too long a history. I nevertheless hope that the impact of what follows will succeed in shaking the overwhelming coherence of Lacan's formulation of the subject as "barred": as original as it may have been and remains, it is presented here along with some of the little fellows with whom it was at school, so to speak, in a playground that could be a rather suspect place. We may perhaps have a clearer view at the end of this of how it shifts the Freudian notion of the unconscious that psychoanalysts—thus taking a fatal path—always reify too much.

The making of the subject

When Lacan takes into account that he has to start working through a new conceptualisation of an object different from the specular object he has used since the mirror stage and, correlatively, of a subject different from the subject he has always emphasised, namely the subject as liar, he has already gone a long way by applying his "theriac" of the real, the symbolic, and the imaginary to the Freudian texts on which he is commenting at the time. By trying to group and articulate conjointly some of the forays he has made, he built what it has become customary to call the "graph of desire" to which he gives a quasi-definitive form right in the middle of the period that interests us here, that is during the year 1960. This movement of synchronic presentation, the scansion of his teaching, is essential to understand the style of his progression. At different points in time the optical schema, the graph of desire, the four discourses and the Borromean knot constitute networks on which Lacan writes more and more relations between the terms that he has either found in Freud and redefined, or invented—and this often to the point of collapsing under the burden of the mass of relations he has to carry. At the time when the question of the subject is about to take centre stage, this subject has already encountered in the course of the construction of the graph many of its determinants and constitutive links with the writings of the fantasm ($S <> a$) and the drive ($S <> D$), but without leading to the change of course that would soon be witnessed. It is therefore appropriate to jettison immediately any excess of linearity that would depict Lacan as progressing uniformly throughout the course of the seminars. Rather, he finds himself facing a palette with which we see him try a particular nuance on a particular day, and another nuance on another day, until "it gels", until a lucky expression or a fortunate formulation happens to set for a while the trembling of the commentary.

During the months of April and May 1959 (when this investigation starts), Lacan is keeping to himself quite a precise montage of the subject in its relation to the demand that he has already addressed in a lecture on 9th May 1958 under the title "The signification of the phallus" that he would use and complete with a decisive point. He has also successfully completed a long commentary on *Hamlet* and even more importantly a re-evaluation of the key term "mourning"[5] that, although it is not the place here to elaborate on it, would frame his new conceptualisation of the object. It therefore matters to me here to emphasise the importance of the *layering* {*feuilletage*} of the notions on which Lacan is constantly working, so as not to weigh down what will follow in the linearity of the narrative he unfurls for a short time by means of a strange "little narrative" {historiole} with the view of *setting the stage* {*mettre en scène*} for what would appear to his future students to be banal but that he still has to build from scratch: the weird idea that between two signifiers there is room for a subject.

The word "subject" is indeed omnipresent during all the first years of the seminar, and the importance already given to the signifier could lead to thinking that the direct mutual contribution between one and the other had to result in the formula that articulates them together. Not at all. The fact that from the start the subject is linked to speech and language does not corner it in such an inescapable definition since what constitutes it as such during those first years is none other than its capacity in the relationship it has to another subject to lie. On 25th May 1955, for instance, Lacan was already stating:

> That said, we the analysts, must not overlook our basic assumptions—we think there are subjects other than us [and] that authentically intersubjective relations exist. We would have no reason to think that if we didn't have the testimony of the characterising feature of intersubjectivity, that is: that the subject can lie to us. That is the decisive proof. (1991)

From 1953 to 1959 this argumentation is central, and there is an undeniable coherence in bringing into play, albeit very classically, the subject as instance of truth, truth that cannot go without its perennial acolytes: lie and deceit.

A first shift is initiated at the end of the first trimester of 1959. It consists in a tightening of the argumentation developed by Lacan in

"The signification of the phallus" (1977b). In the commentary on *Hamlet* (February and March 1959), he has already reworked the formulation in many ways, supporting it on previous writings proposed at the time of the construction of the graph of desire, and this ends up in the presentation of a short "dramatic" sequence, a scene during which an event would happen that by itself would decide the positioning of the subject in its native link to the signifier and to the object of the drive. It is appropriate here to follow Lacan in his very narrative tone since he seems to present as a stage in the development of the child that which constitutes a thesis one would like to qualify as metaphysical, in the same way that he had introduced as ultimate detail of the mirror stage the turning of the child toward the adult beside him, thus decisively modifying the value of the ego ideal.[6]

Caught in the "labyrinths of the demand", what is at first called "the child" is actually engaged with the Other in a relationship weaved by the signifier since the satisfactions he expects from that more or less maternal Other have to be articulated in language. If there were only that, one could say, there would be nothing but communication. But a bouncing effect {rebond} animates the matter from the start: since the Other called upon appears most frequently as able to respond *or not*, the fact that he does respond takes the value of a proof of love;[7] by the same token the response to the demand is divided up into a satisfaction value and a proof of love. All this is already present in "The signification of the phallus", but what has now been added is that this mythical child will want to find in the Other the signifier that would represent him as subject and would thus prove the good will of the Other towards him, [and] prove the fact that the subject is indeed the addressee of the love manifested by the responses to his demands. But, in this new demand, a "common tragedy" (Lacan, 1958–1959) will strike both the subject and the Other: it is strictly impossible for the latter to supply such a signifier. He does not have it. He has nothing of the sort available to him. Why? Because he too is a subject. The clearest formulations about intersubjectivity emerge at that point in the seminar when Lacan is in the process of setting the stage for that "little narrative".[8]

> It is in so far as the Other is a subject as such, that the subject at
> that moment establishes himself, and can set himself up as subject,
> that there is established at this moment this new relationship to the
> Other by which he has, in this Other, to make himself recognised

as subject. No longer as demand, no longer as love, [but] as subject. (1958–1959)

One is faced here with a situation that would later become unthinkable: a subject dealing directly with that big Other and expecting to be recognised by him as subject. The fact that the Other is, at that time, also conceived of as subject—a subject deprived of what allowed him to warrant [or] to block the value of his acts, to spare them the perpetual sliding of signification, this fact is based on a previous statement according to which "There is no Other of the Other". There is no undefined parade of subjects, but a strange confrontation in which the Other, submitted by the subject to the question of veracity of what he utters, would make manifest what usually remains veiled: his fundamental incompleteness. He who is defined as "the treasure trove of signifiers", capable of developing as many [signifiers] as required and then some, is not even capable of producing the one signifier that would prove the address of his love or of his good will, and would then have the value of signifier/sign for the subject he cares about.

This subject, still a long way from being defined as "represented by a signifier for another signifier", thus comes up against the dramatic point of the signifying order that Lacan then hastens to make the pivotal point of the key concept of "castration", using it to read *Hamlet* as well as *Totem and Taboo* as a generalisation of the Oedipus [complex]. And in this new stumbling encounter he connects two different and interrelated events: on one hand, at the level of the symbolic chain, in this sudden evanescence of the Other, the subject vanishes [and] is struck by a characteristic *fading*; and on the other hand, in this situation where the symbolic ends up failing, the means at hand of the imaginary order are summoned. This average subject finds himself caught in (and supported by) a mechanism particular to psychosis such as Lacan conceives of it since his seminar on the theme,[9] namely that, to face up to the radical deficiencies of the symbolic order, the only recourse is imaginary. This point remains delicate, and Lacan, on 20th May, gives three "examples" of this inherently enigmatic "object-cut":

If what is in question is that the object in the phantasy is something which has the form of a cut, how are we going to recognise it? […]. In the relationship which brings it about that the $ at the point where he questions himself as $ can only manage to support himself in a series of terms which are those which here we call o, qua objects in the phantasy, we can in a first approximation give three examples of it [...]. The first kind is the one which we habitually call rightly or wrongly, the pre-genital object. The second kind is this sort of object which is involved in what is called the castration complex and you know that in its most general form it is the phallus. The third kind is perhaps the only term which will surprise you as being a novelty, but in truth I think that those of you who have been able to study carefully enough what I wrote about psychosis will not find themselves all the same essentially upset by it, since the third kind of object fulfils exactly the same function with respect to the subject at his point of failing, of fatigue, is nothing other, and neither more or less than what is commonly called a delusion, and is very precisely the reason why Freud, from almost the beginning of his first apprehension, was able to write: "These people love their delusion as they love themselves" (*Sie lieben also den Wahn wie sich selbst*).

We are going to take up these three forms of the object in so far as they allow us to grasp something in their form which allows them to fulfil this function to become the signifiers which the subject draws from his own substance to sustain before himself precisely this hole, this absence of the signifier at the level of the unconscious chain. (1958–1959, pp. 8–9)

With the conjunction of those two events, the importance of the formula of the fantasm: $\$<>a$ is raised to a new level. From then on, it [the formula] writes the conjunction/disjunction of the subject struck by the bar (*fading*) and of the object (*a*) that, although always imaginary as the specular other was from the beginning, takes on in the course of the sessions of May 1959 a value of cut that makes it formally akin to a subject also on its way to being conceived of as a cut.

Thus, from then on, right at the centre of the "common tragedy", there is the movement of the subject apprehending himself first with the available means on board of the symbolic, in other words the resources of the signifying chain in its relation to the Other. The "little narrative" has taught us that at that crucial point those resources cannot not be lacking—that's the way it is. But in the face of this symbolic failure, the "function of narcissism" as "an imaginary relation of the subject to himself" (1958–1959) is summoned as in psychosis, setting the fantasm astride between the symbolic and the imaginary, between unconscious chain and specular model. Thus Lacan ends up speaking of "what happens at the level of the mirror stage, namely the inscription, the situation where the subject can put his own tension, his own erection *in relation to the image beyond himself that he has in the Other*". It is only once those precisions are made that a strange "fatigue" of the subject can be revealed in correlation with an unexpected author in this context:

> I am alluding here to Maine de Biran's contribution in his very subtle analysis of the role of the feeling of effort. The feeling of effort, in so far as it is thrust forward being grasped by the subject from two sides at once in so far as he is the author of the thrusting, but as he is also the author of what contains [...] here is something which when linked to this experience of tumescence makes us perceive the way there can be situated there and be brought into play at this same level of experience as something through which the subject experiences himself, without nevertheless ever being able to grasp himself [...]. If effort cannot be in any way of use to the subject for the reason that nothing allows it to be imprinted with a signifying cut, inversely, it seems that this something whose mirage-like character whose unobjectifiable character at the level of neurotic experience, which is called the fatigue of the neurotic, this paradoxical fatigue which has nothing to do with any of the muscular fatigues that we can record on the level of facts—this fatigue in so far as it responds, is in a certain way the inverse, the sequel, the trace of an effort which I would call signifyquantity {*significantité*}. It is here that we can find this something which in its most general form is that which at the level of tumescence, of the thrusting as such of the subject, gives us the limits in which the possible consecration in the signifying mark has vanished. (1958–1959)

Strange connection: why does Maine de Biran appear at that important time in Lacan's progress, at the point where more than anything it is a matter of establishing a new status for the subject conceived of as a cut in the signifying chain? What in the Biranian *cogito* might be able to capture Lacan's attention? One has to read that passage again to find an anchoring point that may make of the Biranian subject at least a distant cousin of the one Lacan is then in the process of hatching: "That through which the subject experiences himself yet without ever being able to catch himself". This formulation echoes what can be read in an earlier text of Lacan on the mirror stage such as it was rewritten in 1949 and published in *Ecrits*. What was then the relation of the "subject" (2007a) to the image in the mirror?

> For the total form of his body, by which the subject anticipates the maturation of his power in a mirage, is given to him only as a gestalt, that is, in an exteriority in which, to be sure, this form is more constitutive than constituted, but in which, above all, it appears to him as the contour of his stature that freezes it and in a symmetry that reverses it, in opposition to the turbulent movements with which the subject feels he animates it. (Ibid.)

The reflexive grammatical form can here serve as a guide: the subject "experiences himself" {"s'éprouve"} without this inscribing him in any possession of himself since it is the animation of the image that, in its fundamental exteriority, triggers this quasi cenesthesic experience. In his narrative stand Lacan has to offer to this evanescent subject the moment—elusive and fragile—when he would be there "such as he is" {tel qu'en lui-même}, endowed with a reflexivity—at least a grammatical one—when in fact it is after all a matter of conceiving it outside of any "himself", outside of the reflexivity that happens to be the inalienable property of most of the subjects that the history of philosophy has seen parade, to offer it to a (specular) identification that would introduce it into the reflection (image), the reflection (thought) and the reflexivity.[10]

In relation to this point, Maine de Biran is a fortunate help in that the positioning of the subject Lacan aspires to be from the start [and] contrary to the Cartesian ego, embedded in the body. He therefore comes up with a peculiar *cogito* in which two elements are given conjointly that can nonetheless be distinguished when elaborated on but that cannot be separated or ranked, not on the axis of time nor on the axis of logical priority. To understand the notion of "effort" (of which there is nothing mechanical) one has to pose *at the same time* on one hand a subject that animates a will {volonté} and on the other hand a resistance that this will reveals without at any point anticipating it in any way.

In his *Promenade avec M. Royer-Collard*, Maine de Biran writes that one has to go back to this intimate fact, this inevitable collusion, if one wants to be able to understand "another secondary duality reputed primitive", the one of subject and object in knowledge in general. For prior to founding in reason his "primitive fact", de Biran stumbles against an irreducible reality: sensation exists indeed and appears primary, but it is not possible to follow in every point Condillac or the Ideologists, Destutt de Tracy and the others, since a sensation accedes to the status of "fact" if and only if a subject exists to actively apprehend it.[11] No consciousness, no fact. Throughout all these cogitations on the theme, he does not renege: when I decide to act, I do not act like a sleep walker who is not present to his acts and only passively executes "the blind movements of instinct". He is then prepared to follow Cabanis and a few others who are happy to imagine two quite different centres in the brain: one linked to reactive movements, the other to voluntary initiative. But the medical hypothesis eventually seems gratuitous to him: in his view it is limited to materialising, through a supposedly real division of the brain, what is up to that point only an ideal distinction between different modalities of action whilst the phenomenon of reflection continues to be inexplicable. But de Biran is among those who support an irreducible heterogeneity between thinking subject and material organs, thus confirming the thesis he has already developed in his *Memoir on the dismantling of Thought* (*Mémoire sur la décomposition de la pensée)*, namely that no physiological hypothesis is capable of explaining what *effort* is: organic phenomena added to organic phenomena never give a sense of consciousness and even less of effort.

With this notion of effort—that took some time for him to isolate in its foundational value—Maine de Biran holds an element of psychic life that is simply a relation between two terms *neither of which is reflexive.* In this relation, two poles can nonetheless be distinguished by abstraction: on one hand a motor determination where the real cause of the effort is manifested; on the other hand a muscular sensation that marks the end point of the willing {vouloir} by encountering the resistance it triggers, but the most important is to acknowledge the fact that neither of these poles possesses a proper reality through which they would both enter into a relation. What is real in effort is from the start the link, the immediate connection between those two polar opposites, and Maine de Biran is getting closer to his cogito when he indicates that the primal fact is a relation between two terms that are distinct without being separate.

> There is only one fact—he writes[12]—made of two elements, only
> one relation with two terms of which one cannot be isolated from
> the other without changing its nature, without passing from
> concrete to abstract, from relative to absolute [...]. In asserting a
> connection, I am not saying between two facts but between two
> necessary elements of a same fact, we only express the primordial
> fact of consciousness, we do not go any further.

With his conceptualisation of the fantasm—through which, like never
before, Lacan wants to conjoin his $

 linked to the *aphanisis* in its relation
to the big Other and the new meaning he is conferring to his "object
a"—he holds an element akin to the calibre of the Biranian effort: in
it the subject becomes object, *however without ceasing to be subject*, and
this becomes conceivable inasmuch as both have the same (still quite
enigmatic) status of "cut". Due to the unforeseen evasion of the Other
summoned to answer in truth—in other words at the symbolic level—,
this subject (so narrativised {narrativisé} in this presentation) has no
other way out than to put forward the imaginary value that Lacan has
already called for some years "the object little *a*", this acronymous letter
accounting for its specular origin, when the first "object" with which
the subject identified himself during the mirror stage was nothing but
the image in the mirror, the little other laid at the foundation of the self
{fondement du moi} and its functional unity. Strange marriage, to the
eyes of the future Lacanians, between the fantasmatic organisation that
conditions the subject, and the mirror stage where the *self* takes root;
but it is indeed by conjugating both in this affair where subject and
Other face each other in their recognition as subject that Lacan manages
to proceed toward what gives to subject and object their same formal
making {facture} as cut.

   In his 1938 text on "The family"[13] Lacan was not able at the time
to avoid the ambiguity between the little other, his fellow creature
{ce semblable}, and the object in the sense of the Freudian narcissistic
investment. In those days his mirror stage forced him to confuse them,
(or) at least to give them the same status, the same composition and the
same imaginary value. But now, in the dynamic where the subject in his
relation to the Other is not able to have his nature of subject recognised
on the symbolic level through which he is represented—tied as he is
to the signifying production—he stumbles in his essence, and, unable
to overcome the *fading* to which he is again submitted at the symbolic

level, he ends up producing *himself* in the imaginary value he supposed he has for the Other, for the one (male or female) who has failed him in his ambition as subject.

The deceit of this all too well narrativised presentation comes from the fact that it institutes in a succession of events what can only be given in an immediate conjunction, and similarly one could think that, in the Biranian cogito, a subject first has to be posed who undertakes a vol- untary act, then immediately discovers that he has to fight a degree of resistance. Even without a quasi-concomitance, one would at least have a logical succession. However, it is not so, not for Maine de Biran, nor for Lacan.

The former knows that ranking, in one way or another, his primal duality, he would fall back either into the rut of the Ideologists and the sensualism of Condillac, or into the solipsism of the Cartesian ego he wishes to escape: he therefore holds firmly to his "primitive fact". For his part, Lacan is not as threatened by antagonistic trends, but neither can he let a subject pre-exist to the point of holding up on his own. He knows that "subject" is only ever but a *relative* term, and he has no intention of going soft on that, so much so that where the subject might cease to be suspended to the signifying chain, at the time when the Other falters, far from existing folded over [and] curled up on his solipsistic being as subject, he has no other recourse than to offer him- self of his own accord to that Other in the imaginary value to which he is reduced for that Other. The emblematic figure of this violent bidding {mise aux enchères} is the lover who kills himself for feeling rejected without appeal: as I am dead for you, here is my dead body.

This imaginary congealment only takes on its singular subjective value if it is inserted within the symbolic suspension that Lacan built from scratch in the course of his commentary on *Hamlet*. In doing so he gave body to his writing of the fantasm—$\$ <> a$—by attributing to each of its two terms the maximal distinction he can: the first one, $\$$, struck by the bar, blocked as he is in that moment in his demand of recogni- tion as subject that leaves the Other speechless; the second one, a, that, even though it is rooted in the specular image à la Lacan, is no longer confused with it since it is in the process of acquiring a value of cut that makes him closely connected with the dramatic and painful scansion of the subject (*cf.* the three "examples" of cuts mentioned above).

The little genesis to be found in Lacan about the making of the subject—which pushed him to such narrative developments—implies that the *new look* subject he is trying to hold together only achieves its new status once a stasis is established whereby it [the subject] is linked to the "object" in the same way it has been at the time of the previous specular identification. The faraway echo of the famous "you are this" operates a welding without precedent between symbolic determinations and imaginary values, welding of which it is important here to note that it also constitutes the basis of semiotic functioning: to determined symbolic elements (most often letters and sounds), distinct imaginary values (most often meanings) are conjoined, sometimes with a wholly metaphoric flexibility, more often with a near cadaveric rigidity.

Seen from this angle, the fantasm constitutes a swirling {tournoiement} that prevents a "blocking" of the subject either on its symbolic value or on its imaginary value since one is nothing without the other. If one can venture that the fantasm imposes itself as the most singular psychic formation for a given individual—at the same time result, then matrix, of his history if there is one {s'il en est}—, one also has to accept that this singularity is itself a composite. If one is then allowed to approach it, and even perhaps to describe it as Freud attempted to do with Leonardo da Vinci[14], this fixation, as precious as it may be, does not allow one to situate in it a "subject" element that would be separated from its "object". Here one comes up against a certain quantic limit beyond which it is useless to venture.

> I agree that this session has been perhaps one of the most difficult of all of those that I have addressed to you. [...]

Says Lacan on 20 May 1959, before concluding:

> It is at the level of the cut, it is at the level of the interval that [the subject] is fascinated and that he fixes himself to sustain himself in this instant at which properly speaking he envisages himself and he questions himself as being, as a being of his unconscious. (Lacan, 1958–1959)[15]

The "signifier as such" {le "signifiant comme tel"}

Lacan went as far as he could in his approach of the term "subject", but the term signifier remains quite opaque. One may know that for Saussure—who, if one can say so, owns the term—there is no signifier in nature; the reality, the acoustic or verbal image of a sign, never wanders out of this other reality—the reality of its signified. Both constitute the element "sign" that is only thus severed by linguistic analysis. Lacan is aware of the problem and launches, in the lessons of November and December 1961, into a clear distinction between sign and signifier that could make a case for the subject he is promoting.

The first character convoked for this operation is none other than his dog Justine as representing "never to take him for another". Not only is she sensitive to her master's signs, not only does she know how to produce signs herself (hunger, affection, etc.) but nothing, it seems, exceeds the regular functioning of those signs. Inversely, he says, the analytic rule institutes a "pure speaking subject" {sujet pur parlant} as one says "pure pork pâté" {pâté pur porc}, and in this case, this pure speaking subject "ends up always taking you for another". Pleasant argument, but without real power.

Things get more complicated with the study of the logical statement "A is A" through which the identity of the letter with itself is asserted in equations {calculs}. It is essential to postulate that at each occurrence of the letter A in a formal reasoning we are dealing with the same entity. But is this a self-evident fact, one of those truisms of which logicians and mathematicians seem to be so fond of at the beginning of their work, or on the contrary a constructed reality, and in this case on which basis? Lacan decides on the second possibility: "We can see that it is only insofar as the 'A is A' ought to be questioned that we can advance the problem of identification".

It is indeed important to question the logical {logicienne} equivalence for the good and simple reason that it does the work {effectue le travail} that Lacan means to give his subject in the operation of *identification*—this time symbolic—that he presents as "the spontaneous assumption *by the subject* of the identity of two quite different appearances". In relation to this he refers to a story found in folklore in which a servant recognises a little mouse as the reincarnation of his recently deceased master; but to support the same thing he could also have used the very Freudian "fort-da", the appearance/disappearance of Freud's grandson's reel. To consider identical two different appearances does not imply at all that they are homologous on the basis of a global resemblance as in the (deceiving) case of the letter "A"; for its part, the mouse has nothing of the master except… a certain way of visiting the property, the ploughing instruments, an entire behaviour that is sufficient for the servant to *identify* it as a reincarnation of the master—which will be corroborated some time later by the master's ghost. From then on the question rebounds (one should not forget that we are here hunting for a "signifier as such"): what does shape each of the occurrences that the subject is invited to identify? Lacan follows several different paths so important is it for him to be convincing on this point.

The first is rather Saussurian. Since the definition in the *Cours de linguistique générale* makes of the signifier an element of a battery in which it is only different from all the others, its definition rests on no "itself" [and] does not imply any reflexive identity. It is therefore useless and incorrect to believe that one defines the letter "A" in a tautological movement. In an alphabet like ours, it is only allowed to say: A is not B, is not C, is not D, etc., without (to follow Lacan) balking at "A is not A" when we reach it a second time.

The second utilises Lacan's sinologist knowledge. He produced two different writings of the same phrase: "These two series, he comments straight away, are perfectly identifiable, yet at the same time do not resemble each other at all". And it would be the same, he adds, for two series of elementary marks, of "sticks": the more I will apply myself to make them resemble each other, the more I will fail. What do I identify as "the same" when the resemblance is missing? On which basis can one conceive of an identity that would not be imaginary?

Here appears the third example, at the same time funny, dramatic, and decisive. Lacan relates having visited the Saint-Germain museum and having found in the Piette room a reindeer bone that particularly stirred him. Prepared by the notice presenting an object showing a series of marks going back 17,000 or 20,000 years, Lacan observes "a series of little sticks, first two, then a little interval, and then five, and then it starts all over again. This is why," he continues, "addressing myself by my secret or public name, your daughter is not mute. Your daughter is your daughter because if we were mute she would not be your daughter". These are not words that any visitor could utter; only someone whose current preoccupations seek the emergence of the signifier in the long gestation of humanity. In all modesty Lacan admits: "I'm not saying that it is the first appearance", but "in any case [it is] a definite appearance of something of which you can see that it is altogether distinct from what can be designated as qualitative difference". The contiguity of marks constitutes them as a series, making it possible to differentiate them not from the singular form of their tracing but from the sameness of their formal equivalence. There was already sameness with the two series of Chinese writing, but with them one could still think that this identity rested on their meaning {sens}, identical through different calligraphies. With the reindeer bone, meaning has disappeared and sameness remains at a higher level of formality.

In front of these marks {coches} *of which he knows instantly that he knows nothing of their referents and that nonetheless he cannot not consider signs*, Lacan suddenly has the feeling of being faced with the "signifying difference", the "pure difference". In as much as they no longer refer to anything, those marks only give the sign of a subject[16] (marker) and give rise to a subject (reader), both separated by some twenty millennia. Emotion due to this brutal imaginary fraternity but at the same time captured by that which, in the sign thus "erased"[17] from its referent (and therefore from its signified) can only count as pure presence of the very act of counting, act of which each mark {coche} is here nothing more than the simple reiteration. The sameness of those marks {traces} is only linked to the repetition of the act that inscribed them. In the museum glass case each one of those marks does not by itself represent anything for anyone, does not mean anything to anyone, but it is articulated to others to make a series, and this series implies a subject—through which we are approaching the point of emergence of the canonical formula.

What remains to do is to differentiate *sign* and *signifier*. Given that their relations {rapports} have just been redefined and that, far from the Saussurian conjunction that *systematically* coupled signified and signifier in the unity of the sign, the reindeer bone disassociated them to show that referent and signified can be dropped and the signifier remain by itself without the "subject effect" {l'effet sujet} disappearing, is it not time to singularise sign and signifier with independent definitions and thus cease to explain one by the other and the other by the one?

The end of the lesson of 6th December says it clearly for the first time: "How could the formula of the sign be modified in order to understand what is at stake in the advent of the signifier? Contrary to the sign, the *signifier* is not what represents something for someone, it is *what precisely represents the subject for another signifier*" (1961–1962).[18] As for the "sign formula" that was his starting point, Lacan had already used it in the expression that Charles Sanders Peirce[19] had already given it, but it was only then that he succeeds in "modifying" the formula in such a way as to arrive at what he has been floundering about for some years. On that day he finds out the right expression but only after having succeeded in purifying this new subject from any substantial dimension whatsoever by taking away from it all knowledge, and impoverished the signifier to the point of seeing in it nothing but the unique trait[20] that any symbolic element manifests and whose marks on the reindeer bone have become the paradigmatic example.

We shall not make ourselves dizzy here by investigating the verb "to represent for" that Lacan draws from the classic definition of the sign to the one he has just managed to forge by modifying the two "actants" of this verb ("sign" and "someone" both reduced to "signifier" whilst "something" is being supplanted by "subject") for we have already arrived at a situation on which Lacan remains very quiet (followed in this by the great majority of his commentators for the last fifty years) and that it would be better to clarify without further ado: since there is now a new subject, what to do with the old one, the lying subject caught in the nets of intersubjectivity? Is the latter to disappear in the rubbish bins of history, to become a draught one had to go through all the better to overtake it, or does one have to keep its place warm? Are they in harmony or mutually exclusive?

A bit of reflection is enough to realise that they have to coexist since the lying subject is the subject of the sign (deceitful by principle since he presents himself as designating something other than himself) and that it is not possible to do without the sign or the subject attached to it. How to conceive of the coexistence of two subjects so different in their functioning? The lying subject and the barred subject: the same or not the same? No pragmatic investigation will be able to answer this question, and just to have such interrogation implies the unfolding of a whole battery of associated terms without which the term subject has no chance of sustaining itself or only in a constant homonymy where everyone is lost without even knowing it.

I do not think it is possible to articulate them by only searching the seminars and by multiplying the quotes that seem to speak of one or the other or both. To gage correctly the options Lacan takes in his elaboration of a new subject, it is indispensable to see that they can't be reduced to the Freudian and psychoanalytic ground on which they are presented but have already played their part under other skies and other colours.

Notes

1. *Translators' note*: the same meaning is found in English: cf. *The Shorter Oxford English Dictionary* (Third Edition), Oxford, OUP, (1933) 1964, Vol. II, p. 2058 (III, 3, c.).
2. Anyone who might doubt this can read the following lessons spread over several years: 16th January 1973, 11th June 1974, 15th November 1975, 11th May 1976 and 15th November 1977.
3. *Translators' note*: In English in the original text.
4. *Translators' note*: the original French text uses the abbreviation CQR—Complexe Question-Réponse.
5. On this point read the critical commentary by Jean Allouch in *Erotique du deuil au temps de la mort sèche*, Paris, Epel, 1995—passage translated into English in *Erotics of mourning at the time of dry death* in *Invention in the Real*, Papers of the Freudian School of Melbourne, volume 24, Karnac Books, 2012.
6. On this point see Guy Le Gaufey (1997). *Le lasso spéculaire*. Paris, Epel, pp. 92–105.
7. The Other, in so far as she is here someone real, but who is evoked in the demand, finds herself in the position of raising this demand, whatever it may be, to another value which is that of the demand for love as such, in so far as it refers purely and simply to the presence-absence alternative". Jacques Lacan, "Desire and its Interpretation", lesson of 13th May 1959 (translation by Cormac Gallagher from unedited French manuscripts).
8. That he will conclude in any case, sensing that he went a bit far in the narrativity, with the following statement: "You must not think that I am in the process of attributing here to some larva or other all the dimensions of philosophical meditation".
9. Argument reworked in different forms in "On a question preliminary to any possible treatment of psychosis". In: Jacques Lacan, (2007a) *Ecrits*. Bruce Fink (Trans) NY, London: W. W. Norton & Co., p. 470. "It is around this hole, where the subject lacks the support of the signifying chain, and which need not, as can be observed, be ineffable to induce panic, that the whole struggle in which the subject reconstructed himself took place. […]. For in the field of the imaginary, a gap had already recently opened up for him in response to the absence of the symbolic metaphor […]."
10. *Translators' note*: in French there are two different words for the English word *reflection*: *reflet* (mirror reflection) and *réflexion* (thought process).
11. This position will be decisively found in the argumentation of the Latin Averroism.

12. All along his argumentation on this point, Maine de Biran—sometimes saying it and sometimes not—often leans on the classical maxim: "*Aliud es distinctio, aliud separatio*".

13. Reworked later under the title "Family Complexes" (J. Lacan, *The Family Complex in the Formation of the Individual*, www. Lacaninireland.com).

14. And other authors as well. In relation to this, see the studies of writers presented by Catherine Millot who aims to circumscribe the fantasmatic font from which entire works were able to be written. See: *Gide, Genet, Mishima, Intelligence de la perversion*. Paris, Gallimard, 1996.

15. *Translators' Note*: we have left out the last paragraph of this chapter as it ends on the notion of the distinction between the active, passive, and reflective form of verbs so particular to the French grammar as to make it impossible to translate into English.

16. Lesson of 20th May 1959.

17. On the "erased" ("*les effaçons*"), see the lesson of 6th December 1961 (in the *Identification* seminar) and also Guy Le Gaufey, *L'incomplétude du symbolique*, Paris, Epel, pp. 164–165.

18. This quote, as all the previous ones left in the text, was taken from the lesson of 6th December 1961.

19. That could be found, in substance, in *La logique de Port-Royal* as it so closely corresponds to the classical functioning of the sign.

20. Also called "unary" in an attempt to translate the *einziger Zug* in the second Freudian identification.

CHAPTER FOUR

Father of function, fact, fable … and fiction

Megan Williams

> I buried my father in my heart.
> Now he grows in me, my strange son,
> my little root who won't drink milk,
> [...]
> little grape, parent to the future
> wine, a son the fruit of his own son,
> little father I ransom with my life.

This is an extract of a poem by Lee Li-Young entitled "Little Father" (2001). To ransom is to pay something in order to save, to sustain, to keep alive, something cherished which is stolen or threatened. In this case, the ransom paid is the son's life. For Sylvia Plath perhaps, who also wrote about a father, and who committed suicide shortly after, the daughter's life.[1] It is an old story, the Christian story: something of the child's life is transferred to the side of the father, who in consequence continues undiminished. Abraham is ready to sacrifice Isaac; Christ drains the cup proffered by his father.

Why would one want to keep a father alive? Would that not, as this poem suggests, subvert the natural order? The speech of poets and of patients says that they do. And they make clear, between the lines, that the life which is sacrificed is a sexual life. It's an old story, a Freudian one: desire sacrificed to an ideal; the life one might *have* sacrificed to what one chooses to *be*, following a father.

Li-Young puts into poetry what Freud described as a momentous loan, in which the child subject, struggling to obey his father's prohibition of sexuality, resolves his conflict by internalising the prohibiting agency itself. He sets up the father inside in two forms that correspond to the latter's commandments: the ego ideal that commands *be like me* and the superego that commands *don't be like me*—in possessing the mother (Freud, 1923b, p. 34).

Lacan suggests that the story doesn't start with prohibition. Rather, the speakingbeing borrows a father to protect against the anguish of her helplessness in the face of something of her own flesh which never ceases demanding and which only she hears, without knowing what it wants of her. If this unknown jouissance that tickles and burns incessantly becomes able to suppose for itself an object (Lacan, 1974), it is because the father names one, concurrently with the "No!" which prohibits it: that mother with her roots in jouissance (Lacan, 2007b, p. 78). It is for this protection against helplessness—the protection of turning that unknown demand towards a known object—that the child loves the father. The child pays the ransom, then, in order to be protected from her own heart, in whose place she buries her father. What she doesn't know is that he doesn't know those words whose writing will never cease to incite her flesh; that there is no dissolution of this helplessness.

The paternal function thus gives bones to that flesh with its roots in jouissance. If Freud heard from his patients that the child's love for the father extends back into *pre-history* (Freud, 1923b, p. 31), it is surely because of this Moebian intrication of the child's time with her father's. How could such a momentous loan be returned?

Even if it could, the intrication does not end there. In Sylvia Plath's well-known poem, "Daddy", a girl tells her dead father that she tried to kill herself in order "to get back, back, back to you. I thought even the bones would do". Lacan observes that, for speakingbeings, the bones won't do; that we clothe them with a fable, promoting a father who doesn't know what he says into *The* Father who does; the un-authored voice of the unconscious into that of God the Father. If the subject accepts a father's prohibition of sexuality, Freud argues, it is in order to accede, one day, to what one imagines he has. But "one day" never comes—the sexual rapport never ceases to not be written. Lacan suggests that the fable of an exceptional Father, a *Great fucker*, is the subject's way of hiding from this void by ascribing it to the failings of her own, quotidian father, the little father *who fucked the kid up* (1992, pp. 307–308).

In thus confusing the lack in the Other with her own, particular misfortune, the subject signs up to the ransom of a fable which is doubly castrating—she adds Imaginary to Symbolic castration by taking the fault in the Other as her own. She trades the anguish of helplessness for guilt and shame. Lacan says, "[…] if we are sufficiently cruel to ourselves to incorporate the father [to bury him in our hearts], it is perhaps because we have a lot to reproach this father with":

> The perpetual reproach that is born at that moment [of the dissolution of the Oedipus complex] … *remains fundamental in the structure of the subject*. It is this imaginary father and not the real one which is the basis of the providential image of God. And the function of the superego in the end … is hatred for God, the reproach that God has handled things so badly.
>
> I believe that that is the true structure of the articulation of the Oedipus complex. (Ibid.)

Applying these words—*remains fundamental in the structure of the subject*—to the reproach, the plea for the father to return as *someone who would really be someone*, and the living of the fault as one's own, we can say that they do not cease to be written—and necessarily so, since they are written to fill the void of the impossible which does not cease to not be written. Nick Flynn writes, in a poem entitled "Father outside", of an insensible father that his protagonist cannot cease thinking of, imagining an encounter where he will finally know what to say so that it would reach something he hopes for and has always been disappointed in:

> I want to believe
> that if I get the story right
> we will rise, newly formed,
> that I will stand over him again
> as he sleeps outside under the church halogen
> only this time I will know
> what to say.

His poem ends with: Even now, my father is asleep somewhere. If I followed the river north I could still reach him.[2]

What to do, then, with this complex knotting that we call a father? How to return that which was borrowed; to cease the writing that never ceases? Is a transformation possible? I will briefly address two moments of Lacan's work that speak to this question.

The first is from 1960, the time of the Name-of-the-Father, of the paternal function as bone, word, and exception: a formulation in which the Symbolic surmounts the Real.[3] The Father's "No!" bars something of jouissance, and his Name knots this lack in the Other to the phallic signification of seeking. As Freud had already elaborated, however, that which is buried is not dead: unsatisfied by the Oedipal metaphor, its opaque demand never ceases to threaten the subject with helplessness, *Hilflosigkeit*. Lacan used the term *laisseul*.[4]

Laisseul is a neologism that can be heard phonically as *les seuls*, those who are sole, or structurally as a holophrase composed of the past participle of the verb *laisser*, to leave alone, and the adjectival noun *seul*, sole or alone; thus meaning those who have been left alone. Lacan refers to speakingbeings as *laisseuls*: those who, because of speaking, are sole; each one singular. If we hear this as *laissé seul*—left alone—and also hear evoked the construction commonly made with the verb *laisser*, *laisser tomber*—to let fall—we might think of ourselves as abandoned, let fall, left in the lurch, and even as the *seul*/sole one in that state. Here we revisit what I outlined above: the subject going beyond the paternal bones to a father-fable of the God who has left him in the lurch; the subject defending against helplessness by assuming the lack in the Other as his own, particular failing or that of his own, little father.

In 1960 Lacan comments on the change an analysis might bring about in terms of this defence against helplessness:

> At the end of a training analysis the subject should reach and should know the domain and the level of the experience of absolute disarray […] a level at which anguish is already a protection […]. Anguish develops by letting a danger appear, whereas there is no danger at the level of the final experience of *Hilflosigkeit*. (1992, p. 304)

To experience helplessness without defence would be to let fall the Imaginary fable and the accompanying reproach, confronting the lack where the Symbolic provides bones but neither meaning nor author for the speaking flesh. It would, I propose, be to hear *laisseul* not as *laissé seul*, a singular misfortune or failure, but as a universal state, the nature of things which is the nature of words (Lacan, 1998, p. 73) which are spoken by an Other who lacks: that is, that speaking beings are by nature *les seuls*, those who are alone because of the singular way in which speech has written on their flesh.

Another answer Lacan gives, in 1975, is that, through analysis, one might "knot oneself otherwise",[5] a reference not only to the Borromean Knot but to the Oedipus complex, and thus to the father. Lacan specifies that knotting oneself otherwise makes the Real surmount—though not dominate—the Symbolic.[6]

I would say that making the Real surmount the Symbolic is what Lacan himself does when he knots the Oedipus otherwise, emphasising the Real of what a father can be for a subject, and thus transforming his own theory. Where in 1960 the father entered the Oedipus complex primarily as Symbolic element, as Name and function, in 1975 *The Father* becomes *a father*, his *Name* becomes *naming*, his function that of being a model: the model of a symptom. Naming and being a model are Symbolic functions, but the model of a symptom exemplifies how to make do with the Real of jouissance without knowing its meaning or even what one is doing. Desire here becomes no more than a pathway in which a father who is not master of it, but subject to it, makes do with what the tatters of the discourse of his own pre-history have written into his flesh—and without their acquiring meaning: without the lack in the Other being closed. This father knows neither his own cause nor what the Other wants. He appears to the child not as the "great fucker" who possesses and satisfies the mother, but as one who dares to approach a woman, without knowing her desire. This father knows one thing alone, I would say, reading two texts of Lacan together: how to allow *lalangue* to suppose an object (1974) and to elect a woman into that place. And this that he knows, he doesn't know. "It" knows: "it" that speaks in his flesh, against which he is helpless, contingently finds its cause, which he names the mother of his child. He who possesses the phallus, instrument of seeking, becomes he who finds, in a contingent encounter, resulting in love.

A father thus ceases to be imagined as author-ising. He becomes one for whom, at least once, that which never ceases not to be written in the Other, ceases, in a naming, not to be written. If analysis can bring about a re-knotting, then, it concerns knowledge allowed to function in its singularity: unconsciously and without author or mastery.

The transference is another relation in which the cause which never ceases not to be written comes, in a contingent encounter of love, to cease not being written. In transference the *laisseul* is not entirely *seul*, since what speaks through his flesh is *heard*—not by an Other who knows, but by an analyst who accepts hearing without understanding what she hears, responding with a voice speaking from the place of the oracle without that place being inhabited; without the void being filled. As that which speaks through the *laisseul* has no identifiable author, neither does the response he hears, leaving him the option of author-ising it by doing something with it.

I propose that this hearing might sometimes be enough for the subject to grasp and assume the knowledge that she or he is not *laissé seul* but simply one of *les seuls*; not left in the lurch but one instance of the universal condition of being *seul*. This is a similar formulation to that which the Lacan of the first theory made about castration (1956–1957).

To assume being *seul*: what would that be? If that which comes to be written in an analysis is not a knowledge that could function as an ideal or be written in a permanent, theoretical form, then in what sense could we say that it comes to be written? Perhaps one could refer here to fiction following an unnamed author cited by Gerald Murnane, who wrote of writing as the task of coming to say *that which only he can say*.[7] To say that which only he can say is to speak as *seul*, solo, singular. The author makes clear that these things which only he can say are not known in advance nor especially clever or striking: simply that, through writing, and without knowing it, he will say that which is singular to him. This saying, then, is contingent; a momentary opening or disclosing which cannot fill the void in the Other, and yet in which something, momentarily, ceases to not be written.

Perhaps we could add to this the possibility of a fictionalising of one's father: the fable of *a father that authorises* (from pre—to post-history) becoming the fiction of *a father that only I could have had*. Fable becomes authorship. The change here is less transformation than, as Lacan says, re-knotting, since there is a difference only of resonance or register between *the father only I could have had* said as a reproach to fate, and *the father only I could have had* said as acknowledgement of the invention one has made from the tatters of fleshy discourse that one has been left with. The latter makes of authorship the only authorisation possible.

This fiction operates a knotting in which the singular Real of the subject, in being assumed, surmounts the Symbolic through a contingent saying which is heard and allowed to function. The change is thus twofold: the *impossible* Real which does not cease to not be written does cease, for one *contingent* moment, to not be written; while as a consequence, the Symbolic-Imaginary, which has *necessarily* until then not ceased to be written in the father-poetry of reproach, guilt, and shame, ceases to be written, in a moment of time. Through this, something else becomes *possible*.

Notes

1. Plath committed suicide four months after writing this poem.
2. Published on the website of the Academy of American Poets, poets.org.
3. Lacan asks in 1964, for example, "What grounds [psychoanalysis] as a praxis? What is a praxis? [...] It is the broadest term to designate a concerted human action, whatever it may be, which places man in a position to treat the real by the symbolic." In: Lacan, J. (1979 [1964]). *The Four Fundamental Concepts of Psychoanalysis*. J. -A. Miller (Ed.), A. Sheridan (Trans.), UK: Penguin, p. 6.
4. "[...] this animal parasitised by the symbolic, the bla-bla [...] they dream of not being the only one *(les seuls)*. This has them by the guts. Let us write them *laisseuls* to evoke *let them alone (laissé seuls)*, in this parlance." Lacan, J. (1975). *The Seminar, Book XXII RSI*, seminar of 11.3.1975. C. Gallagher (Trans.).
5. "For being knotted otherwise is what is essential to the Oedipus complex and it is how analysis operates." In: Lacan, J. (1975) *RSI*, seminar of 14.1.1975, op. cit.
6. "What is psychic reality for Freud? It is the Oedipus complex [...] it ties the three, but at a minimum. To dispense with a fourth, to obtain the Borromean knot, it suffices to make, at two points, pass above what was below. In other words, the real must surmount the symbolic. The surmounting of the symbolic by the real at two points is quite precisely what analysis is about. Be careful not to take this term *surmount* in the imaginary sense, believing that the real has to dominate here." In: *RSI*, ibid.
7. The two passages to which I refer appear in two of four paragraphs which Murnane indicates are citations from the work of a Hungarian author whom he does not name. It is probable that the author in question is Sándor Márai. M. G. (2012). *A History of Books*. Sydney: Giramondo, p. 117 & 119.

CHAPTER FIVE

Get knotted

Malcolm Morgan

Is it possible, however, to give the *sinthome* the status of a fourth dimension? And what would the consequences be for the other three? The death of Lacan has left these questions still to be answered.

—*Allouch*, 2007, p. 20

G et knotted. I take my title from the vernacular of my childhood. So, at the outset, my title speaks of something that whistles down through the contours of my history. Something is already knotted to a way of speaking that precedes me. Here though, this "Get knotted" is taken up by me and used—I give it my own, idiosyncratic purposes. It is now more than a charged erotic imperative. It speaks of a different urgent call. Syphoning off Lacan's theory of the Borromean knot, it offers something to my theorising of the end of an analysis. This is what is at stake in my "get knotted", the way one knotting can sponsor the emergence of another.

I stumble in mid speech, and say "three" when I mean to say "four". There are four children in my family. It's just a slip, but the missing "one" is me. The full weight of this casually erupting absence collapses upon me. The knot of history tightens to a point of extreme density.[1] *Hic et nunc*. For Lacan the density of such points is best shown in the tightening intersection of three lines, not the traditional slippery overlap of two. It is in these moments of an analysis, where history, in the guise of the signifier, stakes its claim on the subject that the four chords of the Borromean knot tighten to an inescapable point. There, I appear where I am not.

Lacan explores the move from three to four in his seminar on James Joyce in 1975–1976. It has weight for him as well. He says, commencing the year's work,

> I have contented myself with the 4 and am very glad of it, because I would surely have succumbed to 4, 5, 6. Which is not to say that the 4 in question is any less weighty for me. (1975–1976a)

For Lacan this "4" involves theorising the inclusion of a missing chord into the knot of his "3"—Real, Symbolic, and Imaginary. He spends the year's seminar exploring the implications of weaving this fourth ring, which he calls the *sinthome*, through his Borromean knot of 3. This knot of the *sinthome* reveals itself as the chain that grips the subject in his tongue tie. Throughout his seminar of 1975–1976 Lacan works to develop a viable showing of the four ringed Borromean knot.

Imaginarily, the three ringed Borromean knot is a stable figure. It derives its figurative stability from the image of the triangle. We invariably show this three ringed Borromean knot resting on its base, never perched precariously on its apex, nor tilted, as if toppling. What would that do to our imagining? These conventional pictures of the three ringed Borromean knot privilege its imaginary stability, and, I argue, make it more difficult to think about the properties, and utility, of a four ringed Borromean knot. We rarely show the inelegant, four ringed B knot, and when we do, it is always within the context of what I've called a running repair to a failed three ringed knot. This fourth ring has come to be understood primarily as a way of showing a repair to a broken three ringed Borromean knot that speaks to the questions posed by psychosis. By confining our thinking in this way, we miss what the fourth ring might have to offer other questions, such as our theorising the end of the analysis.

Zentner refers to this "mending a failure" in his paper "The exile of James Joyce—après le mot le déluge". He says,

> [...] a problem posed in his seminar *Le sinthome* is that of Joyce's
> Ego as mending a failure. But wouldn't that in any case be that this
> is none other than the "normal" situation? To know that the ego is
> a symptom? (2004, p. 328)

For Zentner, the problem is that we might think that there is a show-ing of any Borromean knot that does not represent something that fits within the concept, "mending a failure". Joyce's or anyone else's ego is a symptom, and a symptom is an attempt at mending a failure—an attempted self-cure for the dis-ease of language. The beguilingly strange thing about Joyce is that it is language itself that is deployed so successfully to "treat" this dis-ease. And without recourse to psycho-analysis. With Joyce, the illness, unaided, treats the disease. Zentner's argument provokes the question: what is shown by the intact three ringed Borromean knot? What is the nature of the coherence and con-sistency given to the disparate psychic elements, Real, Symbolic, and Imaginary in the three ringed Borromean knot? It is certainly not the divided subject. This is better shown, as Zentner indicates, in the four ringed Borromean knot. Pereira (2004, p. 211) claims that the three ringed Borromean knot shows how the three "registers" of the real, the symbolic and the imaginary—previously designated by Lacan as "essential for human reality", function within a knotting and chaining. What is "essential for human reality", however, may bear no relation to the truth of the human subject. Whether approached as "regis-ters", "psychic elements" or "dimensions", the consistency shown by this functioning within a knotting is deceptive. It can be argued that essential to human reality is the deceit of a smoothly functioning sub-ject—apparently integrated registers, psychic elements, or whatever, operating synthetically, and grounded in a guarantor of their authen-ticity. Lacan, with Heidegger in mind,[2] questions what the truth of the human subject is. The truth of human being is essentially evanescent. It is unendurable. It emerges as it fades in the act of speaking. There is no human reality for the $ beyond this.

With the intact three ringed knot as an apparently coherent and stable contextual starting point, the "mending a failure", when applied to the four ringed Borromean knot, confines thinking about the func-tion of the fourth knot, (however construed, as either ego, *sinthome* or, "Name of the Father"), to considerations of its possible place within the description and treatment of psychopathology—specifically psychosis.

From this three ringed starting point, the idea of psychosis can be understood as an inaugural failure of a three ringed Borromean knot. In this scenario, the fourth ring comes to the possible rescue—re-knotting the broken knot, and thereby allowing a functioning of the failed subject as a repaired subject. The problem here, however, moves us once again, to the question posed above: if the subject is always already divided, what is this three ringed knot showing before it is broken?

There is another possible understanding of the fourth ring—as re-knotting the transiently unravelled Borromean knot, rather than knotting the never formed, or otherwise irretrievably broken Borromean knot. This possibility may help to differentiate between the four ringed knot that indicates a psychotic "patch", as in a patch for a failing software program, and a different four ringed knot that speaks to the un-knotting and re-knotting indicative of the course and end of an analysis—a different kind of re-pairing. That trajectory could allow for a showing of the work of an analysis which charts the movement from symptom to *sinthome*—that signature of one's place in the world, a way of speaking with one's own voice.

In *Seminar XX, RSI*, the year before the *Sinthome* seminars, Lacan says:

> The Borromean Knot consists strictly insofar as three is the minimum. … The remarkable thing, a fact of consistency, is that you can add an indefinite number of rings—it will always be true that, if you break one of the rings, all the others however numerous, will be free.

He continues,

> This property alone homogenises all that there is of number after three. […] The Borromean knot will always carry the mark of the 3. (1974–1975)

All numbers beyond three, within the Borromean context, are what Lacan calls, "homogenised"—that is, any disparate elements are merged together beyond three. They become undifferentiated. Figure 1., "Knot becomes Chain", shows a picture of a Borromean chain from which you may sense what Lacan means by this word "homogenise".

The "mark of the 3" that Lacan speaks of is this property of a minimal condition for the establishment of a viable Borromean knot. The third ring does not so much knot the other rings, as allow the possibility

Knot becomes Chain

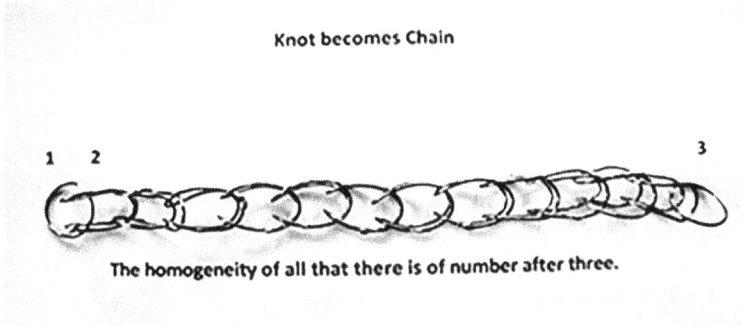

The homogeneity of all that there is of number after three.

Figure 1. Knot becomes Chain.

of an inter-weave between all three rings such that they become jointly knotted. It is this weave that produces what we misleadingly call the knot. This sharing of all three in the knotting is, I think, one way of understanding the "common measure" of which Lacan speaks.[3] Because it is an "at least three", all "more than three" versions of the knot are marked by this "at least three". This makes it all the more difficult to derive a version of the knot that is, for want of a better term, a "natural" four—un-marked by this "at least three".

So, to take our bearings: the Borromean knot requires an "at least three", but is not limited to three. Three can become four or more, though when this occurs, the beyond three remains marked by the three, and the illusion of order within the three is disrupted by additional rings. At the end of the text of the December 10th 1974 seminar there is inserted, not another ring, but what is called a "Marginal note for Figure 3". This note starts with the following remark:

> It is obvious [!][4] that this kind of Borromean chain has an "end"—without which it is un-knottable one by one. As soon as this chain is longer, if only by a single round, the round that closes it here must double itself at the other end of the open Borromean "chain". [...] Whence the privilege of the three linked chain, which as we will see, distinguishes it from the four linked chain, where the order begins to be no longer any whatsoever. (1974–1975)

What is Lacan saying here? The four ringed Borromean knot loses the privileged "common measure"[5] of the three. The "order" of three begins to be disrupted—there is only disorder. The two end rings of the four, or more, Borromean knot are different from the homogenised rings interposed between the closing rings (see Figure 1.). Instead of order and consistency, "there is no longer any order whatsoever". Another problem is that with rings beyond three the knot reveals itself as a chain, and in order to close the chain, requires two untwisted rings to lock it at either end. It no longer shows the deceptive triplicity of the three ringed knot.

In the *Sinthome* seminar, the year following the *RSI* seminars, Lacan constructs various Borromean knots with four rings. This fourth ring is his attempt to show, what he calls, the *sinthome* woven through, and thereby knotted to, the registers that comprise Lacan's three—the Real, the Imaginary, and the Symbolic. It is crucial to recognise that whilst Lacan's starting point for this weaving of a fourth ring is the three rings that constitute his three ringed knot, they are not already knotted. His goal is to start with four, not three. The previous three merely lie one atop the other—with the Real on the bottom, covered first by the Imaginary, then both these covered by the Symbolic. They are together, but not linked. This starting point is not three in the way that an intact three ringed Borromean knot is three. It is into, and through, this non-connecting assembly of registers that Lacan attempts to weave his fourth ring, the *sinthome*, and so construct the four ringed Borromean Knot that Zentner claims shows us "another way of the Borromean knot rather than the application and extrapolation of the ('mended') Borromean Knot for a 'restitution' of a supposed psychosis of Joyce" (2004, p. 323, fn. 67). What is at stake here is precisely what Allouch alludes to above—the possibility of a fourth dimension (the *sinthome*) taking its place within Lacan's Borromean topology.

For the most part, Lacan relates his four ringed Borromean knot to the enigma of Joyce's writing, what he calls Joyce's *sinthome*. Through this weaving of a fourth ring into the de-constructed three ring Borromean knot, Lacan attempts to show the place of Joyce's writing in, what I'll call, the coherence, or perhaps we could say, the consistency of his life. Lacan also presents this four ringed Borromean knot as an evocation of how any *sinthome*, not only Joyce's prodigious talent, can operate in conjunction with Lacan's other three—the Symbolic, the Imaginary, and the Real—to create an end to an analysis and indicate the presence of a psychoanalyst.[6] Lacan even proposes that his invention of the Borromean, knot as a presentation of the real in his theorising, is his working *sinthome*. The knot of the *sinthome* enables something to operate that otherwise, either might not function at all, (psychosis), or perhaps only function to sustain the futile suffering of a symptom. The *sinthome* offers a possibility of a functioning that moves beyond mere suffering or madness.

Oscar Zentner has written extensively on the question of Lacan's theorising of the Joycean *sinthome*. He argues,

> Among the manifold consequences of the encounter with the work of Joyce we should also mention that the chain writing and the Lacanian Bo-knot of three were repaired and perfected by the Joycean Bo-knot of four with its *sinthome*, ego or name of the father. This repairing, [...] far from indicating psychopathology, appears to be the unavoidable structure of the speaking being. (2007, p. 283)

For Zentner the four ringed Borromean knot constitutes the appearance of "the unavoidable structure of the speaking being". This is not, therefore, a statement about the *sinthome* either as repair that allows what is called psychosis to function, or as a possible end of an analysis, but a display of the dilemma of the subject divided by language who must make do with castration.

A repair clearly implies damage made good. Something is broken in the three ringed Borromean knot that is repaired by the insertion of the fourth ring—the Joycean *sinthome* ring. But, "repaired" and "perfected" is a curious pairing of concepts. Things are not usually perfected as a result of a repair. Is there a clue here concerning a possible move away from the myth of the intact three ringed Borromean knot, which is broken and then repaired, towards a comparison of one version of a four ringed Borromean knot—the symptomatic knot—with a separate version of a four ringed Borromean knot—the *sinthomatic* knot? This could then be another way of comparing—or re-pairing—the Borromean topology, which turns away from the repair as mere deficit management towards a capacity of a speaking being to speak with their own voice, and recognise this as such.

So, we have the proposition, supported, in part, by Zentner's argument, that the idea of the *sinthome* might have broader application, beyond Joyce's illustrious *sinthome*. The *sinthome* may be a way of referring to how a subject, forever entangled in the cogs of language, functions symptomatically. The starting point, therefore, for this symptomatic functioning, could be shown by a four ringed Borromean knot which is knotted by a fourth ring—the symptom. The course of a psychoanalysis, then, could be thought of as the transformation of this fourth ring from symptom into *sinthome*. It may be that this transformation is not possible without something like a violent rending of this fourth knot as symptom, and its re-weaving as *sinthome*. This is one way of thinking of the risks associated with undertaking a psychoanalysis. This process of the de-knotting and re-knotting of the four ringed Borromean knot as *sinthome*, confronts the analysand with that implacable clarity that emerges in an analysis taken to its conclusion.

How can one get from the four that reveals a speaking being, to the four that reveals the end of an analysis? This is the move from symptom to *sinthome*. This investigation positions its questioning at the level of the singular experience of each subject. The four ringed Borromean knot brings us closer to the particularities of each speaking subject. This can be sensed in the insertion of the proper name—Joyce—when we speak of the Joycean Borromean knot. This could, perhaps, just as easily be the Smith or even Morgan Borromean knot, or any other speaking subject who dares to take their psychoanalysis to its conclusion. Of course, the irony in this statement, as Zentner indicates, is that Joyce did not undertake any kind of analysis, let alone one that reaches its conclusion, yet his work is presented as:

> [...] *"par excellence"* the paradigmatic example of what can be expected of an analysis: *to make do* with the symptom-creation, [...]. (2007, p. 329)

The four ringed Borromean knot, therefore, opens to something of the singularity of the functioning subject—the psychoanalytic subject, and charts the course of an analysis to its conclusion where symptom emerges as sinthome.

In the seminar of 18th November 1975 Lacan says,

> [...] the fact is that starting from four, what is figured is the following, namely, that you will have the following relationship. Here for example, the Imaginary, the Real and the Symptom [...] and

the Symbolic, and that each one is interchangeable with the others.[7]
(1975–1976, p. 14)

We must hear in this statement the words, "starting from four". When you start from three you have to insinuate a fourth where it doesn't belong, unless something is broken. When you start from four "each one is interchangeable with the others", it has its own consistency and the symptom/*sinthome* its own place.

I began with an imperative, "Get knotted", and by the end I have reached a point where I think I've argued that there is no urgent need for this imperative—the speaking being is always already, unavoidably knotted to his history. The question posed is whether there is a way, through the Borromean topology, to show something of how that knotting allows something else to function. Late in his year's work, and in response, finally, to a question from his audience that he thought was worth responding to, Lacan finished his answer with the words,

One can moreover do without it provided one makes use of it.
(Ibid., p. 10)

The *sinthome* then, is this capacity to make do with a doing without—that capacity, not just to live without, which is the barren field of privation, but to make something of this living without function—a writing that draws upon that which does not cease to not be written.

Notes

1. Pereira refers to a "point of density" in his paper, "Real, symbolic, and imaginary: the times that bind", In *Papers of the Freudian School of Melbourne*, Anguish & Erotics, Vol 22, 2004, page 201. This "point of density" is, in the present context, also a "point of destiny"—the grip of history revealed to the subject in his slip. Lacan, J., refers to this gripping point, in Seminar 22, *RSI*, 1974–1975, Jack Stone (Trans.), Lesson of 10th Dec 1974. " […] the essence of the Borromean knot, […] is […] determining, gripping, a point as such."
2. See Heidegger, M., *The Essence of Truth*. Ted Sadler (Trans.), Continuum, 2002. Heidegger works the concept of truth as αλετηια in relation to Plato's Cave Allegory in Part 1, The Clue to the "Essence of ΑΛΕΤΗΙΑ".

3. Lesson of 10th Dec 1974, p. 8.
4. Exclamation mark inserted by translator.
5. The Borromean knotting gives an illusory "common measure" to the registers real, symbolic and imaginary "I have only found one way to give a common measure to these three terms, real, symbolic and imaginary: it is to knot them as a Borromean knot." Lacan, J., Ibid., p. 8.
6. Lacan, J., Seminar 23, Lesson of 13th Apil 1976, "[…] the psychoanalyst cannot conceive of himself otherwise than as a sinthome. It is not psychoanalysis that is a sinthome, it is the psychoanalyst" p. 10.
7. Lesson of 18th Nov 1975, p. 14.

CHAPTER SIX

About psychoanalysis

Madeline Andrews

> To talk and write about silence is what produces the most obnoxious chatter.
>
> —*Tezuka*, quoted in Heidegger 1982, p. 52

These are the words of the Japanese academic and once member of the Imperial University of Tokyo, professor Tezuka, who in the early 1950s met with the German philosopher Martin Heidegger, and in a publication, *On the Way to Language* (1982), plays the part of his interlocutor. This paper takes up a question which, not without bearing upon questions of silence, has generated copious amounts of obnoxious chatter for more than a century and which nowadays, continues to do so, namely, the question: "What is a psychoanalysis?"

From the outset of approaching this question, whenever we set foot on the slippery terrain of *talking about* psychoanalysis, the object of our inquiry seems to slide from under us. On account of this problem, I shall broaden the landscape a little towards obtaining sufficient ground. This will entail considering some of the difficulties associated with talking about silence, talking about philosophy, talking about love, and talking about discourse. The last of these, talking about discourse, is of central concern to psychoanalysis, as discourse is the necessary entry point to any approach to the unconscious—an unconscious which one so often hears, psychoanalysis is all about. In what follows, Tezuka's cautioning will be disregarded and the risk of more obnoxious chatter undertaken, in order to determine what speaking about psychoanalysis might yield.

Tezuka's words delimit a silence that obtains its status in relation to speech. Silence distinguishes itself as a product of discourse and not the reverse, for the latter notion would confer upon silence the status of an aural void underpinning language. Silence refers to an absence of sound, and for the speaking being, this is principally defined by the clacking of tongues. As distinct from an intolerance for silence that characterises the broader field of clinical discourse, psychoanalytic discourse is shot through with a repertoire of silences—silences that irrupt, insist, and demand to be filled—arresting, forestalling, and marking the vacillating utterances of the sessions. This dynamic occurs in a peculiar discursive arrangement that privileges the speech of the patient—the encounter between a psychoanalyst and an analysand. The silent anticipation of the psychoanalyst holds a particular place in relation to this encounter, which begins with an open invitation for the patient to speak freely. Does this silence bear any resemblance to the silence that Wittgenstein, at the conclusion of his *Tractatus*, resigns himself to with the following statement: "Whereof one cannot speak, thereof one must be silent"? (1992, p. 189) It is this silence, "whereof one cannot speak" that the present inquiry puts into question in relation to the discourse of the psychoanalyst.

Tezuka's statement implies the paradoxical effect of talking about silence. Talking about silence invariably misfires, as anything said about it demonstrates a contradiction by way of the sound issuing from the speaker's mouth. When apprehended as a lack in relation to speech, silence infers muteness. Thus, one can speak of its effects, but speaking about what silence is, seems to be a losing game. Likewise, speaking about discourse leads to a parallel contradiction. It carves a hole around the speaker, subtracting the speaker's voice from the discourse it aims at. Freud observed something similar in the structure of the drive— a bypassing of the object in the circulation of the drive around its object—an invariable near miss. Given that psychoanalytic discourse takes its orientation from this elusive object (the object, cause of desire), there seems to be every indication that talking about psychoanalysis is an inevitable exercise in futility. In response to this type of impasse, Lacan showed that the object of psychoanalysis obtains its inscription in language through a logical rather than representational operation, unconstrained by the conventions of ordinary discourse.

Something that a colleague drew my attention to some time ago strikes me as being relevant here. She noted that despite the vast expanse of psychoanalytic literature produced by psychoanalysts, the proportion of texts directly addressing the question of what a psychoanalysis is, appeared to be surprisingly limited. Whereas the pens of these analysts flowed freely with regard to *what a psychoanalysis was not*, their ink ran conspicuously dry *vis-à-vis* what its affirmative status might be. Her observations reflected a similar experience of my own. For how often had I encountered descriptions of Lacanian psychoanalysis that laboured the negative with statements such as: "psychoanalysis is *not* a therapy, *not* a technique, *not* science, not a philosophy, *not* a religion", and so on. In 1961, Lacan spoke to the problematics of speaking about psychoanalysis to a lay audience as follows:

> I take up again before you my difficult discourse, more and more difficult because of the aims of this discourse [...]. Moreover, to speak about unknown terrain when it is a question of our own, of the one which is called unconscious, is still more inappropriate because what is in question, and what constitutes the difficulty of this discourse, is that I can say nothing about it which does not take on all its weight precisely from *what I do not say about it*. (1960–1961)

In Lacan's address, he attributes the difficulty of speaking about psychoanalysis to its aim, which as we have thus far determined, invariably misses its object. In addition, his reference to "what I do not say about it" implies an effect of transference, which confers upon the knowledge of the psychoanalyst a strange significance. Lacan defined the structure of knowledge as paranoid. Although he claimed that this applied to discourse generally, it was not without acknowledging that its effects are intensified in the presence of the psychoanalyst and by a resistance in analysis, which accentuates the veiling of the object (ibid.). In *Lacan Love*, Jean Allouch designates this "paranoisation" as having the structure of the "discourse of the interpreter" (2007, p. 143). As such, the subject gripped by his passion posits an unknown knowledge in an other supposed to know. This supposition, when addressed to an analyst, has the effect of conferring upon the discourse of the psychoanalyst the status of a sign (to be interpreted). Speaking of this paranoid amour, Lacan referred his audience to Freud's analysis of the joke concerning a man travelling to Cracow, the logic of which amounts to the following: "You say this, but I know perfectly well that it really means something else."[1]

The difficulty of speaking about psychoanalysis has thus far shown itself to be a two tiered problem. Firstly, because *speaking about* psychoanalysis can get rather *round about* and secondly, due to an effect of transference such that whatever the psychoanalyst has to say about psychoanalysis will be interpreted on the basis of *what he does not say*.

In his seminar of 1964, Lacan referred to an "antinomy of reason", which equivocates the position of the speaking being. He proposed that language is a deception in which the subject is never where he appears to be and at one and the same time, implicated where he is not. Taking the statement, "I am lying" as an example; Lacan demonstrated a "twisted logic", which situates the subject paradoxically in opposing positions (1979 [1964], p. 139). For if I say, "I am lying", the statement is false at the level of meaning (a liar cannot speak the truth), yet at the level of the utterance it is logically true (speech as the lying truth). Thus, Lacan showed that the subject is divided in language between two irreconcilable localities: the "I" of his statement and the "I" of his enunciation (ibid.). In Freud's 1937 paper, "Constructions in analysis" (1937d, p. 59), his reference to two separate psychic localities (one historical and the other, fictive) is underpinned by the same antinomy of a double registration that has no relation at the level of representational sense. Lacan maintained that the neurotic's misrecognition of this non-relation is what he pays for with his being and his suffering—the suffering of the symptom, which in attempting to reconcile this non-relation, calls out for an interlocutor. Furthermore, he proposed that the interlocutor best equipped to respond to this call without being deceived is a psychoanalyst.

Now having taken into consideration the elusiveness of the object of psychoanalysis and that fact that the discursive means of approaching it is characterised by deception, it would appear that our original question, "what is a psychoanalysis", has been undercut by a more fundamental question, namely, "can psychoanalysis speak for itself?"

Towards pursuing this more elementary question further, I now want to turn to the philosopher to whom Tezuka made his address concerning silence in 1953, Martin Heidegger. Notably, Heidegger devoted himself, amongst other things, to interrogating the question of being and on that basis the question of what philosophy is. I refer to something he published, *The Fundamental Question of Metaphysics*, in the same year, 1953 (2000). The following is an English translation which, for the purposes of this inquiry alone, I have tampered with by taking the liberty of replacing every reference Heidegger made in it to "philosophy" with the term "psychoanalysis":

> [Psychoanalysis] is essentially untimely because it is one of those few things whose fate it remains never to be able to find a direct resonance in their own time, and never to be permitted to find such a resonance. Whenever this seemingly does take place, whenever [psychoanalysis] becomes fashion, either there is not actual analysis or else [psychoanalysis] is misinterpreted and, according to some intentions alien to it, misused for the needs of the day.
>
> [Psychoanalysis], then, is not a kind of knowledge, which one could acquire directly like vocational and technical expertise, and which, like economic and professional knowledge in general, one could apply directly and evaluate according to its usefulness in each case.
>
> But what is useless [...] what is untimely [...] will have its own times. This holds for [psychoanalysis]. Therefore we cannot determine what the task of [psychoanalysis] is in itself and in general is, and what must accordingly be demanded of [psychoanalysis]. Every stage and every inception of its unfolding carries within it its own law. One can only say what [psychoanalysis] cannot be and what it cannot achieve. (2000, p. 9)

In approaching psychoanalysis, via Heidegger in this way, I am not suggesting that the theory of psychoanalysis is a philosophy, rather, that philosophy might furnish the theory of psychoanalysis in some way, although the question remains as to what extent this might be possible. Curiously, when we apply Heidegger's words to the situation of psychoanalysis today they seem surprisingly apposite. In 1967, on the rare occasion of acknowledging Heidegger's influence upon his work Lacan stated that:

> "In language man dwells". What Heidegger meant by that is not what I am going to talk to you about this evening, but, as you can

see, I have to sweep up in front of the monument. "In language
man dwells" […] even when it's extracted from Heidegger's text,
it speaks for itself. It means that language was there before man, and
this is obvious. Not only is man born into language in precisely the
way he is born into the world; he is born through language. (2008a,
p. 27)

Although the development of Lacan's work did not continue in the
same direction as Heidegger's, the mark of a definite influence is apparent in Lacan's earlier seminars. The following is taken from a public
lecture he delivered in 1958:

This passion of the signifier now becomes a new dimension of the
human condition in that it is not only man who speaks, but that in
man and through man *it speaks* [*ça parle*], that his nature is woven by
effects in which is to be found the structure of language, of which
he becomes the material, and that therefore there resounds in him,
beyond what could be conceived of by a psychology of ideas, the
relation of speech. (2005, p. 217)

Lacan's *ça parle* is an axiom, which as such, invites interpretation and
at one and the same time refuses a definitive answer. The "it speaks"
is indicative of a jouissance, which confers on the speaking being who
dwells in language something more than the mere repetition and contingency of a discourse imposed upon him. In the returns of speech,
a speaking that implicates the analysand as complicit in his suffering
and affected by it, lies the potential for an encounter, which at the limits
of this discourse, yields a surplus. The way that Lacan works *ça parle* as
an axiom of psychoanalysis converges upon a fragment of jouissance:
the force of a remainder that insists as singular.
    In his seminar on transference, Lacan proposed that the psychoana-
lyst is capable of bearing what is imposed upon him in the transference. Thus, if he carries a knowledge at all, it is to do with the strange
logic of a love, in which the analysand supposes in him precisely what
he does not want to know and cannot access rationally or relationally
speak of. What distinguishes a psychoanalysis is that the analyst recognises this love as the proxy and device of an unknown knowledge.
The analysand who submits to the fundamental rule of free association articulates more than he knows in an erotics of speech, which in

sur-passing ordinary parlance and categorisations of sense, does not abdicate the unspeakable to silence. When faced with a demand for knowledge concerning his method, from a public outside the delimited field of his consulting room, an analyst might conclude that is safer to say nothing, and thus, to lapse into silence. Alternatively, he might resort to the promise of a cure guaranteed by the touting of credentials and professional affiliations. Neither of these responses can be considered consistent with psychoanalysis properly speaking.

In 1967, Lacan addressed a different lay audience:

> Is psychoanalysis purely and simply a therapy, a drug, a plaster, a magical cure or indeed something that can ever be described as a cure? At first sight, why not? The only problem is that it is certainly not what psychoanalysis is; of all plasters, this is one of the most fastidious to have to put up with. Despite that, if people do commit themselves to this hellish business of coming to see a guy three times a week for years, it must be because it is of some *interest in itself*. Using words you do not understand, such as "transference", does not explain why it lasts. (2008, p. 12f)

If Lacan's grammar veers towards the negative here (i.e., "certainly not what psychoanalysis is"), this "not what it is", is nevertheless supplemented by reference to an *"interest in itself*. The object of the transference is implicated here, as an interest yielding a return, which in this case, is the return of the analysand to the sessions with his complaint and the insistence of its remainder—his irreconcilable, implacable, singular relation to jouissance. In the supposition of the analysand, in the erotics of the discourse that he addresses to the psychoanalyst, the jouissance that has the measure of his suffering exceeds itself.

Throughout his seminars Lacan employed the terms "love", "transference", and "supposition" interchangeably. According to Jean Allouch, these references to love were fragmented, inconsistent, and did not aggregate into a theory of love (2007). He proposes that Lacan's approaches to love were variations, in which the fallacy of *speaking about love* was strategically avoided. For to speak about love is a fallacy in that it can only approximate love, *referencing what it is not* and thereby diminishing it. We have encountered the same antinomy of reason at play in speaking about silence and speaking about psychoanalysis. Thus, as distinct from speaking about love or psychoanalysis, Allouch attests to the necessity of abiding by one's idiocy (one's mother tongue), namely, abiding by the necessity of *speaking psychoanalysis,* noting that the Greek term *idios* refers to the singular—that which belongs only to each thing (ibid.). This *idios,* funded by a surplus of jouissance, is exemplary of a love speaking in its own name. If psychoanalysis can speak for itself, it is recognisable here in the nominating of an excess, which funds language with its élan vital. What is transmitted via the *ca parle* of psychoanalysis distinguishes itself as a way of speaking that traverses the silent reaches and transcendent heights of discourse stripped of its erotic intensities. In this regard, psychoanalysis takes its departure from philosophy and particularly from the silence to which Wittgenstein resigned himself at the frontier of the unspeakable in 1918.

To enter into an analysis is to enter into the fray of the word; words that are never exhausted; words that burn into the tongue and etch into the walls of the consulting room. Lacan was one who addressed himself to walls: the walls of the asylum, the wall of language, and the impossibility of saying it all.[2] To enter into an analysis is to encounter that wall, via the awkward necessity of an obnoxious chatter. It is to forgo the consolations of knowledge and the rattling teeth of cadaverous doctrine—to experience the plaintive echo and cutting call, the froth, the seduction, and violence of the spoken word. To enter into an analysis is to tarry with the question of "who speaks?" and "to whom?" It is to risk the consequences of associative speech, tremulous speech, desperate speech, raw speech—the whirlwind and disorientation of the otherness of language. To enter into an analysis is to risk encountering, in the articulations of one's suffering, the returns of that speech. It is to encounter where one is implicated in the urgency of an address, gutted of mastery and sense. This goes further than articulating any doctrine of psychoanalysis insofar as the *interest in itself* of psychoanalysis returns to the necessity of breaking silence.

Notes

1. Lacan's reference is to a joke recounted by Freud in *Jokes and Their Relation to the Unconscious*: One Jew asks another, "Why are you telling me, 'I am going to Lemberg' unless—since I know you are already going there—you want me to think that you are going to Cracow?". See *The Four Fundamentals of Psychoanalysis The Seminar of Jacques Lacan.*

XI. A. Sheridan (Trans.). J. A. Miller (Ed.). New York: W. W. Norton. p. 139.
2. Pivotal to this address was Lacan's reference to a poem by Petronius Arbiter in *The Satyricon*, see, "The function and field of speech and language in psychoanalysis" (1953). In: *Ecrits*. A. Sheridan (Trans.). 1977. London: W. W. Norton. p. 77.

CHAPTER SEVEN

Anaesthesia

David Pereira

L et me begin with the clear proposition that psychoanalysis most particularly differentiates itself from the field of medicine and psychiatry in locating itself within an aesthetic field. Before proceeding I will need to define, for my purposes, what I am referring to as a field of aesthetics. Firstly, you will notice that my claim is that it is "an" aesthetic field, not "the" aesthetic field; not simply for the purposes of maintaining the obvious equivocation between aesthetics and anaesthetics. The reason will become more obvious as we proceed, but at the outset I want to be clear that the relation with aesthetics within which I want to implicate psychoanalysis is not one in which it conventionally and recurrently becomes ensnared; a contribution of psychoanalysis to aesthetics within which analysis and interpretation is proffered concerning artists' motivations or the creative impulse as such, or upon works of art as products of sublimated sexual drives, much as Freud, to use Lacan's judgement, grotesquely engages in at times. Freud's views concerning aesthetics, in this regard at least, join with a dominant current of thought which found clear expression in Schopenhauer's argument, naïve in its idealism, that aesthetics has the function of disarming a certain excess or surplus of sexual interest and desire.

Neither, in situating psychoanalysis within the field of aesthetics, do I want to be detained by matters of taste, and judgements concerning the beautiful. Lacan's analysis on this subject gives impetus to mine only insofar as it allows us to situate aesthetics as already further advanced than ethics and the good along the path of desire and its barrier to jouissance. There is sufficient funding for my argument in Lacan's observation that the field of the beautiful is never far from judgments of pain and pleasure; the parameters which are of greatest value to the argument I will endeavour to develop.

The entry point into this field of aesthetics then, as my title forewarns, is anaesthesia—an indispensable medical device. In "Sexuality in the aetiology of the neuroses" Freud introduces the question of anaesthesia in attempting to draw a corollary between medical investigations, and sensitivities around taking a sexual history in psychoanalysis. He notes there that:

> It is not true that interrogation of his patients and knowledge about sexual concerns give the physician a dangerous degree of power over them. It was possible in earlier times for the same objection to be made against the use of anaesthetics, which deprive the patient of his consciousness and the exercise of his will and leave it to the doctor to decide whether and when he shall regain them. And yet today anaesthetics have become indispensable to us because they are able, better than anything else, to assist the doctor in his medical work; and among his many other serious obligations, he has taken over responsibility for their use. (1898a, pp. 264–265)

Important for my argument in this juxtaposition, is that anaesthesia becomes that which weds the practice of psychoanalysis to the physician's duty—to the ethical practice of medicine. The taking of a sexual history becomes medicalised, numbed, neutered; in effect anaesthetised. This is also the function which Freud tends to accord to aesthetics—a pacification which maintains an essentially anaesthetic function. Such is clear in "The Claims of psychoanalysis to scientific interest" where Freud refers to sublimation as the fulfilment of wishful phantasies under the transforming work which "softens what is offensive in them [...]" (1913j, p. 187).

In Freud's earlier observations concerning hysteria however, we find the possibility of further opening our interrogation of anaesthesia.

In these early observations anaesthesia, and more often than not hemi-anaesthesia, forms one of the hysterical stigmata through which this neurosis was able to be recognised and confirmed. The stigmata comprise convulsive attacks, hysterogenic zones—what Freud describes as "supersensitive areas of the body" (1888d, p. 43) and "disturbances of sensibility" (ibid.).

These "disturbances of sensibility"—which for our purposes we might call aesthetic disturbances—consist, for Freud, in *anaesthesia* or *hyperaesthesia*. Herein lays the interest of hysteria to us with regard to the phenomenon of aesthetics as delimited between the parameters of anaesthetics and hyper-aesthetics. The hysterical symptom is both an anaesthetic and a hyperaesthetic device.

It is worth considering Freud's argument more closely here. On the one hand we find the hysterical symptom, in its anaesthetic aspect, is configured as a prophylactic response to the threat of a certain excess of stimulation. Freud contends, for example that a woman who is impotent, that is, really anaesthetic, is not as susceptible to anxiety neurosis as a sensitive woman, inasmuch as she has a remarkable tolerance for the excesses of stimulation" (1895b, p. 102).

Freud also notes, however, in a somewhat contradictory fashion that young women who have remained anaesthetic during their first sexual experiences are more prone to anxiety neurosis, which resolves upon the anaesthesia giving way to what he refers to as "normal sensitivity" (ibid., pp. 99–100).

On the one hand therefore, the anaesthetic aspect of the symptom takes up the duty of the doctor; it is medicinal, though not necessarily curative. The doctoring of the symptom carries its anaesthetic function as a retreat from excessive excitement and sensation. Such a retreat occurs in line with the pleasure principle, which on this occasion is in line with the medical principle as it informs the duty of the doctor.

The curative, on the other hand, may be understood to proceed in the reverse direction; in the direction of the restoration of sensibility and sensitivity, even if it labours under the limit of "normal sensitivity." Beyond the limit of "normal sensitivity" governed and limited by the pleasure principle, the medical principle, is the other pole of aesthetics in hysteria, hyperaesthesia. In all instances, given the reciprocal relations between anaesthetic and hysterogenic zones, anaesthesia may be replaced by hyperaesthesia producing an "extraordinary refinement" Freud writes, "of sensory activity" (1888d, pp. 44–45). "Normal sensitivity" has been supplanted here by "extraordinary refinement of sensory activity". The hysterical symptom, therefore, embodies a division with respect to aesthetics. On the one hand, the numbed hand, it is an anaesthetic device. On the other hand, the one prepared to engage with the excess, we find it to be a hyper-aesthetic device.

This same interplay is seen in another of Freud's preoccupations around the time of his investigations on hysteria, his use of and experimentation with cocaine resulting in the publication of the monograph *Uber Coca* in 1884. What drew my attention to this work was a recent book by Howard Markel concerning the cocaine addictions of Freud and the American surgeon William Halstead in which he contends that:

> Freud had published an extensive review of cocaine's potential therapeutic uses. His central experimental subject was himself. But as impressive as his work was, Dr Freud neglected to describe cocaine's most practical application: it was a superb anaesthetic that completely numbed a living being's sensation to the sharp blade of a scalpel.

He goes on to say that:

> Cocaine thrilled him in a manner that everyday life could not. He wrote romantic, often erotic letters to his fiancée, dreamed grandiose dreams of his future career, walked about the streets of Paris, visited museums and theatres, and attended sumptuous soirees— all under the influence. (2012, p. 6)

Now, the reference to "Dr. Freud" is striking here as Markel more often than not opts for the less formal "Sigmund" or more neutral "Freud". The use of "Dr." draws our attention once again to what is supposed to be involved in "doctoring"—the indispensability of anaesthesia, which Freud appears to have somewhat neglected in this case.

Markel is puzzled by this and asks himself why. He, justifiably I think, is unconvinced that it was Freud's haste to be the first to publish his discovery which led to an apparent oversight. What he concludes is the most probable explanation, which runs counter to the anaesthetic "doctoring" tendency, is that Freud was dominated by the "deliciously exhilarating effects of cocaine—the high rather than the physical numbness" (ibid., p. 84). Nonetheless, Markel regards Freud's sensorial hyper-aesthetic rather than numbing anaesthetic preoccupation as a "colossal mistake"; a colossal mistake, however, which clearly distances psychoanalysis with respect to the indispensable hallmark or medicine. The question which it now raises for us is what then is indispensable for psychoanalysis which no longer has access to the medical dispensary even though Freud at this stage, still held a key to a dispensary of sorts.

Freud's own views on the question of why he apparently neglected the anaesthetic properties of cocaine are indicated in the monograph itself where he writes that:

> To many doctors cocaine seemed destined to fill a gap in the medicinal resources of psychiatry, already known to have sufficient methods at its disposal to reduce the heightened excitement of nerve centres, but being aware of none, which would raise them from a state of reduced activity.

Later, in a lecture held at the Psychiatric Society on 5th March 1885, Freud once again affirms this position, asserting his interest in the intoxicating rather than anaesthetising properties of cocaine.

Although Freud eventually abandoned the use of cocaine around 1896, he retained, I would argue, an interest in a hyper-aesthetics afforded by intoxication. In a letter to Fliess of March 11th 1900, Freud writes that:

> After last summer's exhilaration, when in feverish activity I completed the dream [book], fool that I am, I was once again intoxicated with the hope that a step towards freedom and well-being had been taken. (1985, p. 403)

The medicinal had not obtained the better of Freud. The intoxicating effects of cocaine had not given way to anaesthesia but rather to a hyper-aesthetics of language and dreams; psychoanalysis operating under the influence of the intoxicating effect of language driven through the delirium of free association.

We strike here the possibility that whilst anaesthesia, by Freud's own word, is "indispensable" for medicine, then by the argument which I am prosecuting, intoxication is "indispensable" for psychoanalysis, which hence always operates under the influence.

Let us take our bearings at this point. We have identified two positions with respect to the field of aesthetics. The first is the position of anaesthesia; underwritten by the seriousness of an interpretation of aesthetics as a calmative which produces a suppression of the will. Occupying this place in the aesthetic field is the psychologist, the physician, the psychiatrist, and sometimes, why not, the psychoanalyst; any indeed who pledge aesthetics to a sublime morality, whose formula in this instance is an anaesthetic concoction.

The second position with respect to aesthetics is one which moves to a hyper-aesthetics and takes intoxication as its "indispensable" precondition. This is the position in which psychoanalysis is differentiated and distinguished, articulating itself as a hyper-aesthetics of tragedy. The tragic is at the forefront of our experience as analysts, Lacan contends, as a consequence of the fact that the good, the function of ethics, radically fails to sublimate, calm or anaesthetise an excess which gives rise to a jouissance involving us in the question of whether we want to be cured of what ails us (1992, p. 243).

In what sense, however, tragic? It is with Nietzsche that we find the clearest exposition of the intoxicating relationship between aesthetics and tragedy; ideas which are being formed and developed all the way from *The Birth of Tragedy* published in 1872 through to his last writings. The Nietzschean tragic, not unknown to Lacan, who rejects the Aristotelian cathartic purging of fear and pity, is not to be found on the side of the depressive, or of a subduing anaesthesia. "Tragedy does not teach resignation" (1968, p. 434), asserts Nietzsche.

Rather it is the figure of Dionysian man who, in establishing the indispensable precondition of aesthetics as intoxication, "overlooks no emotional sign, he has the instinct for understanding and sensing in the highest degree, just as he possesses the art of communication in the highest degree. He adopts every skin, every emotion: he is constantly transforming himself" (Nietzsche, 1998, p. 48). Nietzsche describes the experience of the intoxicated aesthetic state as follows:

> "The sensations of space and time are altered: tremendous distances are surveyed and, as it were, for the first time apprehended; the extension of vision over great masses and expanses; the refinement of the organs for the apprehension of much that is extremely small and fleeting [...] 'intelligent' *sensuality* [...]". (1968, p. 421)

We find here an anticipation of Freud's definition of hyper-aesthesis in hysteria as an "extraordinary refinement of sensory activity". Tragedy involves such a hyper-aesthetic state which invokes an always dissolving amalgam of pain-cum-pleasure in which our enjoyment is suffered and our suffering enjoyed. For Nietzsche, the origin of tragedy is to be found in this joy; a joy whose "indispensable" precondition, as we keep repeating, is a hyper-aesthetic intoxication. This is the experience of the tragic which is at the forefront of analysis.

Now, for Nietzsche, this aesthetic state is the "source of languages. This is where languages originate: the languages of tone as well as the languages of gestures and glances" (ibid., p. 428). The intoxicating influence of language comes closer and closer to sound itself, to the purest of aesthetic experiences, that of music. Do we not also hear in this the seed from which might grow the tree out of which will be born the fleshy fruit *lalangue*? But that will have to be for another time.

For the moment I will simply reiterate that it is in this passage from anaesthetics to the intoxicating hyper-aesthetics of language that psychoanalysis will differentiate itself from the net of other "psychs", with which it otherwise runs the risk of family resemblance, by constituting itself as a tragic experience. Tragedy, in Deleuze's commentary on Nietzsche, is "an aesthetic form of joy, not a medical phrase or a moral solution to pain, fear or pity". He draws from Nietzsche, brilliantly, a function which might be the best one could hope from an analyst, the function of the truly aesthetic listener, the one who leaves behind the anaesthetics of his "moral sublimations and medical purgings" (2006, p. 17).

PART II

FROM THE CLINIC

CHAPTER EIGHT

The discomfort of psychoanalysis

Madeline Andrews

"We ask what we are, gradually, addressing the problems we struggle with: how to be involved in things and participate in them without getting trapped in them."

—*Foucault*, 2007, p. 124

Upon reading these words of Michel Foucault, in his an essay entitled, *For an Ethics of Discomfort* (ibid.), I was reminded of the discomforts of psychoanalysis. In particular, I was reminded of the awkwardness of a situation that the psychoanalyst increasingly finds himself in nowadays, namely, when he is called upon (explicitly or implicitly) to service the demands of psychiatry. The psychoanalyst encounters such demands in his public practice, but also at its peripheries in private practice. Presently, a culture of productivity saturated with commodities surrounds his practice, but the desire of the psychoanalyst has no correspondence whatsoever with the desire for products. When the discourse of the psychoanalyst has the effect of unfettering desire from these very chains of production, which extend and reproduce it under new names, it is sometimes reviled for the discomfort this produces in those habituated to avoiding discomfort.

For the psychoanalyst, the question of what we are is registered through a listening, tied to the object of the analysand's address, which as cause of his desire brooks neither exchange nor displacement. "What we are" in psychoanalysis manifests as the supposition of a cause, whenever an analysand addresses the question of what he is, to a psychoanalyst. In the desiring productions of free associative speech that an analysis produces, the intimacies of a way of speaking capable of abandoning itself, loosed from the comforting balustrades of economies of exchange, re-productions of rational sense and self-recognition take effect. The psychoanalyst in procuring this effect, bears witness to the symptom that desiring speech produces, intervening in the transference to place it in the service of its greatest potential. As such, the discourse of psychoanalysis differs from the discourse of medical science, as the aspirations of the latter converge upon a conceptualisation of the symptom as the organic cause (of a disorder), which demands a formula for cure. Conversely, in psychoanalysis there is no formula, for the symptom of psychoanalysis is apprehended as an effect of language, which the treatment intensifies rather than cures. In the absence of a cure—in the absence of any possible cure for desire, a psychoanalysis procures from the desiring productions of speech, a residue of jouissance that falls outside this economy.

At the interface of psychiatry and psychoanalysis there is often a patient—a patient confronted with the task of navigating two discrete discourses, namely, one that prescribes and one that does not. Whenever a doctor, his standard prescriptions having fallen short of their aim, prescribes for his patient a psychoanalysis, he assumes his patient will be capable of traversing the unbridgeable gap between medical science and psychoanalysis. The demands of the doctor, the demands of the state, the demands of a patient who identifies as sick, are frequently brought to the psychoanalyst's consulting room upon a raft of misguided assumptions. For at the limits of scientific know-how, the psychoanalyst is frequently misapprehended as an alternative therapist who is expected nonetheless, to function as an extension of the status quo in sympathy with the aspirations of medicine and psychology.

A man comes to see me. He tells me he has no investment in living and that years of previous treatment have failed him. He says he wants to die, but against his will, something is keeping him alive. The sessions are at a preliminary stage and his anxiety is at a pitch. He expresses strong reservations about speaking with me. After doing so for a time, he lets me know that he shared his misgivings with his referring physician. She advised that he ask me for strategies. I continue to invite him to speak. Dissatisfied, he reiterates a complaint, oft repeated, and tied to a rigid set of beliefs associated with a long and fraught conflict with institutions. He wants me to be answerable to this. Whilst acknowledging that his dogged pursuit of a cause associated with this conflict has exacerbated his suffering for years, he insists that he cannot relinquish it. As he begins to hear in the articulation of this demand, the shackling of his desire to an impossible place, it precipitates a crisis.

At this point, his physician contacted me. Noting that since the referral her patient had ceased calling her between appointments, she urged me to continue. However, before ending the call she added a rejoinder—an imperative statement veiling a demand that I practice something other than psychoanalysis in response to her patient's discomfort, namely, a prescription bearing the false promise of a cure. Her appeal was that I mitigate any risk, even to the extent of dumbing down the risk of the symptom speaking. Here is an example of medicine calling upon psychoanalysis to provide something it cannot.

There was once a time-honoured line held between the doctor and the psychoanalyst, historically respected and held intact. This tacit divide was based on an agreement that whereas the doctor prescribed, the psychoanalyst did not. In recent times, a consortium of psychiatrists and psychologists, in making themselves the emissaries of a new trend, recruited one another to collaboratively servicing and promoting a strictly prescriptive form of therapeutics. Under the auspices of this unprecedented handshake, pharmacotherapy and "strategic psychological interventions" were paired off, extensively researched, and promoted as the combined treatment of choice for almost every form of human malaise. As is now well known, funding and regulatory bodies motivated to preference practices promising quick, measurable, outcomes have since enthusiastically endorsed this formula. Consequently, non-prescriptive practices have increasingly fallen into disrepute in the estimation of these agencies under suspicion of a failure to produce evidence.

Yet in the midst of such change, the open-ended, explorative drift of a mode of inquiry traditionally germane to the hypothetically determined sciences, seemed to abruptly turn a corner, charging headlong into the straights of a commodity driven industry. A plethora of standardised, didactically administered treatments promising "consumers" quick symptom relief now floods a field more recognisable today as a market than a profession. Manualised treatments misrepresented as psychoanalytic form part of this fast track servicing philosophy. Thus, a set of new expectations surrounds the psychoanalyst who has always worked alongside, but never in conformity with, prescriptive practices. We cannot eschew the fact that under the ruse of requests for psychoanalysis, demands for therapeutic responsiveness are often relayed to the analyst's consulting room. Nor the fact that negative transference and the difficulties associated with it readily seize upon such expectations, which must be disappointed from the outset.

The recent enthusiasm for prescriptive therapeutics extends from a revived emphasis on the concept of "mental man", which reached its nadir under the influence of Descartes' philosophy in the seventeenth century. In his early seminars, Lacan critically appraised this ontology and particularly, the influence of its vestiges upon psychiatry and post Freudian psychoanalysis. The conceptualisation of man as a universal subject pitted against his objects forms part of this philosophical legacy. Descartes' *cogito,* acknowledged by Lacan as a pivotal moment in the history of philosophy and science, established the ontological subject as a less god-fearing and more clandestinely religious being—his truth bearing belief having slipped under the veil of the indubitable evidence of his ideas. The Cartesian subject of doubt thus obtains his certainty in a solipsism, in which an irreconcilable difference is shunted into the synthetic holding bay of a disembodied ideal. It is this Cartesian subject of certainty that the Freudian unconscious subverted. The psychoanalyst, in bearing witness to the effects of speech directly on the body, the body as penetrated, carved up, and intensified by language, encounters a body that has no correspondence to the medicalised body. Freud deciphered these effects in the symptoms of his hysterical patients, which exceeded the threshold of the pleasure principle (a libidinal economy of minimum displeasure).

In the 1980s, Michel Foucault contrasted the structure of Cartesian truth-production, with a different modality of truth (i.e., *techne*) privileged by the pre-Socratic Greeks.[1] The following is taken from a lecture given by Foucault in Berkeley in 1983:

> It would be interesting to compare Greek parrhesia with the modern (Cartesian) conception of evidence. For since Descartes the coincidence between belief and truth is obtained in a certain

> (mental) evidential experience. For the Greeks, however, truth does not take place in a (mental) experience but in a *verbal activity* namely, *parrhesia*. It appears that *parrhesia* in this Greek sense can no longer occur in our modern epistemological, framework … If there is a kind of "proof" of the sincerity of the *parrhesiastes*, it is his courage. The fact that the speaker says something dangerous— different from what the majority believes—is a strong indication that he is a *parrhesiastes*. (2001, p. 112)

Parrhesia, (translated from Foucault's French rendering of the Greek term as "true speech" and "free speech"), refers to a verbal encounter in which the truth of the speaker is put to the test. For example, the *parrhesia* of Socrates entailed the game of eliciting a truth from the unwitting mouth of his interlocutor (i.e., lover, Sophist, slave), whereas for the Cynics, *parrhesia* was a scandalous affair, in which the *parrhesiastes* was expected to expose himself to enormous risk. In addressing a king with an unpalatable truth, for example, the *parrhesiastes* undertook the risk of arousing the ire of a despot and being condemned to death. Diogenes is said to have taken this risk in addressing Alexander the Great.[2]

Lacan proposed that the neurotic takes flight from the truth of his desire, perpetually deferring the risk of an encounter with what is inadmissible to consciousness. The pursuit of the truth of "mental man", reflected in a renewed cultural preoccupation with sense data, cognitions, and rational norms does not countenance an end to this flight. In *The History of Sexuality*, Foucault writes of a "new way of philosophising: seeking a fundamental relation to the true […] in the self examination that yields through a multitude of fleeting impressions, the basic certainties of consciousness" (1990, pp. 59–60). Some neuroscientists are presently pursuing these certainties with renewed vigour.

The discourse of the psychoanalyst does not yield this type of self-examination, but rather, a way of speaking, which at the limits of the desire for self-recognition, veers towards a form of self-dismemberment (dis-identification). Lacan unequivocally speaks to the distinction between self-conscious psychology and psychoanalysis in his seminar of 1965:

> Our starting point, our given, which is not at all a closed given, is the subject who speaks. What analysis contributes is that the subject does not speak in order to tell his thoughts. There is no world,

the intentional, the significant reflection at whatever level it may be—this grotesque, infatuated personage who is supposed to be at the centre of the world, predestined for all eternity to give it its essence and reflection. (1964–1965)

The contemporary "psy" clinic with its associated technologies attends to silent bodies that cogitate and self-report, but which say nothing of that which escapes this cartography. Here, the suffering of the affected body is apprehended as an unregulated system of excitations and if this extends to the patient's erotic life, as a functional or moral dilemma. In the absence of risky speech, those excesses of the body that resist therapeutic regulation frequently return to the psychiatric clinic in the form of an hysterical risk. As such, the imaginary body-at-risk strives to claim its symbolic pound of flesh in disarticulated acts of self-starvation, mutilations of the flesh and suicidal gestures. It is in response to these urgencies that the psychiatrist is called upon to assess, monitor and control a different type of risk and if need be, by invoking statutory law.

The psychoanalyst, however, has no such recourse in the face of the risk he undertakes in exposing himself to the force of these excesses in the transference. In Lacan's 1960, *Discourse to Catholics*, the psychoanalytic body is *tête-à-tête*, not with cognitions, but with the effects of language on the body:

> The subject fades but does not end—beneath the signifying structure. Indeed, what intention shows is that this structure is already there before the subject begins to speak and makes himself into the bearer through speech of any truth whatsoever, before he lays claim to any recognition whatsoever. The Thing is thus that which—in any living being that discourse comes to inhabit and that offers itself up in speech—marks the place where he suffers from the fact that language manifests itself in the world. In this way, being appears everywhere that the Eros of life encounters the limits of its unitive impulse [*tendance*]. This impulse toward union is, in Freud's work, at an organismic or biological level, as they say. Nevertheless, it has nothing to do with what is apprehended by biology, the newest of the physical sciences. It is a mode of eroticized capturing of the body's principle orifices. (2013, pp. 41–42)

One of these orifices to which Lacan refers is the mouth, but in the mouthing off of interminable sense data, preconscious thoughts, and repertoires of sexual sense, the symptom's singular relation to the body speaks poorly if at all. The therapeutic prescription presupposes the symptom as a reportable cluster of measurable bio/psycho/social dysfunctions, which can be classified and regulated. In adhering to the conceptual armoury of the evidence base and its standard bearer the outcome measure, the therapeutic prescription conforms to a sliding scale of mental health, which valorises the ideal of the happy, healthy, normal individual. This bracketing out of the effects of language upon the body distinguishes the symptom of psychological medicine as ideationally circumscribed and foreign to the symptom of psychoanalysis.

The recent roll out of new government guidelines and funding arrangements in Australia was introduced against the background of a tide of publicity concerned with unprecedented rates of mental illness. The best intentions of this scheme (aimed at increased treatment access and efficacy) were bolstered by new developments in biotechnology, a platform of associated research findings and new knowledge claims promoted by neuroscientists, neuropsychologists, and cognitive scientists.[3] These studies produce an imaginary mapping of the body— the body scanned, measured, and graphed, as surpluses and deficits of intensity. Images of the brain, synaptic systems, cellular reactions, and genetic code, statistically analysed and hypothetically linked to inventories of behaviour, are in turn being utilized in the generation of more and more classifications of mental disorder. This diagnostic juggernaut would not have been possible however, without the allure and authority of the bell shaped curve and its gold standard truth bearer, the normal range. In addition, the myth of the normal individual, if measured and maintained in perpetuity, produces a steady surplus of supply (codes of abnormality) and with its corresponding coefficient of unserviceable demand, a perceived need for more treatment. When placed on the conceptual grid of the signifying binaries: abnormal/normal; ordered/disordered, mental health research statistics can be very generative.

The following quote is taken from Georges Canguilhem's 1943 essay, "On some problems concerning the normal and the pathological":

> The impetus behind every ontological theory of disease undoubtedly derives from therapeutic need. When we see in every sick man someone whose being has been augmented or diminished, we are somewhat reassured, for what a man has lost can be restored

to him, and what has entered him can also leave. We can hope to conquer disease even if it is the result of a spell, or magic, or possession; we have only to remember disease happens to man in order not to lose all hope. Magic brings to drugs and incantation rites innumerable resources for generating a profoundly intense desire for cure. (1991, p. 19)

In the 1940's, Canguilhem developed an innovative method of critiquing the philosophy of science, which departed from traditional approaches to historical research. His genealogical method introduced a particular way of mapping the formation of scientific concepts and the dominance of particular concepts over others in the history of physiology. In Canguilhem's work, the scientific concept emerges from a flux of discursive accidents, errors, and disjunctions intercepting with cross currents of cultural and political forces. In his "Essay on some problems concerning the normal and the pathological", Canguilhem examines nineteenth century attitudes to the theory and treatment of disease. Central to this work is his study of the invention and codification of the concept of the "normal state" in the history of physiology.

When Canguilhem's work is revisited in the context of recent times, a striking parallel can be seen between events that influenced the conceptualisation of pathology in nineteenth century physiology and twentieth century psychiatry. Under the influence of Canguilhem, Foucault pursued a genealogical analysis of the latter. During the periods mentioned here, the concept of the normal has been zealously applied and notably, this has occurred against a background of revived enthusiasm for therapeutics, broad applications of new biotechnologies, a renewed emphasis upon research, and the privileging of evidence-based practice over practice-based experience. In the 1900s, the theory of the lesion came into prominence under such conditions, and according to Canguilhem, radically altered the conceptualisation of disease in the discourse of medicine.

Canguilhem argues that the modernisation of the microscope, in making it possible for pathology to be newly perceived as an *observable phenomenon* in a cell, produced a radical shift in the discourse. At the time, earlier perceptions of disease as a structure of signs indicating disequilibrium in systems of the body, were side-lined by a theory of the symptom, which localised pathology at the level of the cell (trauma in a cell) and thus, redefining the symptom as the cause of disease.

Pathology was now attributed to a paucity or excess of excitement in a tissue. Canguilhem notes that to accommodate the new theory, a sliding scale of measurement (the hyper/hypo scale) had to be introduced, which displaced the standard fixed-point scale of measurement and that for the new scale to function, an ideal state of tension needed to be defined. For this purpose a *mythical benchmark was arbitrarily selected and nominated as the "the normal state"*, obtaining its corroborating measure of proof in the recently established and celebrated statistical methods of the day (based on the distribution of *the normal curve*).

As such, the concept of the pathological was pitted against the normal, then eclipsed in the signifying binary, normal/pathological in the administration of the ideal body (rid of abnormalities). The pathological as a distinct conceptual entity was thus displaced by the concept of the abnormal state. The inheritance of this signifying binary can be seen in contemporary psychiatric nosologies (spectrums of disorder) and popular psychological tests (sliding scale questionnaires) in which phenomena are identical save for quantitative variations. Canguilhem outlines this as the effect of a binary signifying series plugging back into itself to become a circuit:

> Every conception of pathology is based on prior knowledge of the corresponding normal state, but conversely, the scientific study of pathological cases is an indispensable phase in the overall search for the laws of the normal state. (1991, p. 51)

Now Canguilhem, before Foucault, also looked to the Greeks for a point of comparison, finding in Hippocratic medicine a different approach to pathology. During the early Hellenic period, he notes, disease was understood dynamically in terms of a disturbance to the fluidity of the humours of the body. Canguilhem writes:

> In this case, disease is not somewhere in man, it is everywhere in him [...] external causes are the occasions but not the causes.

Further noting that for the Greeks,

> Disease is not simply disequilibrium or discordance, it is, and perhaps most importantly, an effort on the part of nature to effect a new equilibrium in man. Disease is a generalised reaction designed

> to bring about a cure; the organism develops a disease in order to
> get well. Therapy must tolerate and if necessary, reinforce these
> hedonic and spontaneously therapeutic reactions. (1991, pp. 40–41)

When I read this passage, I was immediately reminded of Freud's reference to the "negative therapeutic reaction" in his 1923 paper, *The Ego and the Id* (1923b). Freud refers to an inverse reaction, observable in many of his patients, namely, a "resistance to recovery". Freud attributes the negative therapeutic reaction to unconscious guilt, but since Lacan, we might think of this reaction in a less morally stricken way, as an effect of the affected body's resistance to interpretation. The resistance to cure might be thought of as a hedonic and spontaneous articulation of that aspect of the symptom specific to psychoanalysis. The psychoanalyst's response to resistance embodies his attitude to therapeutics for he knows that he must tolerate his patient's hedonic and spontaneous reactions. Via the exigencies of speech, the work of an analysis is a form of procurement, which differently to cure, places the symptom in the service of the treatment. This is not so much a work of restoring equilibrium, but a method of propagating the risk of a true speech act, which does not defer in desire to what is inadmissible to consciousness. What I am proposing is that the psychoanalyst's procurement of the symptom (as a spontaneous rather than dysregulated intensity) is far more in keeping with one of the treatment principles of classical Hippocratic medicine, than those of the paradigmatic psychiatric cure.

In 1943 Canguilhem observes that medical thought:

> Has never stopped alternating between two representations of
> disease—between two types of optimism—always finding some
> good reason for one or the other attitude in a newly explained
> pathogenesis". (1991, p. 41)

These oscillating optimisms to which Canguilhem refers, I shall crudely attempt to summarise in brief. The first is an attempt to normalise the pathological and the second, to imitate it as a natural reaction. Canguilhem qualifies the mimetic aspect of the latter Hellenic approach in terms of an action that is, "not to merely copy an appearance, but to mimic a tendency and to extend an intimate movement" (ibid.). Now the psychoanalyst, might be thought of as a mimetic artisan of sorts, for in lending himself in the transference to the mythical benchmarks of the analysand's being, he or she participates in a type of deception, which supports the possibility of speaking from an other place, which abandons them.

Conversely, the symptom of the "mental man" of capital is highly commodifiable and poised for the comfort of promises. In order to be, however, the subject of the cogito has to have—he has to have more and more knowledge to temper his dis-ease. The evidence base offers him constant supply; an epistemological chain of production that requires more and more research to shore up the surplus of doubt it produces, and more and more consumers to service its aims. When the disturbance of an other scene makes itself felt—in the anomalies of mental man's dreams, blunders, and the strange irregularities of his erotic life, something falls outside of this economy of exchange. Nevertheless, with his disposable capital, mental man can acquire more commodities, more identities, and more vital signs of happiness to shore up his doubt. If it continues to disassemble, he can always turn to a steady stream of opinion polls, satisfaction surveys, personality tests, and rating scales to determine whether he is on the winning side and what he can do to alleviate his discomfort. His disorder can be classified. His intensities can be regulated. He can be spared the malaise of his angst.

Alternatively, he might find his way to a psychoanalyst's door without prescription in hand, quaking at the knees as he knocks. There, in the service of extending the most intimate movement of his suffering, beyond any presuppositions regarding what ails him, he might demand a difference. There, he might encounter in the invitation to speak, the anticipation, open ears, and presence, of a psychoanalyst.

Notes

1. Foucault defines the ancient Greek *techne* as a spiritual technique of the self. The significance of truthful practices changed over time but remained consistently inscribed in the socio-political milieu of the polis until 4 AD. See: Foucault, M. *Fearless Speech*. J. Pearson (Ed.). Los Angeles: Semiotext(e), 2001, p. 112.
2. Diogenes of Sinope (404–323 BC).
3. In 2006 a new COAG Action Plan on Mental Health was agreed to, and as part of this plan, the *Better Access to Psychiatrists, Psychologists and General Practitioners through the Medicare Benefits Scheme* was introduced towards addressing a perceived shortfall in affordable psychological

treatment services in Australia. See: Department of Health and Ageing (2007). *National Mental Health Report 2007: Summary of Twelve Years of Reform in Australia's Mental Health Services under the National Mental Health Strategy 1993–2005.* Canberra, Australia. Department of Human Services.

CHAPTER NINE

The wall of the body

Michael Gerard Plastow

Emma is an adolescent girl who dedicates her life to the Other, to keeping her mother alive for instance, since the mother threatens to kill herself if Emma leaves her. When asked what she can claim as her own, she replies that the only things that are hers are her tattoos. She shows me what she refers to as her first tattoo, the signature of her father on her wrist, a father who killed himself some years before. She tells me about her most recent tattoo. This girl, who has been unable to sustain her place in the educational system, has nonetheless recently read Freud's *Civilisation and its Discontents*. Subsequently she had the word *Eros* inscribed on her lower back. It seems that this writing and its reading is all the more necessary when the wall on which it is written is at risk of crumbling, when this shoreline does not function well, when it needs to be shored up, by the writing and reading of such letters of love.

Lucy, a young adult woman in analysis, recounts that she goes to visit her parents. Her father for the first time notices that she has a piercing in her tongue. She says: "My father freaked out." Silently he begins to beat his head against the veranda post. He does so until his head begins to bleed. If the piercing in the tongue is one sort of writing, a type that marks out a hole in the tongue, a hole in language, is the bloodstain as a response from the other's body another sort?

In analysis today we are presented with piercings, tattoos, cuttings, and markings as a private writing on the body. We are also aware of other contemporary related phenomena such as branding, scarification, stretchings, and other markings of the body wall. We can certainly add to these the socially sanctioned circumcisions that still take place. Whilst such writing on the body attempt, literally, to deal with the excess of sex, they fail in this endeavour. The multiplication of such writings and markings of the body do not put an end to one's suffering. But is there another sort of writing, a public writing, a letter on the post, or a mark on the wall, which we can discern? Here we will endeavour to answer this from psychoanalysis in which there can be an efficacious way to write something of this excess, by a movement from the private space, that of the body, to a public space.

The writing is on the wall

We are all familiar with tattoos on the knuckles of hands, on one hand the letters of the word "love", on the other those of the word "hate". Such writings are often inscribed on unsavoury characters. But it is the unsavoury character of each one of us that is evoked. All of us love and hate. Here we literally have writing on the wall of the body, different writings of love. Tattoos are often composed of letters, even letters of a foreign alphabet, characters devoid of meaning. Many converge on the holes of the body, whether it is the navel, the nether regions of the lower back, or the pubic area, which, despite the retraction of bikini lines and the display of underwear brands, continues to remain private. Even the wrist is a potential hole as it is always possible, in language, to slit one's wrists.

We encounter a different form of writing in the piercings. These often attempt to define one of the orifices of the body wall, those places where the borders of the body circumscribe the place of the object: thus there are piercings around the ear, the eye, the nose, the mouth, the nipple, the navel, the vagina, the penis, and the anus. These are also places of a certain ex-timacy, where the outside of the body is continuous and contiguous with the inside and vice-versa. These markings are attempts to inscribe the imaginary modalities of the object *a* on the wall of the body.

But our patients do not just write on the body. Some write on other walls with graffiti, marks that produce writings. Some place marks on the walls, marks that attempt to produce a naming, an identity, through the device of tags. What else do we find on the wall? There are many signs including those of advertising. On one side of the wall we find a private writing; on the Other side we find public notices.

Lacan also attempted to read what was written on the walls. In Baltimore he read the "Enjoy Coca-Cola" (1970, p. 194) of the superego. He reads on the walls, "Smoking Prohibited" which he characterises as "a tactical error," and "*Liberté—Égalité—Fraternité*" which he says is "indecent" (2008b, p. 70). In the protests of 1968 many political slogans appeared on the walls of Paris. Included in these were phrases such as "the walls can speak" [*les murs ont la parole*] or "let's be reasonable: let's ask for the impossible" [*soyons raisonable: demandons l'impossible*]. Lacan makes specific reference to such writings in *From an Other to the other*. "There," he says, "the relation to truth was evident. Truth was spread over the walls" (1968–1969, p. 37).

In the seminar *Of a Discourse that would not be of the Semblant*, Lacan also referred to *Civilisation and its Discontents*. Here he speaks of the marking of the body in initiation rituals:

> These […] rituals include […] let's call them manipulations, opera-
> tions, incisions, circumcisions that aim to and put their mark very
> precisely on the organ that we see functioning as symbol in that
> which, through analytic experience, is presented to us as going well
> beyond the privilege of the organ, since it is the phallus, and that
> the phallus, in so far as it is, to this third that is ordered, all that, in
> the end, is an impasse to jouissance. (1971, p. 64)

These marks, then, are the means by which castration is inscribed on the body and mark the impasse to jouissance and thus the barrier to the sexual relation. This impasse is, on the one hand, a limit to jouissance, a jouissance that at times threatens to overwhelm and engulf the sub-ject. At the same time the phallus also inscribes its own modality of jouissance, that of speech and signification.

In *The knowledge of the psychoanalyst*, Lacan hears himself saying "I am speaking to the chapel", that is, to the walls of the chapel in which he is speaking, beyond the participants of the seminar. He contends that he had "always spoken to the wall" (2008b, p. 47), addressing himself to the very structure of the chapel, to the structure and limits of speech and language. The walls are the place from which the voice, the sound of the voice, can resonate. This *reson*-ating evokes for Lacan the *raison* of reason, but also the *res*, the thing. And the voice is also resonating from the walls of Plato's cave, which in Lacan's hands become the walls of the mouth. This oral cavity now resonates with sounds that make up the voice, no longer the play of shadows, the negative images of Plato's cave. What resonates is the *res* of the voice as object *a*.

And if Lacan speaks of the voice resonating or repercussing off the wall, we can perhaps speak of other modalities of the object *a* in their collision with the wall. We have spoken of a letter of love written in blood. We might say that the letter on the Other side of the wall is written *in* the Other's body as we might say that something is written in ink.

And all that is written on the wall reinforces it. And what is written are letters (1972–1973, p. 92). Perhaps the wall is composed only of letters, letters being the concrete support of the signifier. The wall is thus a concrete wall. The wall here is one that is a barrier to the real, but on which is already written a letter of love, the letter *a*. One cannot speak of love but one can endeavour to write it. Love, *l'amour*, becomes here *l'(a)mur* (1971–1972, p. 58), the (*a*)wall. Love then is intimately associated with the wall.

A wall, generally, has a door, *adore*: I (*a*)door you. Lacan says: "I am going and once again I will write on the door"—the door of the bedroom in which he has placed us—he says:

> [...] the following sentence: "The jouissance of the Other [...] of the body of the other that symbolises It—is not the sign of love".
> (1972–1973, p. 13–14)

In the version of the seminar *Encore*, the one "established" by Miller, this is left as an apocryphal but definitive statement. This severely truncated and distorted rendering is, of course, faithfully repeated in Fink's translation. Strangely, though, in a footnote Fink speculates on the meaning of this phrase, without referring to the fact that the text here is deficient. But Lacan continues—and this elaboration of his statement is missing from the "official", or rather, officious, version. He proposes:

> It is not the sign and it is nonetheless the only response. What is complicated [...] is that the response is already given at the level of love. And that jouissance, by virtue of this fact, remains a question. A question in so far as the response that it can constitute is not necessary in the first place. It is not like love [...]. (1972–1973, p. 14)

Here there is a complication and a question that are both elided in the published version of the seminar. Love is necessary but jouissance is not, at least it cannot be circumscribed by the necessary.

Lacan notes that it is precisely this jouissance of the body, of the other's body, that he called *l'(a)mur*. He states:

> *L'(a)mur* is what appears in bizarre signs, on the body, and which comes from beyond, from the outside [...]. (1972–1973, p. 13–14)

The "outside" is something he says that we thought we would find through the microscope in the form of the *germen*, the germ cells evoked in Freud's *Beyond the Pleasure Principle*, as pertaining to the real of the body. Lacan notes that "the body carries the traces of this: there are traces on the (a)wall" (1972–1973, p. 15). These traces are the traces of life which are at the same time the traces of death.

One side and the Other

In our patients we can hear the accounts of the writings on the body as an attempt to inscribe a paternal function. We could put forward that the current prominence of these markings is an attempt to inscribe an order in the contemporary fashion of the failure of the name of the father. Such a mode, it seems, is left in the hands of the individual when social forms of the name of the father, both religious and secular, are in decline. Even circumcision is not what it used to be. And the name of the father, in any era, can only ever fail to apprehend the real. In other words these inscriptions, these love letters on the wall of the body, are rendered necessary as an attempt to domesticate the real precisely in the place where the signifier fails. And this real, such as emerges from the body, threatens to overwhelm us. There is a another jouissance that lurks.

And like in other initiation ceremonies, the marking of the body of our patients at times occurs when the subject is confronted by their sex, by an excess. There is a jouissance, a suffering of the body that threatens to spill over and in regard to which a cut or a mark must be made. Only writing can do what the signifier cannot. The mark endeavours to tame the excess, to place a limit on this real of the body. And in this encounter with an excess, the subject cannot come out unscathed.

If this first type of writing is the writing of a symptom by an attempt to locate the phallic signifier, there might be another type of writing that can occur in an analysis. This is a writing that might be read in the marks on the body of the Other, or those left on the wall. On one side of the wall there is the private writing of a symptom, an inscription of the phallic function. Such an inscription is necessary, necessary says Lacan, "in so far as it *does not cease to be written*". But this "necessary", he proposes, "is conjugated to the impossible, and this *does not cease to not be written*, is its articulation" (1972–1973, p. 108). And if on one side the inscription relates to the phallus, on the Other it pertains to the impossible writing of the signifier of the lack in the Other.

On the wall was written, "Let's be reasonable: let's ask for the impossible". On one side is the reasonable which is the side of meaning, of signification. But contained in this voice of reason is the reson-ating of the voice, the voice as object *a*. Here is a sound stripped of meaning, of signification, a groaning that no longer even pertains to the phoneme. Thus on the other side is the impossible to attain, the body of the mother, the *res* or *Das Ding*: a forbidden jouissance. Lacan asks:

> Is it that, on the other side, something cannot be attained which would tell us how, what up until now was only lack, gap in jouissance, would be realised? (1972–1973, p. 17)

If we are speaking of a writing that might be effected, an Other type of writing, it is indeed a strange type of writing. As we have said it is a writing of what does not cease to not be written. In other words it is a writing that fails, a writing that can never reach its term. This of course does not absolve us of the task of writing.

It is a writing, and indeed a reading, of letters, not of words or signifiers. In one way, for Lacan this writing was a writing of what is not necessary, what has no sense. It has only ab-sence, non-sense, or even in-de-cency. It is a writing of particular letters: a, S1, S2, $, S($). The wall then is also the surface of the writing of the mathemes, it is a topological surface. The Borromean knot is written on the wall. This is a public writing through which an unknown knowledge might be transmitted, a knowledge that has no signification.

In the *singular* analysis, the name of the father can be established. This name of the father is necessary for signification and private meanings. It proceeds by what is *said*. But, according to Lacan:

> That one is saying remains forgotten behind what is said in what is
> heard. (1973, p. 5)

Here the *saying* is an act that we can take as a type of writing, a writing
of the impossible: that which might irrupt in an analysis. That is, this
saying is able to leave a trace, a trace that might be transmitted. And it is
in this *saying* that a change of discourse can occur. Such a passage may
even mark the end of an analysis.

This *saying* is no longer of the field of signification. It is therefore by
the same token no longer in the field of the subject. There is no author
even if a subject might answer to it, to take responsibility for what can
be passed on, or transmitted, of an analysis. Here we can situate a passage from the private to the public. It is also here that we can locate
Lacan's comment that one can do without the name of the father "on
condition that one makes use of it" (1975–1976b, p. 55).

And one might make use of this passage in the *passe*, a *passe* that
attempts to transmit something that makes no sense *via* the voice and
via a writing, through a *saying*, through what might be heard from
this *saying*. The *passe* then is an attempt to overcome the impasse of
signification.

In this there is a movement from the private consulting room to the
wall of the public space. This is a passage of that which leaves a trace by
its failed attempt to be written. It is one thing to write the symptom. It
is another to attempt to produce a public writing or reading that might
put this symptom to use.

CHAPTER TEN

The gift of speech: beyond ambivalence

Sarah Jones Ferguson

To be heard or not to be heard

The patient is speaking, but I cannot hear his words. They mumble along inaudibly. I ask whether he might speak a little louder. He pays no heed. He pauses, then proffers again his very, softly uttered speech.

For a period of time in most of the patient's sessions the volume of his speech would similarly diminish. Infrequent requests that he speak louder remained unacknowledged. The content of these words ostensibly making as little effect as the content of his words, which I could not hear. What did impress itself was a disabling of the giving and receiving of speech. Yet at other times this patient spoke out audibly, and in moments was far from unmoved by something that I had said. His preference to periodically render impotent the reception of speech had the effect of evoking considerable ambivalence in the transference, which appeared specifically to respond to the potency of speech. What is it that could provoke this response to giving and receiving speech?

The experience of working with this patient initiated a study of speech in psychoanalysis, taken up in terms of the actions of giving and receiving. A broader question suggests itself in this regard: how might giving and receiving function in psychoanalysis? I approach the inquiry with reference to Mauss' influential essay first published in French in 1924, *The Gift: the Form and Reason for Exchange in Archaic Societies* (1990); Lacan's paper, "The function and field of speech and language in psychoanalysis" (1977a, p. 30–117) published in 1953; and Volume I, "Consumption" (1991a) of Bataille's three volume work *The Accursed Share,* the first volume of which he published in 1949; along with several references to Freud. Mauss' work and subsequent anthropological texts, such as those of Lévi-Strauss, were significant for Bataille and Lacan, as is evident in the two texts I discuss here. Lacan's paper and volume one of *The Accursed Share* were published within several years of one another and both address the notion of the gift, which suggests that taking up the import of Mauss' essay was prevalent at the time. These texts remain relevant, as they bear upon the current question that arose in the work with my patient who presented with such remarkable ambivalence over giving and receiving speech in his psychoanalysis.

The gift

Mauss' essay, *The Gift,* contests the theory that exchanges of goods in archaic and some extant societies occur for the purposes of barter: that is, to supply for the practical needs of each group. Rather, the significant act in social exchange is to give. Mauss discusses how social structures on every level are constituted by giving and receiving gifts, referring to this as a "system of total services" (1990, p. 5–6). This system creates and perpetuates the legal, governing, economic, social, and moral functions of a society. Alliances between people and groups, marriages and rank in social relationships are all instituted through giving gifts. Mauss writes:

> Such exchanges are acts of politeness: banquets, rituals, military services, women, children, dances, festivals, and fairs, in which economic transaction is only one element, and in which the passing on of wealth is only one feature of a much more general and enduring contract. (Ibid., p. 5)

Stressing the obligation that accompanies giving and receiving, Mauss notes that it is not simply that receiving obligates a recipient to give a return gift: people must give and they must receive (ibid., p. 13). He considers that despite modern forms of contract, sale and money, the more hidden morality of the gift endures as a foundation of human society.

The term "potlatch" is derived from the meanings, "to feed" and "to consume". It has come to refer to the purely sumptuary destruction of wealth, often in the expression of hostile rivalry with another of similar status (ibid., p. 6). Acts of destruction at the potlatch are often sacrificial, with the aim of giving to the gods or spirits. Quoting Brown, Mauss notes:

> [...] nobody is free to refuse the present that is offered. Everyone, men and women, tries to outdo one another in generosity. A kind of rivalry existed to see who could give the greatest number of objects of the greatest value. (Ibid., p. 19)

Mauss discusses extreme and moderate forms of potlatch: the former expresses an intense, agonistic attitude, while in the latter those who are entering a contract might seek to outdo one another in their gifts.

The magical force in every creature along with his honour is connoted by the Polynesian term, *mana*, which has been translated as "authority" or "wealth" (ibid., p. 38). *Mana* also refers to the force of things: a force contributed to by the assumption that in giving something a part of the giver himself is incorporated in the thing. Mauss discusses how *mana* acts as the imperative that a thing received will be given to another. Since the gift possesses part of the giver, receiving it is to accept part of his nature, substance, and spiritual essence (ibid., p. 12). Thus one must give back to another person what is part of him: the gift must be passed around or circulated. According to Mauss "to retain that thing would be dangerous and mortal" (ibid., p. 12). Thus the guarantee that gifts will be reciprocated lies both in honour, the pledging of one's name, and in the nature of the thing given.

We also find in Freud the notion of giving a part of oneself with the gift. At a certain point the child is obliged by the mother to produce his faeces, and these are construed by the child as part of himself: they have separated off from his body, and can be given to the mother, and thus become for the child his "first gift" (1933a). In asserting that money is equivalent with faeces Freud underpins that which has value and can be exchanged with the unconscious, infantile sense of the first gift.

The gift of speech

Both Lacan and Bataille confirm Mauss' argument against the primacy in human interaction of redressing a need or deficit. In Lacan's discussions of the gift of language in "The function and field of speech and language in psychoanalysis" he does not explicitly reference Mauss' work; however, we find in other contexts that he takes care to separate the relation of need from that of desire (1977a, pp. 281–291). Below I discuss in some detail Bataille's concept of general economy, in which he similarly aims to dissuade the reader of the notion that what is essentially at issue is the supplying of goods.

In presenting the view that psychoanalysis takes its spring from speech and language, Lacan contests the psychoanalytic milieu's neglect of symbolic relations, and its disregard of Freud's focus on speech in the psychoanalytic session. In writing, "the law of man has been the law of language since the first words of recognition presided over the first gifts" (1977a, p. 61), Lacan aligns speech with the process of giving gifts in early societies. The gifts that enabled bonds between early communities were a part of speech: "Gifts, their act and their objects, their erection into signs, and even their fabrication" were even designated at times with the same name that designated speech (ibid., p. 61). Lacan emphasises that the objects that were given were destined to be useless in themselves, or at least superfluous in their abundance. This suggests the aspect of emptiness of the gift in itself, as with the signifier in itself, which enables their symbolic designations.

Speech is posited by Lacan here as a gift of language; while speech itself is also the gift:

> [...] it is in the gift of speech that all the reality of its [psychoanalysis'] effects resides; for it is by way of this gift that all reality has come to man and it is by his continued act that he maintains it. (1977a, p. 106)

In other words for what is *to be* it relies on acts of speaking. The issue that I principally want to draw out here is that *to give* is posited by Lacan in a relation of equivalence with *to speak*. The notion of the gift contains the process of giving and receiving along with the objects themselves: in this instance words are given. At this point in his work Lacan stresses that it is from the gift of speech that both the effects of psychoanalysis and reality ensue. It is pertinent to differentiate giving from what is given, similarly to Lacan's notions of the saying and the said. The import is not firstly accorded to *what* one says or gives, but to the act of giving and receiving speech. It is questionable in the light of this, what manner of saying is implied by the completely indistinct words that my patient gave.

Two points about speech emphasised by Lacan are that it is addressed to another, and it makes a demand: speaking to the other makes the demand that he hear and reply. Replying would thus constitute a return gift. I find this later condition palpable in working with those psychotic patients who shy away from the demand intrinsic to speaking. More striking than neurotic ambivalence, the psychotic's response in these instances is suggestive of a primary difficulty with assuming the conventions involved in speaking with others, and no less with those involved in giving and receiving.

Receiving

Receiving poses a particular challenge as regards the gift, which I will discuss in this section. Lacan stresses the condition of speech as something originally received: the instruments of communication are received from the field of the Other, whereby the subject "receives first of all his own message in an inverted form" (1962–1963). Speaking requires that there has been an appropriation of language: in essence, repeated inaugurating acts of receiving and replying.

The relation to receptivity is an aspect of Freud's concept, *Bejahung*, which is translated as affirmation, but maintained in its specificity by often appearing untranslated from the German. In the paper "Negation" Freud writes that the primitive *Bejahung* is the preference to incorporate or eat a thing that possesses "the 'good' attribute" (1925h, p. 239). Negation is the preference to repress something or to spit it out. A predominance of negation in the psychoses points to a non-functioning of the inaugurating *Bejahung*. The gift of speech and all the reality that it creates appearing in many respects to be refused. Ambivalence over receiving and giving speech, more the province of the neurotic, evinces both affirmation and negation, desire and hostility.

Taking up these concepts in his seminar *The Psychoses* Lacan maintains that the effect of the *Bejahung* is subjection to "primitive symbolisation"

(1993, p. 82). In this context he writes: "We do indeed receive something in receiving speech" (ibid., p. 84). There is a particular density of this "something" that is received at the point that the subject affirms the gift of speech, and it is only possible within the purview of this paper that aspects of it are drawn out.

A passage in Aristotle's *Nicomachean Ethics* is pertinent in the manner in which it prefigures Mauss' proposals regarding the gift and the institution of rank or hierarchy in social relationships. With reference to the virtuous and proud man we read:

> And he is the sort of man to confer benefits, but he is ashamed of receiving them; for the one is the mark of a superior, and the other of an inferior. And he is apt to confer greater benefits in return; for thus the original benefactor besides being paid will incur a debt to him, and will be the gainer by the transaction. (Aristotle, 1998, p. 92)

Superiority or status and power accrue for the one who gives and a debt and potentially shame for the one who receives. Thus the original benefactor must be repaid with interest, as Mauss expresses it. Reciprocating a gift "in turn will give the donors authority and power over the first donor, who has become the last recipient" (Mauss, 1990, p. 12). In Mauss' study it is both the spirit of the object and the implications of having become a recipient that bear upon the return gift.

In relation to the obligation to receive a gift or accept an invitation Mauss emphasises that people do not have the right to refuse. There is a lawful and moral duty to share in the meal at which one is present. To fail to accept would be to reject the bond of alliance and commonality (ibid., p. 13). In principle every gift is always accepted and reciprocated with interest. To refuse to receive a gift might reveal that one is afraid of the requirement to reciprocate, and of the substantial loss of prestige that would ensue from not reciprocating worthily.

By giving or accepting a gift in archaic societies the person enters and commits himself to a social process, in which the sense of *oneself* is less individual than it often is in current western societies.

> If one gives things and returns them, it is because one is giving and returning "respects"—we still say "courtesies". Yet it is also because by giving one is giving *oneself*, and if one gives *oneself*, it

is because one "owes" *oneself*—one's person and one's goods—to others. (Ibid., p. 46)

Mauss emphasises the sense of indebtedness: if one has something, essentially it is because one has received the thing. The return gift is owed, with all the import of giving and receiving the part of the self that attends the gift.

Potlatch is comparable to contemporary practices involving vying with one another in giving presents of thanks, banquets, and weddings. Through use of the German term, Mauss claims, "We still feel the need to *revanchieren*" (ibid., p. 7). *Revanchieren* has two related senses: to return an invitation or reciprocate a favour; and to take one's revenge or pay back. The way the gift functions following Mauss' study it accomplishes both senses: it reciprocates a gift already received, and it takes revenge on the giver by rendering him as one who has received. Mauss writes:

> [...] all these institutions express one fact alone, one social system one precise state of mind: everything—food, women, children, property, talismans, land, labour services, priestly functions, and ranks—is there for passing on, and for balancing accounts. (Ibid., p. 14)

The most recent recipient carries for a period of time the largest burden, because he has indebted himself, and committed himself to passing on gifts to others. The motive identified here though, the balancing of accounts, is specifically pursued by giving more than one has received.

Lacan also discusses the passing on of goods in early societies.

> Identified with the sacred *hau* or with the omnipresent *mana*, the inviolable Debt is the guarantee that the voyage on which wives and goods are embarked will bring back to their point of departure in a never-failing cycle other women and other goods, all carrying an identical entity [...]. (1977a, p. 68)

It is not the objects in themselves that identify them with each other; it is their sacred *hau* or *mana*, which is itself constituted at least in part by the ubiquity of debt. The import of this process is that the debt is not absolved or balanced out through the cycle of giving and receiving.

What is sacred in the *hau* or *mana* appears more as the condition that the force that attends receiving a gift cannot be finally accounted for, even by reciprocating with interest.

Malinowski's translation of the Trobriand people's language of gifts interestingly refers to the flesh with which one commits oneself. The "opening gift" commits the recipient to make a reciprocating gift. This is the "clinching gift", which is sometimes called *"kudu,* the tooth that bites, that really cuts, bites through and liberates" (Mauss, 1990, p. 26). An insufficient return gift, one that bids for time to give more, is a *basi* that merely pierces the skin, but does not bite. In this account we see the recipient bound to the first donor at the level of his flesh. The notion of becoming liberated by that which cuts or bites through can be read as trenching on what finally the subject cannot be liberated from.

Considering survivals of the ancient morality of the gift Mauss notes that charity is wounding for the recipient: "Our morality strives to do away with the injurious patronage of the rich almsgiver" (ibid., p. 65). He concludes that the unreciprocated gift still makes the recipient inferior, and we still feel the urge to give back more than we have received.

Returning to psychoanalysis I will make brief reference to Freud's encounter with the "bedrock" of the psyche (1937c, p. 252), in which he describes from the experience of his practice a process of giving and receiving. He repeatedly encounters a refusal by his patients to receive from him. For a woman it is the refusal to receive his interpretation of the impossibility of her claim of the phallus. The position of the man is more evocative, as it bears upon the difficulties accompanying receiving that I have been addressing. Freud bemoans:

> At no other point in one's analytic work does one suffer more from an oppressive feeling that all one's repeated efforts have been in vain [...].
>
> The rebellious overcompensation of the male produces one of the strongest transference-resistances. He refuses to subject himself to a father-substitute, or to feel indebted to him for anything, and consequently he refuses to accept his recovery from the doctor. (Ibid.)

For the man an impasse arises over receiving from another man in a position of authority, as an effect of the castrating implications of taking up a passive attitude towards him. The man eschews his indebtedness;

however, with this, does he not also avoid the love and work that he might take up with others?

Bataille: energy finally can only be wasted

Much of Bataille's writing addresses the experience of intimacy. *The Accursed Share, An Essay on General Economy, Volume 1: Consumption* (1991a) presents a conception of intimacy that I propose arises from beyond the poles of indebtedness and an impossible liberation. For Bataille intimacy occurs in the realm of the sacred, with a luxurious and wasteful giving.

In a similar vein to Mauss, Bataille affirms that the essential motivation for economic exchange is not to supply for a deficit of goods; rather, "It is not necessity but its contrary, 'luxury', that presents living matter and mankind with their fundamental problems" (ibid., p. 12). The essence of the problems posed by luxury is that economic processes are ultimately "subordinated to giving" (1991a, p. 25).

In the general economy that Bataille presents, his "Copernican transformation"[1] of thought, economic production always yields an excess of wealth. An impulsion moves inescapably towards the dissipation or loss of the excess wealth, which finds its primary source in the abundant energy provided by the sun without any requirement for exchange or return. We read:

> I will begin with a basic fact: The living organism, in a situation determined by the play of energy on the surface of the globe, ordinarily receives more energy than is necessary for maintaining life; the excess energy (wealth) can be used for the growth of a system (e.g., an organism); if the system can no longer grow, or if the excess cannot be completely absorbed in its growth, it must necessarily be lost without profit; it must be spent, willingly or not, gloriously or catastrophically. (Ibid., p. 21)

Catastrophic expenditure includes war with its enormous consumption of resources and human life. Growth, as the expansion of a system or reproduction of an organism, is termed productive expenditure. It is the province of the isolated individual, with overall human interest being a multiplication of isolated interest (ibid., p. 181). The movement within the general economy determines and surpasses the individual; similarly, growth and production are surpassed by unproductive expenditure with its movement toward dissipating wealth in a profitless loss.

Through these terms Bataille works the thesis that energy finally can only be wasted. Luxurious giving, the wasting of energy, spending for no purpose lends itself to an experience that shocks and disturbs. It is "the return of life's immensity to the truth of exuberance" (ibid., p. 76).

It is on this point the Bataille takes a different direction to Mauss. Mauss studies the way the gift produces a total network of obligatory giving and receiving, with its unavoidable indebtedness and repayments. In the potlatch a mass of goods is given to others or destroyed. It is a practice involving a luxurious dissipation and loss of wealth, while what is gained are alliances, the indebting of others and rank. For Bataille this is an initial attribution of meaning to the excess that must be wasted: "One might even say that potlatch is the specific manifestation, the meaningful form of luxury" (ibid., p. 76). The lie of the rich is their uniting of ostentatious squanderings of wealth to rank and status. An important concept is introduced in this regard: the potlatch and its modern day forms achieve a *"servile use of the negation of utility"* (ibid., p. 77, my italics). About the paradox of his own production Bataille says:

> [...] writing this book in which I was saying that energy finally can only be wasted, I myself was using my energy, my time, working; my research answered in a fundamental way the desire to add to the amount of wealth acquired for mankind. (1991a, p. 11)

Nevertheless, he maintains that life's exuberance is destined to revolt against productive expenditure and the servile use of the negation of utility.

Bataille opposes to purposive giving a reckless, wasteful expenditure, without recourse to meaning or utility—except it occurs to me, the aim that Bataille valorises, which is experiencing the intimacy of sacred communion. This wasteful expenditure can be found in the human labour and resources required to build the pyramids and churches and to create elaborate, splendid ornamentation. Bataille discusses how the morality and values of earlier eras promoted the unproductive glory of art, festivals, and churches. Capitalism, supported by Protestantism, turns away from luxury, as it extols the gainfulness of all things and human effort, such that in current times a glorious deed is justified in terms of its utility (ibid., p. 29). Bataille's proposals regarding intimacy revolve around the assertion that the primary meaning of squandering wealth is to break the chain of utility and efficacious actions (ibid., p. 120).

It is precisely the negation of the utility of things that constitutes the realm of the sacred. The sacrificial object is torn from its profane position and restored to the order of the sacred, and in so doing the previously useful thing is restored to the realm of intimacy. In human sacrifice the victim is removed from his profane functions in the world: he is consecrated and thus comes to embody the accursed share (ibid., p. 59). Sacrifice destroys the sacrificial object; however, what is essentially destroyed are the ties to the world of meaning and value. The sacred arises from this destruction, not necessarily of the offering in itself; rather, a definitive destruction of its utility. What has been set apart in this way, according to Bataille, cannot be restored to the profane order.

Both intimacy and the deepest nature of the subject are permeated by the quality of the sacred. Bataille writes: "Servile use has made a *thing* (an *object*) of that which, in a deep sense, is of the same nature as the *subject*, is in a relation of intimate participation with the subject." (1991a, p. 55) Man similarly becomes a thing, when he is conceived in terms of his labour and value is placed on future results, rather than on the truth of the present moment. This is a degradation that man longs to escape: "In his strange myths, in his cruel rites, man is *in search of a lost intimacy* [...]" (ibid., p. 57). Bataille suggests that it is for the experience of intimacy that man pursues that which will destroy, if only for the duration of the experience, his connections to his significance and value.

Consumption is a means of expending energy in which the thing consumed is lost and destroyed. Bataille posits the subject's existence as a being of consumption: "The subject *is* consumption insofar as it is not tied down to work" (ibid., p. 58). Unconcerned about holding onto things for future use, "I can at once, in disorder, make an instantaneous consumption of all that I possess" (ibid., p. 58). Consumption allows separate beings to communicate: the intimacy of the subject is particularly revealed in consuming immoderately. Bataille qualifies this by asserting that the notion of a separate being arises only from the "real" world, which is antithetical to intimacy with its moderation, reason, and lucidity.

What Bataille is presenting in this book, he claims, is something that repels, that people strive to avoid. The general economy of exuberance and dissipation is able to effect a "violent movement, sudden and shocking, which jostles the mind, taking away its tranquility" (ibid., p. 11). To individual blindness, and despair, he opposes "a strange, exuberant, simultaneously beneficent and disastrous sense of wealth" (ibid., p. 181). Man does not want to know that he cannot escape the movement impelling towards profitless expenditure, the effect of his ignorance being that he is unable to bring about in his own way what he will inevitably undergo (ibid., p. 23). An ethical consideration arises from this work, when Bataille maintains that "monstrous disorders" ensue, when people do not know how to consume the energy that they have (ibid., p. 16).

In this paper I have discussed the implication of the gift in changing positions of obligation, status, and responsibility; and in a fundamental *Bejahung*, which is creative of the subject. An important consideration is the wish to elude debt and obligation, a wish in effect for liberation from the force of the gift. The patient speaks; his words are inaudible. Speech is given, while it is also withheld. The patient hears. Does he affirm, receive, refute or parry these words? He quietly ignores what I have just said, in order to ask that I might hear what he was saying. Exploring the gift and its foundation in the gift of speech leads to this consideration of the transference: that there is enacted there one or more economies or styles of giving and receiving along with the ambivalence provoked by the gift. The patient who had often spoken of not getting himself heard gave the incomprehensibility of his words in the transference, this presentation appearing replete with an ambivalence that erred on the side of the wish for liberation.

Giving for no purpose points to a beyond of ambivalence. Bataille offers an account of what might remain when psychoanalysis eschews the purposive quality of the therapeutic, and when it opens itself to a beyond of symbolic relations: speech might be given in a spirit of wasteful and luxurious expenditure. Bataille evokes the destitution of the subject that is tied to its ideals and articulable functions in its world. The strange, forbidding experience of luxury suggests that the economy of indebtedness might actually be preferred over the shock and disturbance of intimacy. Nevertheless, a certain obscurity imbued my patient's expenditure of speech as a soft, murmuring intonation: words given in the transference precisely such that any possible utility ensuing from their sense was negated.[2]

Notes

1. An allusion is suggested here to Freud's Copernican revolution, which Freud presents in a series following Darwin's challenge: "But human megalomania will have suffered its third and most wounding blow from the psychological research of the present time, which seeks to prove to the ego that it is not even master in its own house [...]". *Introductory Lectures on Psycho-analysis*. Lecture XVIII Fixation to Traumas—The Unconscious. Vol. XVI, Standard Edition of the Complete Psychological Works of Sigmund Freud. J. Strachey (Ed. & Trans.). London: Vintage, 2001, p. 285.
2. I would like to thank Linda Clifton for her reading of a draft of this paper.

CHAPTER ELEVEN

The grammar of sex: verb or noun?*

Alicia Evans

There's a knock on the door; it's my three pm analysand. I open the door and he stomps in, past me, without looking, then into my consulting room where he stomps over and then sits almost upright on the couch. Occasionally on the way in, he announces "bathroom" and makes his way to the bathroom, before returning to brush my presence aside as he moves directly to the couch.

He talks almost non-stop, rarely straying from the topic. When there is a momentary pause and I speak, sometimes he speaks directly after me; it's like I haven't spoken. The sessions are difficult to finish because he keeps talking; I manage to squeeze in "We'll need to finish there". As I rise, so does he, and he races me to the door. On the way out he mostly stares straight ahead as he walks past me and out the door; sometimes there is a gruff glance on the way past.

I recall the first time he came to see me. He couldn't achieve what he wanted from life; he was alone and lonely. I didn't think he'd return after the first appointment as there was no rapport between us. Indeed,

---

*An earlier version of this paper was presented at The Freudian School of Melbourne's 2012 "Homage to Lacan".

it seemed that there was nothing between us. But he came back and he comes back after every session.

Clearly then, there is something between us. It is working for him, he tells me; things are better since he has been coming to see me. He tells me this before Christmas, as a gift. Of course, whether there was a therapeutic effect or not was not at issue, at least not for me. What was at issue for me, what crossed my mind one day as he stomped in past me, was a thought about his sexuality. I wasn't sure what to think of it really, but it crossed my mind.

In this paper, I will explore the notion of "sexuality". For, although I had a thought about his sexuality, I wasn't sure what to think of it. That "it" that I was unsure of, was both this man's sexuality and, beyond that, the whole idea of something called "sexuality". Something about the very notion of sexuality puzzled me.

In order to consider the notion of sexuality, I will turn first to psychiatry to argue that the dominant discourse of psychiatry is very clear about it. Indeed, psychiatry takes sexuality up as part of its domain: that is, psychiatry defines and categorises sexuality (Foucault, 1990). There is the fetishist and the paedophile for example.[1] Psychiatry also differentiates a normative heterosexual sexuality from what deviates from this.[2] But that is psychiatry's discourse on sexuality and I am going to argue for something different from this—a psychoanalytic reading that is outside the classification system of the medical specialty of psychiatry. I'm going to start by considering sexuality in grammatical terms, then briefly consider Foucault's (1990) critique of psychiatry's normalising practices, that is, with respect to the classification of sexuality. In doing this, I will argue for a notion of sexuality that is not a static aspect of personality (as psychiatry would have it) but rather something more dynamic and active—an action, a practice, something one does.

Turning now to begin to prosecute this argument, let me pose the question: what can be made of the word sexuality in terms of grammar? That is, what is sexuality at a grammatical level? We have sex as a verb, as in "to have sex". Or, more grammatically correct: "to sex", if we take the verb in its infinitive form. There is sex as a noun, as in: "What is the sex of the baby?" Then we have sex as an adverb, as in: "She was sexually active". There is sex as an adjective, as in: "It was their usual sexual practice". But sexuality, what is sexuality? Well, in terms of grammar, it's a noun, as in: "What is the sexuality of this person?"

Of note, the word sexuality appears in the titles of Freud's *Three essays on the Theory of Sexuality* (1905d) and Foucault's *The History of Sexuality* (1990). On the other hand, Lacan wrote: "There is no sexual relation". For both Freud and Foucault, in these titles, and assuming no issues of translation, sexuality is a noun. In Lacan's "there is no sexual relation"; the sex word takes the form of an adjective, although of course there is seminar twenty: on feminine sexuality (1998).

Foucault's (1976) *History of Sexuality* appears much later than Freud's *Three Essays* and even after Lacan has given seminar twenty. Foucault knew Freud's work but apparently not Lacan's later work (Foucault, 1977, pp. 194–228). He critiques the idea of sexuality and with it, the discipline of psychiatry (certainly) and the theory and practice of psychoanalysis (possibly). There has been considerable debate about the latter possibility.[3]

Foucault contends that psychiatry had produced an object called sexuality via what he called "scientia sexualis" or, in English "scientific sexuality". During the nineteenth and early twentieth century, this "scientia sexualis" rendered simple sex pleasures a matter for psychiatry and its machinery; sex became something to make talk, to investigate, and categorise (Foucault, 1990). Before psychiatry's gaze turned to sex, Foucault contends that it was not possible to think of someone in terms of their "sexuality". This was because there wasn't such a concept in existence at that time. Before the concept of sexuality arose, the idea was that of the flesh (1977).[4] This seems unimaginable now, that is, that one was unable to think in terms of someone, for example, being considered a transvestite, a heterosexual or a paedophile.

Notice that they are all nouns. "She is a transvestite". This was one of the things Foucault (1990) objected to—this categorisation of the person by the way they experience sexual pleasure. That is, he objected to the way that one could become defined by one's sexual acts. Moreover this was part of Foucault's critique of psychiatry in relation to what he called "scientia sexualis". That is, how one's preferred way to experience sexual pleasure came to form a classification system that could then be pathologised and normalised.

While Foucault's critique is much more extensive than this, it is important to note that he does not advance the idea of an ideal state of sexual practice existing prior to psychiatry's gaze turning to sex (ibid.); for sex pleasures do not exist outside language or history. Moreover,

Foucault argues that psychiatry took over from the church in the governance of sexual pleasure. While the church once governed the sexual conduct of citizens, this became the remit of psychiatry. That is, psychiatry took over the governmentality of sex; a mentality of governing the conduct of others (Foucault, 1998).

I am not going to enter the debate about whether Foucault's *History of Sexuality* was a critique levelled at psychoanalysis, as much as psychiatry, but I am interested in his critique as a means of interrogating psychoanalytic practice. That is, if a psychoanalyst's practice answers to the question of sex in the same way as a psychiatrist's practice, in the way Foucault argued, then perhaps they are the same. If the question of sex is taken up differently, then there is a gap between the psychoanalyst and the psychiatrist on this question.

What is most important in Foucault's critique is how it can be considered in relation to a psychoanalytic practice. That is, one can consider how close, or how distant, a psychoanalytic practice is to that of a psychiatric one on the question of sexuality. For example, in relation to these categories of sexual disorder that psychiatry has nominated: transvestite, fetishist, paedophile, and in previous times, homosexual, and masturbator, I can consider whether I am thinking of the analysand I mentioned earlier in this categorical way. Am I thinking of him as having a sexuality that fits into one of psychiatry's categories?

Returning to my analysand then, I might consider again the question of his sexual practices. Yet I know almost nothing of them as he does not really speak of this. He does not tell me about his sexual practices or his sexual fantasies, either as an adult or a child. Moreover, many of the analysands who I see do not speak of their sexual practices much at all; sometimes not at all. Yet this was clearly not the case with Freud's practice.

When we consider the Wolfman case (1918b), for example, we see Freud meticulously tracing back, as he called it, the analysis to the first years of the analysand's life. This part of Freud's method, the tracing back, he likened to an archaeological dig (1937d). He dug his way back to the beginning to find the lost and deeply buried "objects". Once he found then, he examined them in great detail. He put them into question. "Is this 'object' a phantasy or a memory?" he asked. This digging back, his archaeological method, was part of, what I call, a vertical method in psychoanalytic practice; you dig down.

It is possible that it is because I do not dig down in my practice that I do not find what Freud found in his practice, that is, "the beginnings of human sexual life" (1905d, p. 133). Of course this archaeological endeavour of Freud's—to go back vertically, to discover what is buried beneath—is not his only method. There is also the thread in his work that is more focused on language and symbolic interpretation, as is illustrated by his analysis of his forgetting the word Signorelli and his work on the interpretation of dreams. This thread that is focused on language in Freud's method was taken up and extended by Lacan, perhaps even radicalised by him.

Quite different from a digging down archaeologically (that is, a vertical approach), Lacan took up, what I consider to be, a more horizontal approach to method. This more horizontal approach could be thought of as a language approach. In this horizontal language approach, instead of a tracing back akin to a digging down vertically, there is a reading across the speech of the analysand; a reading that is quite literal. The reading of the analysand's speech by the analyst, in the way the analyst might hear the repetition of a particular signifier is more horizontal than vertical, as is the way the analyst might point to something said in a session.

Indeed if the unconscious is the discourse of the Other (Lacan, 1991) then, the unconscious, as a discourse, is discursive and something discursive is read. In this way the unconscious is produced in the session rather than dug up. This production of the unconscious can be seen in moments when something is produced in speech (Zentner, 2007, pp. 363–370), such as a "slip of the tongue" for example.

Lacan took up this language, or horizontal, method and extended it; this notion of something hitherto unknown coming into the present via speech—something that is produced in the moment between the analysand and the analyst. That is, this non-archaeological or language approach to psychoanalysis is an approach that privileges the production, in speech, of something we might call "unconscious". In this way something unconscious is produced in the consulting room rather than discovered in an archaeological dig. The unconscious then is "more like lightning on the horizon, a singular product of an encounter between analyst and analysand" (ibid., p. 367); so horizontal rather than vertical—in the now, rather than in the past.

Therefore, in these two methods—the archaeological method (the digging back to find something hidden) versus the language method (the disclosure in speech in the session)—there is a juxtaposition of the idea of a thing, a some thing, that lies buried beneath versus something that acts in the moment—a thing versus a doing word—a noun versus a verb. The unconscious, in this way, is not something buried deep down but something that acts in the present.

In this way, the unconscious can be thought of as a verb[5]—something actively produced, in a moment, in speech. This is by way of contrast to how the concept of the unconscious can be thought of as a noun—the unconscious—akin to an absent monument that can be discovered in an archaeological dig (Freud, 1937d).

In a similar way to how the word unconscious can be thought of in archaeological terms as a noun and in language terms as a verb, so too can the word sex. Sex can be thought of as a noun when we think of the sexuality of a person, that is, when their sex practices are categorised so that they fit into one of the known categories: fetishist, transvestite, etc.[6]; when their sexual practices are pathologised in this categorical way—the way of psychiatry. These categories that psychiatry designates are static things that are both constant and defining. But sex can also be thought of as a verb—to sex—to have sex.

When we consider the sex/sexuality question by way of sex as a verb it becomes active and dynamic; it becomes something that expresses itself, not in a categorical way but in a particular way. This idea of activity, a movement that goes with sex, resonates with the following passage from Freud. Although Freud speaks of sexuality, it is not of a categorical sexuality but rather is more akin to this notion of sex as a verb; it acts.

> The individual does actually carry on a twofold existence; one to serve his own purposes and the other as a link in a chain, which he serves against his will, or at least involuntarily. The individual himself regards sexuality as one of his own ends; whereas from another point of view he is an appendage to his germ-plasm, at whose disposal he puts his energies in return for a bonus of pleasure. He is the mortal vehicle of a (possibly) immortal substance—like the inheritor of an entailed property, who is only the temporary holder of an estate which survives him. (Freud, 1914c, p. 78)

Here Freud contends that the act of sex, although considered by the individual to be entirely that of their making, is also not of their making.

Instead the individual becomes a vehicle for something that is passed through them and passed on. The individual, by way of this act of sex, passes on something unknown to them. They act but they are also acted through. Although the word "individual" is Freud's, clearly there is little that is individual in what he portrays.

Another way that something unknown can pass through and become present is via transference. This is in the sense that the "passing through" is a passage from not present to present, via the physical presence of the analysand and analyst. This is in keeping with the idea of transference as "the enactment of the reality of the unconscious" (Lacan, 1979, p. 149). Something is enacted, that is, there is an action that is transference. Further, this "reality" is "sexual reality" (ibid., p. 150) This sexual of sexual reality clearly isn't categorical though, rather it is libido and it speaks of desire (Lacan, 1979, p. 149); a desire that is particular to each one.

Returning to my analysand again, we find that he enacts his way of sexing in a particular way. He brushes me aside, he stomps in, he stomps out, he stomps over—this is his way of sexing and through it both something of his inheritance is disclosed and something particular to him is made present via his presence, that is, in the transference.

Most importantly though, in conceptualising the question of sexuality in this way, that is, as a verb rather than as a noun, we find that my analysand's practice of sex does not fit into a category. It is his particular way to sex and in this way it is not confined nor pathologised, nor made to fit into a binary of normal and abnormal. Therefore we can conclude that when sex is considered as a verb, that is, when the static categorisations of psychiatry's scientia sexualis are dismissed, than both the analyst and the analysand have some freedom of movement, outside of the confinement of the sexual category.

By way of post-script, I notice lately, in the time between when this paper was first thought about and when it was finished, that this analysand's practice of sex has changed. He no longer stomps in, threatening to roll right over me, nor does he talk over me. He leaves a space for me; something has opened up to allow another person a place in his life. Thus we see, quite different from the categorical ideas of psychiatry's scientia sexualis, a sex that acts, sometimes like this and sometimes like that. It isn't confined because it isn't a noun. Sex is a verb. Perhaps there is no such thing as sexuality.

Notes

1. Although, in psychiatric practice a person is diagnosed as having a sexual disorder rather than being described as a sexual disorder, nonetheless the dissemination of the psychiatric discourse into the public arena has led to notions of "fetishist" and "paedophile".
2. As is illustrated by how psychiatric diagnoses are named "disorders". See the *American Psychiatric Association. Diagnostic and Statistical Manual of Mental Disorders, 5th edition, DSM-5*. 2013 Arlington, VA: American Psychiatric Association.
3. For example, Arnold Davidson doubts that Foucault's "History of Sexuality" was an attack on psychoanalysis *per se*, as some have argued. See: Arnold I. Davidson. *The Emergence of Sexuality*. 2001. Massachusetts: Harvard University Press.
4. The systems that imposed normative rules on sex also included the judicial system and the educational institutions. See: Michel Foucault. Preface to the *History of Sexuality Volume 2*. In: *Essential Works of Foucault Volume 1. 1954–1984*, (pp. 199–222). 1998. P. Rabinow (Ed.). Melbourne: Penguin Books.
5. This is perhaps what Lacan refers to when he says: "I do not say that the verb creates. I say something very different because my practice implies the following: I say that the verb is unconscious—therefore, misunderstood" (p. 98). Jacques Lacan. The Seminar, Paris, 10th June 1980. In: *Papers of the Freudian School of Melbourne, 1980*. Oscar Zentner (Ed.). Melbourne: The Freudian School of Melbourne.
6. However, the so-called disorders of sexuality are even more prolific than these broad categories. The *DSM-5* has diagnoses such as "female orgasmic disorder", "premature ejaculation" and "erectile disorder". See *American Psychiatric Association. Diagnostic and Statistical Manual of Mental Disorders, 5th edition, DSM-5*. 2013 Arlington, VA: American Psychiatric Association.

CHAPTER TWELVE

What's not home in homelessness?

Peter Gunn

I am part of a program designed to address chronic homelessness. With the program soon to finish, it is now clear that not all of the participants have been able to be comfortably accommodated. The reason for these outliers is not entirely clear. Certainly there has been no lack of effort, particularly on the part of caseworkers.

Let me give you an example. I will call this man Neville.

Especially at the start of the project, Neville would closely question his caseworker about her reasons. Neville pressed her to give an account of herself: "Why are you taking such an interest in me?"

"There's nothing wrong with me," he says. "I'm not a paranoid schizophrenic, but an intelligent man who has a lot of wisdom." "I've worked it all out." "People are jealous and don't want me to succeed." "It's a set-up: they've hooked me up to heroin; they've destroyed my soul." "I'm heart-broken." "I had a girlfriend in Sydney; she is now a supermodel who has 240 million dollars and lives in London." "My family has exploited me and they are now having a good life in New York and LA living it up." "I'm walking around poor and lonely on this planet."

At other times Neville speaks of everything being pointless, and of being better off on the streets of The Cross. As most of you will know (and certainly it's been in the news quite a lot of late, and for all the wrong reasons), "The Cross" is the Sydney colloquialism for the well-known entertainment or, slightly less euphemistically, red-light, district of Sydney. The somewhat more formal name for this district is "Kings Cross", but even that name does not appear in the official list of Sydney suburbs.

His worker thinks that part of the attraction of Kings Cross may be that it has a "shooting gallery", or, to use the more recent, and more official terminology, a Medically Supervised Injecting Centre. But as well as being a place to where he has safe, and free, access to drugs (i.e., heroin), Neville sees the shooting gallery as a place to socialise. Sydney is Neville's hometown; he grew up there; "I'm a Sydney person," he says.

Neville has gone back to Sydney for extended periods on several occasions during the course of the program. Before setting off at these times he is sad, even to the point of feeling like killing himself.

Having said that, Neville does also say that despite having had his trust broken many times, after more than two years of intensive work he does now have a degree of trust in his caseworker.

Nevertheless, the question posed by this man to his caseworker remains, "What is your interest in me?" If, as a psychoanalyst, I am part of this same program, this is a question which I must hear as also addressed to me. I hear it as clinical supervisor for the caseworker, but it also returns to me just in presenting myself in this program as a psychoanalyst, that is, apart from any consideration of the form of my collaboration.

If some program participants feel put on the spot by the interest their caseworkers take in them, the caseworkers are themselves put on the spot by being asked the participant's question: "What is your interest in me?" It is incumbent on them to say something, as best they can, in response. It is equally incumbent on me to respond. However, as a psychoanalyst, the question returns to me in a more general way. It takes on an even more challenging form: "What is your interest?"

This, indeed, was the very question which the French psychoanalyst Jacques Lacan posed to his audience of psychoanalysts when, in 1977, he opened a section of the Department of Psychoanalysis at the

University of Vincennes in Paris devoted to clinical practice. Lacan said that the section should function as a way of interrogating the psychoanalyst. By means of clinical presentations of various kinds it would put the psychoanalyst on the spot. If, in this forum, he wants to present himself, and to do so as a psychoanalyst, it will be on condition that he makes a declaration of interest.

I see this public lecture as being just such a declaration; it is my response to being put on the spot. If in this way I put myself in the spotlight, I have to acknowledge that that won't take me very far. Even in his consulting room, the psychoanalyst need not expect any glory. If he thinks that is where he will find it, he had better shut up shop immediately and start looking for another job. It is equally the case that if the psychoanalyst chooses to venture out into unfamiliar territory, say, for example, into the bailiwick of the homeless, he need not expect a warm welcome. Indeed, and in keeping with Lacan's logic, it is even more incumbent on the psychoanalyst who presumes to go out into such territory to declare his reasons for being there.

This logic, which is really an ethics, puts me under pressure. It obliges me, in particular, to give my reasons for taking an interest, even indirectly, in this man who I've mentioned, and for taking an interest, even more particularly, in the pressure to which he finds himself subject. After all, it is precisely this pressure which Neville associates to busybodies like me.

So, let me come clean right away and make my declaration, or at least a partial one. My interest is in those who I am going to refer to as *Sykos*. I am spelling this not "p-s-y-c-h-o-s", but "s-y-k-o-s".

This takes us to something else which was written in Paris, but in this case over seventeen years, from 1922 to 1939. It was also written in English, or, at least, in a polyglot in which the English language is dominant. I'm referring to James Joyce's *Finnegans Wake*.

It might seem strange to you that I would adopt such a term, one which, as you hear it, is taken as an insult directed at those who, in more polite speech, are said to have a mental illness. It is of course always dangerous to try to pursue an author's intentions, or indeed their biography, on the basis of their fiction, and all the more so when that fiction is what Northrop Frye has called the "chief ironic epic of our times". But for the purposes of my present pursuit I choose to do so.

I take Joyce to have intended his *Sykos* as an insult. This is not the insult which you might sometimes hear directed at those troubled souls you encounter on the street. This insult is directed rather at those "psychos", psychologists, psychiatrists, and psychoanalysts, who purport to treat those troubled souls.

Joyce's spelling of the word suggests that it is one of the many portmanteau words he constructs in *Finnegans Wake*. In this case it may be a combination of "psycho", with the usual spelling, p-s-y-c-h-o, and a truncation of the Ancient Greek word *Sykos*, s-y-k-o-s, meaning a ripe fig.

Certainly, the suggestiveness of this combination is born out in the passage from *Finnegans Wake* where it occurs (Joyce, 1992, p. 115):

> [...] we grisly old *Sykos* who have done our unsmiling bit on 'alices,
> when they were *yung* [Jung!] and easily *freudened* [Freud!], in the
> penumbra of the procuring room and what oracular *comepression*
> we have had apply to them!

Now, perhaps it's just my own bent, but what this seems to be saying is that, given the nature of the pressure which these Sykos apply to their young, female patients, their interest is decidedly lecherous.

This brings me to something else about my interest in *Sykos*. If I say I have an interest it is, first of all, because I include myself amongst these *Sykos*: that is, I take Joyce to be levelling his accusation at me. It is, after all, clear for all to see that I am indeed one of those grisly old *Sykos*.

At the time however it is likely that Joyce's disapprobation was directed most especially at Carl Jung, the self-styled analytical psychologist. In a letter written to his patroness Harriet Weaver in 1921 Joyce described Jung as amusing himself "at the expense (in every sense of the word) of ladies and gentlemen who are troubled with bees in their bonnets" (quoted in Harari, 2002, p. 169).

But Joyce also had a personal connection with Jung. In 1933 his twenty-six year-old daughter Lucia was diagnosed with schizophrenia. Her behaviour had become increasingly unmanageable. She was subject to what were described as "hysterical episodes" and tantrums, and frequently absconded from the various establishments which were found for her. In late 1934, and despite his reservations, Joyce agreed to her being admitted to the private sanatorium in Switzerland where Jung worked.

As Joyce's biographer Richard Ellmann describes it however, after a few months Jung found that he was "unable to keep his hold over Lucia" (quoted in Ellmann, 1983, p. 679). Echoing her father's own refusal of such pressure, Lucia herself later commented, "To think that such a big fat materialistic Swiss man should try to get hold of my soul!" (ibid., 679).

If then, Joyce directed his insult at those who would contain Lucia, his daughter shared his refusal, his resistance. As a psychoanalyst, I have an interest, as well, in this resistance. Why? Because of what it says about the position … not only of the patient, but also of that particular *Syko* called the *psycho*-analyst.

Allow me to elaborate. To do so I will need to review a little of the early history of psychoanalysis.

As a clinical term, resistance goes back to the very beginnings of psychoanalysis. Sigmund Freud used it for the first time in 1895 in *Studies on Hysteria*, the work he co-authored with his colleague and friend at the time, Josef Breuer. In his Introduction to that work, James Strachey, the translator and editor of the Standard Edition of the works of Freud in English, characterises resistance as the patients' "unwillingness to co-operate in their own cure".

How did Freud deal with resistance? Not by shouting it down (as Freud's teacher, the neurologist Jean-Martin Charcot might have done), nor by suggesting it away using hypnosis (as Freud himself had tried to do). Instead, says Strachey, he treated it as he did other mental phenomena, he investigated it. It was this investigative orientation of Freud which, to quote Strachey, "led him directly into the uncharted world which he was to spend his whole life in exploring" (1895d, p. xvii).

Now, what interests me about Strachey's description is not so much where it takes the patient, but where it takes the doctor, doctor being what both Freud and Breuer were at this time. At the outset, we have the idea of a cure; the doctor brings a cure, first and foremost, for bodily symptoms. After all, this was what these hysterics, as they were called, presented, albeit often in bewildering variety.

Initially, the cure takes the form of massage and warm baths combined with the patients being asked to talk about their symptoms under hypnosis. But Freud finds that this cure that he and Breuer have come up with is one which, for some reason, his patients resist, despite it supposedly being for their own good; that is, despite it being their own cure.

In the face of this, wouldn't we expect any self-respecting doctor to tell the patient to go away, go away himself, or else to keep to his knitting: to keep on applying the same old poultice to the wound? No, this doctor, Freud, not Breuer, is not impotent. He has the courage to *investigate*, that is, to both persist and to go further. But if he investigates in this way he needs to be prepared to venture into uncharted territory.

Studies on Hysteria dates from the period just prior to Freud's invention of psychoanalysis proper. As Strachey puts it, Freud at this point was "at a half-way stage in the process of moving from physiological to psychological explanations" of psychopathology (ibid., p. xxiv).

The majority of the patients Freud was seeing at this time suffered troubling bodily symptoms. These symptoms, however, wandered about, and no organic explanation could be found for them.

It was Charcot, who, in naming the condition these women suffered from, resorted to the old term hysteria, from the Greek for wandering womb. Despite recognising the wandering nature of this condition, however, Charcot held to a physiological explanation. In naming it, he was concerned only to differentiate it from epilepsy. Charcot proposed that hysterics suffer from a "dynamic lesion" in the brain, yet one which, though physiological, is "elusive, changeable, always prone to disappear" (quoted in Didi-Huberman, 2004, p. 77).

By contrast, Freud's work with these patients had increasingly forced him to the conclusion that the cause of hysterical symptoms must be sought in sexual factors. This was despite him initially believing, in common both with Charcot and, indeed, his patients themselves, that this linking of hysteria with sexuality would constitute a sort of insult (1895d, p. 260). For Freud, the cause must lie in the idea of some most intimate and secret sexual event, the memory of which has been "repressed" from conscious thought inasmuch as it is both traumatic and unacceptable.

At the same time, what Freud recognised was that there was something uncontainable in his hysterics' bodily symptoms, something which was being driven to express itself, but could only do so in this way. The symptoms could be read as expressions, in bodily form, of the unacceptable sexual excitation with which they were associated. This, for Freud, was the key to eliciting these unacceptable ideas in speech.

In attempting to overcome his patients' resistance to disclosing the ideas with which these symptoms were associated, Freud abandoned hypnosis. He found it more effective if instead he put his patients into what he called a "state of concentration". In doing so he started from the assumption that something must have occurred to her about her symptoms; he insisted that his patient put these associations into words. She must "say what [comes] into her head, whether it [is] appropriate or not" (1895d, p. 154).

In other words, Freud turned things around. Instead of bringing a cure, he brought only an insistent declaration that he knew that his patients knew. He knew that they knew, as he put it, "everything that was of any pathogenic [that is, disease-causing] significance and that it was only a question of obliging them to communicate it" (ibid., p. 110).

At this time Freud found that he could intensify this insistence by applying pressure, that is, actual physical pressure to the heads of his patients (ibid., 270). But as he went on to develop his theory of the unconscious and, in conjunction with that, the practice of psychoanalysis proper, Freud ceased to rely on any such overt forms of insistence. In fact, Freud came to take a different view both of what insists and of what resists.

What continued to insist however was something which, even in 1895, he recognised as a necessary condition for a psychoanalytic treatment: the analyst must have a "great interest in psychological happenings [as well as] personal concern for the patients [...]" (ibid., p. 264).

Freud came to see that both insistence and resistance are intrinsic to psychoanalytic treatment. Both occur in the context of the prescription to associate, the only prescription which the doctor, now a psychoanalyst, gives to the patient. It is intrinsic to this associating that something insists and, at the same time, something resists.

In this respect insistence and resistance are, you could say, two sides of the one coin. Freud named this coin *transference*.

In his 1912 "Papers on technique" Freud describes the transference as arising as a compromise between resistance to association and what insists there, in that association:

> If we [...] follow a pathogenic complex from its representation in the conscious (whether this is an obvious one in the form of a symptom or something quite inconspicuous) to its root in the unconscious, we shall soon enter a region in which the resistance makes itself felt so clearly that the next association must take account of it and appear as a compromise between its demands and those of

the work of investigation. It is at this point, on the evidence of our
experience, that transference enters the scene. (1911–1915, p. 103)

For the patient, the demand of the "work of investigation" is in the
work of associating, that is, in saying what occurs to him. In other
words, under the obligation to associate, there is a demand implied in
the very act of saying. As was the case back in 1895, this demand, this
insistence, continues to be carried by the analyst's unflinching, investigative orientation. That is, it is carried by the analyst's interest.

This interest on the part of the analyst is either there or not there,
which is equivalent to saying: either there is an analyst present, or
there is not one present. The position of the analyst is not something
which can be put in place by way of a set of practice guidelines. This is
why, sixty years later, in his seminar *Ou Pire …* (1971–1972, p. 8) Lacan
described psychoanalysis as an art, the art of producing the necessity
of discourse.

Let's now come back to Joyce's acerbic insult, *Sykos*. As I said, in
his usage it seems to have been directed at psychoanalysts like me and
other such busybodies. If I must, nevertheless, include myself amongst
those accused, (and in so doing put myself at risk of being seen as a
dirty old man), it is because I don't deny my interest both in what resists
and in what insists with my patients.

Indeed, I have a confession to make. I too have done my bit in extract-
ing some *comepressions* from Alice. I could try to get away with this by
pleading that my interest in her was confined to writing a psychoanalytic paper on Alice Liddell, or at least, on the Alice that she was for
Lewis Carroll, as he portrayed her, both in *Alice in Wonderland* and in his
photographs. But that doesn't cover it. Joyce's accusation still finds its
mark. It puts *me* under pressure and, in so doing, it extracts this further
admission: that I am, as a psychoanalyst, implicated by my interest,
and, in particular, by the interest which I showed in Alice, as I found
her, albeit by way of Carroll's photographic image.

But if *Syko*, in Joyce's coinage, is another of his portmanteau words,
it can also be taken to include something else: *psycho*, that is, *psycho*
with the usual spelling, p-s-y-c-h-o. In this usage it can of course also
be heard as an insult, in this case directed at those who are, to use a colloquialism, off-the-wall. The insult is given force by its allusion to the
psychiatric classification: to say of someone they are a *psycho* picks up
on the psychiatric term *psychotic*.

In appropriating Joyce's term in this way however I am wanting to keep a colloquial flavour, and, in this way, maintain some separation from psychiatric terminology. I am thinking here of the way the French theorists Gilles Deleuze and Félix Guattari appropriate the term *schizo*. That is, in much the same way that the colloquialism "queer" has been appropriated by some in order to distance themselves from the language of officialdom and its classification "homosexual", it is possible to turn the street-insult *schizo* around in order to take some distance from the official designation "schizophrenic".

In my usage Joyce's *Syko* now gives recognition: it recognises the orientation of those to whom it is directed. In doing so it resists, it refuses, the easy path; it refuses the tendency to retreat, to use the familiar categories of official terminology as a fall-back. In other words, if it takes an interest, it does so without implying an immediate interest in re-orientation, in setting the *psycho* back on the right path. Here then, I am using *Syko* to indicate a different kind of resistance to the one Joyce was promulgating: a resistance to immediately categorising off-the-wallness in terms of psychiatric terminology.

This brings us back to the wanderings of Lucia Joyce. After her time with Jung she continued to refuse to be held. She lived a peripatetic life, interspersed with various attempts to contain her.

When one acquaintance, the Irish painter Patrick Collins, met her in Dublin in the summer of 1935, he marvelled at the way she walked, "wearing a camel's hair coat and carrying a stick", as if "she owned the whole bloody world". He saw "great scope in her" (quoted in Loeb Schloss, 2003, p. 332). When he saw her again a few months later however the picture was rather different. She had spent six days wandering the streets of Dublin. Collins now found Lucia filthy and hungry, and being followed by a sinister man who reeked of Jameson's Irish whisky (Loeb Schloss, ibid.).

Now, as a portmanteau word, Joyce's *Syko* can be taken to include one more word, one which also comes from the Greek: *psyche*. This can mean the soul, as well as mind, spirit, breath, and life. However, in its earliest usage, in Homer, it seems to have meant something like free soul.

If we apply this to Lucia it might, at first glance seem to also give recognition to her resistance, and even to warrant adopting Collins' first, and rather romantic impression, of her position, that is, that she embodies a free spirit. But here the adjective "free" refers to the soul as active, but also lost from the body. That is, this is the soul as active, as having force, but in some sense separate from the consciously-willed body, as in a trance. To quote one scholar, the free soul is active in "dreams, swoons, and other types of unconsciousness" (Bremmer, 1987, p. 17).

In this usage *psyche* picks up on the word's etymological connection with another word from the Greek: *psychein*, to blow. Here then it's not a question of recognising resistance, or at least not conscious resistance, but rather of recognising what insists; like a leaf in the wind, *psyche* blows you down whatever road it will.

Who does Collins see at the end of Lucia's walk? Not our glamorous, bohemian heroine who walks as if she owned that world, but rather our lost, destitute and preyed-upon girl. Given that this journey is driven by something which, finally, cannot be articulated, to say more than this is pure confabulation. It is the case however that, however obscure the impulse, Lucia did set off to walk the streets of Dublin, the very same street-scape which provided the raw, and erotic, material for her father's art, though in his case at a distance. Perhaps we can propose therefore that she sought to recreate for herself her father's Dublin. If so, what she finds is that without having a map to start off with, she is blown about like a leaf in the wind.

Let me, to conclude, now go to the "Journey" that brought me here to give this public lecture tonight. I'm referring to "Journey to Social Inclusion", that being the name of the program of which, as a psychoanalyst, I am a part. Clearly, this program has its own imperatives. That very name, "Journey to Social Inclusion", would seem to place the emphasis on participants being brought in from the cold, as it were. It suggests an expectation that, considered as a group, the participants will travel, they will move forward, but that movement will be measured by the extent to which they are enveloped in what is called the social.

But what is it to be enveloped in this world which is called social? Of course we can trot out the usual responses: that it's about being engaged with others, including friends and family, of being able to sustain yourself by having a job. Also, of course, it is usually thought to be about having a home, with all that that word implies about having the capacity to live with others as well as sustain yourself. In summary then, in this context, entering this world of the social seems to be about "getting a life", as the phrase puts it; of joining in the pursuit of, if not the good life, at least of life.

The difficulty is, however, that, as we pull back to consider this social world in terms of the descriptions we've given of it, further questions begin to arise. Each of these words, "friends", "family", "job", "home", and even "life" itself, do not have any very fixed meanings. And once we try to specify those meaning more precisely we find that they slip away even further.

We find that these terms bring with them whole sets of assumptions, assumptions which already carry a certain understanding. This includes even this goal of life towards which one is being asked to proceed. Even in putting the directive in this way, using the phrase "proceed towards …", you might find yourself inclined to insert a goal which, to all intents and purposes, is quite different to life. I'm thinking of the order given in an emergency: "Proceed calmly towards … the exit!"

Beyond any question of sociological variability, or of cultural or moral parochialism, there is then an ambiguity in the meaning of words. And, as we see, this ambiguity can have implications for those who are being addressed, implications which, in some cases, can be deadly.

This is a difficulty which is intrinsic to the nature of language itself. For us humans, this ambiguity of words is part and parcel of the difficulty we have with language, given that language comes to us by way of speech. This was something which Lacan placed great emphasis on, and from early on in his work as a psychoanalyst. In 1953, in a long paper which he gave in Rome entitled "The function and field of speech and language in psychoanalysis", he summarised this difficulty in a neat formulation which he attributed to a tenth-century Indian philosopher by the name of Abhinavagupta. Lacan happened on this author in an article on aesthetics which, as one does, he came across in a journal published in the Indian city of Benares.

In telling us where to go, speech "conveys what it does not say" (2007a, p. 243). Lacan contrasts this with the social life of bees who, having been given directions to a source of nectar by the precise wagging-dance display of a single bee, are then able, as a group, as a "socius", to proceed unerringly to the goal.

If, however, we are given such directions by another, in an apparently similarly precise form, but by way of speech, as in, "You go here, and when you see this, you turn off there", we can immediately recognise that the effect of such an act of speaking might well be to evoke some questioning on our part. Even if our interlocutor says nothing further, we might well become suspicious of his motives: "Why is he directing me to this destination?"

More importantly however, even if these are instructions are ones which we ourselves have come up, having said them, even to ourselves, they might still come back to haunt us: "If this is the destination, the Fate, to which I am being directed so casually, what does that say about my world, my reality, and, in particular, about my direction?"

Speech conveys what it does not say, or, to put this another way, it conveys more than it says. To put this yet another way, you might say that for us humans, inasmuch as our speech is always already enveloped in language, it is social, or, to use Lacan's formulation, speech is always already enveloped in discourse. This is why, as he says, "speech always includes its own reply" (2007a, p. 243). Whenever we speak there is always a response to be heard, even if there is no one there to say it, and even if we're not conscious of it.

In fact, it is this aspect of speech which sometimes haunts those I am calling *Sykos*. At such times the *Syko* refuses, or, to be less respectful, and also more charitable, is unable, to place himself in, the position of the "I" who receives back his own response in this way. Whether or not his act of speaking is vocalised, in hearing it, he does not hear it is as his own. Because he is unable to affirm this voice as his own, what returns to him can be profoundly unsettling.

It might be possible for our *Syko* to do a patch-up job here. This might be done by attributing the strange voice to malevolent other or others who are then his persecutors. However, much like the bees with their nectar, his instructions are then put in the form of a lock-step, goal-directed imperative: "You *must* go here, and when you see this, you *must* turn off there." In addition, the baleful provenance of this imperative is captured by the all-encompassing command: "This is your fate."

In their book *Anti-Oedipus* (1977) Deleuze and Guattari are scathing about any curative approach which seeks to restore the *Syko*'s ability to pronounce that "hallowed word", I. The response of the *schizo*, as they call him, is to say: "they're fucking me over again. 'I won't say *I* any more, I'll never utter the word again; it's just too damn stupid'"(ibid, p. 23). They propose instead that the *"schizo's* peregrinations are [his] own particular way of rediscovering the earth" (ibid., p. 35).

In making these provocative observations, Deleuze and Guattari are not, I think, seeking to minimise the problems of the "schizo", or, as I prefer to say, the *Syko*. Rather, by asserting that his problems are of a different order they are seeking to recognise that his peculiar peregrinations are a quest.

As this not-I who has lost his soul, or, as he sees it, had it destroyed, Neville is indeed lonely walking the earth, but he is, nevertheless, walking the earth. He could therefore be said to be on a journey.

The limitations of this recognition are illustrated by what occurred in the case of Lucia Joyce. Her experience on the streets of Dublin is nevertheless instructive.

Let me tell you a little story.

Like many children of my generation and social background, I was brought up on Robert Louis Stevenson's *Treasure Island*. I'm not sure whether it was my first book, but it was certainly one of my early experiences of the art of fiction. I can't remember my encounter with it very well, but I do recall a sense of being caught up in an exciting, yet perilous, adventure.

I was reminded of this by reading a short essay by Gilles Deleuze entitled "What children say" (1997, p. 61). What Deleuze refers to in fact is an article by Stevenson in which he tells another story: about how *Treasure Island* came to be written. The article is entitled "My first book—*Treasure Island*".

Stevenson tells us that a crucial element in the creative process was when he happened to draw an elaborate and beautifully coloured map of an island, not Treasure Island, but *an* island. That is, he did not draw this map with some idea that this was already his "treasure island", the process was the other way round. It was, as he puts it, "with the unconsciousness of the predestined" that he was led to give a name to this work of art, that name being "treasure island". So-named, it was this drawing which, in turn, led him to begin work on what was, now, the story called *Treasure Island*.

Stevenson's description of this creative process captures something of the wonder of the children who, like me, came to read the story which this map had engendered. I find it quite moving, and I would like to read you an excerpt:

> I am told there are people who do not care for maps, and find it hard to believe. The names, the shapes of the woodlands, the courses of the roads and rivers, the prehistoric footsteps of man still distinctly traceable up hill and down dale, the mills and the ruins, the ponds and the ferries, perhaps the "Standing Stone" or

the "Druidic Circle" on the heath [Stevenson puts these points of interest in quotes]; here is an inexhaustible fund of interest for any man with eyes to see, or twopence worth of imagination to understand with. No child but must remember laying his head in the grass, staring into the infinitesimal forest, and seeing it grow populous with fairy armies. (Ibid., p. 81)

Deleuze makes mention of another map: the one which Freud drew in his case study of 1909 entitled, "Analysis of a phobia in a five-year-old boy" (1909b). In fact, he draws a parallel with Stevenson's creative experience and that of the boy who figures in this case-study, to whom Freud gave the fictitious name "Little Hans".

As many of you know, Little Hans developed a phobia which focussed on horses, particularly those in his immediate milieu, in the streets around his family's apartment in Vienna. He was afraid a horse would bite him in the street.

As Deleuze describes it however, the problem at the outset was that Hans wanted to leave home. He wanted to spend the night at the little girl's apartment downstairs; he wanted to leave the building and go to the restaurant to meet with the little rich girl, and even if this involved passing by the horses at the warehouse.

In the mid-1950s Lacan gave a year-long seminar in which he spent quite some time re-examining this case of Freud. As Lacan describes it at one point, the difficulty which Hans faced was that the passage, the journey, beyond his immediate milieu was at once a necessity and, in his case, an impossibility. In this impasse it was, says Lacan, the hold of his mother which was the impediment:

[...] everything hangs from the point of impasse which has arisen in Han's relations with his mother. We find it indicated at every moment. It was his mother who had assured his insertion into the world up until that moment. We can grasp the crisis that the child then experiences literally translated into the anxiety which prevents Little Hans from going further than a certain circle, within sight of his house. (1956–1957, p. 381)

The map which Freud drew (which in fact appears twice in the case study, in slightly different versions) depicts Hans' immediate milieu: the short section of his street which includes only his house and the warehouse opposite. Lacan added an additional map. This one zooms out to show the whole district in which Hans' house was located, including the railway system.

In the case-study Freud himself observed the tendency for Hans' phobia to proliferate by association, from horses to railways, and indeed everything in the street-scape which could be seen to have colour, that is, interest, excitement. His description of this echoes something of the way Stevenson's coloured map functioned. But whereas in Stevenson's case the imaginative effect of this colouration was an opening-up to the creation of his world, the world of *Treasure Island*, in Hans' case there was a closing-off of his world:

> It has been noticeable for some time that Hans' imagination was being *coloured* by images from traffic, and was advancing system-atically from horse, which draw vehicles, to railways. In the same way a railway-phobia eventually becomes associated with every street-phobia. (1909b, p. 84)

What I conclude from this, in the present context, is that, for all of us, not only the child, if we are not to come adrift, there is a necessity to make an art of the journey, not the journey home, but the journey out-of-home.

In the case of Neville, the interest of his caseworker has been both insistent and consistent. On his side this has produced resistance, but, part and parcel with that resistance, a fragile trust has also been fash-ioned. For me, given that I too have been implicated in it, this speaks of transference.

Might it be that, with the assistance of this transference, Neville, or some such *Syko*, might find himself enabled to take up the necessity of fashioning a patch-work out of his lonely peregrinations on this planet, even if it turns out to be one with more than a few holes? At least in this way his *not-home* might then become his own, peculiar, *out-of-home*.

CHAPTER THIRTEEN

The death of Marat

Jon Kettle

It came to me in a dream. That is one's position in relation to a dream: the one who receives, the indirect object. One receives the dream and it is only through an indirect path that one can not only speak but realise that one has spoken a signifier. This indirect path is a psychoanalysis. This is the text of my dream:

> I was in a room with straight, white painted walls and polished wooden floorboards, upstairs, the kind of old Victorian house that has been refurbished and used by a psychologist, or a psycho-analyst, as a consulting room. I looked around the room and saw at first that there was no furniture in the room and I thought to myself, "How am I going to make everything fit?" I then looked to my right and saw that there was a bed, like a hospital gurney but with the rails at the end rather than the side, on which one of my patients lay. She was lying on her side, facing the wall, with a white linen sheet draped over her torso, running over the nape of her neck and across the small of her back, her black hair falling over the apex of the sheet and hips and legs, voluptuous, draped along the hospital bed; her skin white, luminescent. She was speaking under the demand of free-association and I was sitting on a chair with

four steel legs, a plastic seat and no armrests—not ideally suited for consulting—hunched forward, listening. I then heard two colleagues, both of whom professed an interest in psychoanalysis—one of whom had never entered a psychoanalysis and another that had informed me her psychoanalysis had been interrupted—and they asked me over my right shoulder, despite being physically absent from the room, "Can you do that?" I replied, "Why not?"

Through what avenue might I approach this text: my transference to my patient, competition with my colleagues, psychoanalytic technique? These are all plausible if I were to undertake an analysis of the themes present in the text. I had pondered this dream on the morning of its reception, the image of my patient's white skin returning. As I recounted this dream in my psychoanalysis several days later, the white skin exerted a pressure, it insisted, and I uttered the words indicative of free-association: "It reminds me of …". What it reminded me of was a painting in which a man lay dead in his bathtub, stabbed to death. He was draped over the side of the bathtub, his limbs flowing over the edge, the undulating muscle etched into his flesh, like the mark of a sculptor's hand upon the white marble of a Renaissance statue. I knew the painting that I was remembering was by Jacques-Louis David but its name eluded me. "The death of Marat" entered my mind but I was particularly doubtful; was it not "The execution of Robespierre"? I learnt following this psychoanalytic meeting that my doubt indeed betrayed the truth.

"The death of Marat"—I had not consciously thought nor spoken this title since age seventeen. I was particularly drawn to the study of history in secondary school. In my final year, amongst other subjects, I studied Roman history and Latin, as well as a history of revolutions, in particular the French and Russian revolutions. I had read voraciously of the Jacobins, the Girondins, Napoleon, writings by Caesar, Horace, and Ovid. I had also studied the paintings of Jacques-Louis David and wrote a final examination piece on his painting, "Napoleon crossing the Alps". I had seen the painting, "The death of Marat", during this period of study but had had no further conscious intellectual engagement with it. Why then, fourteen years later, had I suddenly remembered its name, infected as I was with doubt about its relevance?

As I left the psychoanalytic meeting and again spoke, "Marat", I heard my speech, which invoked a slide into "matar", then "martyr".

Through a meeting with speaking, my psychoanalysis, I spoke and then heard a signifier. I met a signifier. The aural and lingual slippage of Marat, matar, martyr, coupled with the association that Marat was exalted as a martyr of the French revolution by the Montagnards after his murder by Charlotte Corday, indicated that this was an encounter with a signifier in my own history. Speaking under the demand of free-association led to this encounter that could not have been revealed through any means other than a psychoanalysis. The signifier that it produced, martyr, speaks of an aspect of my relation to psychoanalysis.

After reaching the end of secondary school, I undertook to complete an undergraduate degree at a university in Melbourne. This required a certain number of subjects be completed within a defined time period, initially prescribed as four years, and my interest was again drawn to history, particularly Russia during Stalin's rule. There was one man, a lecturer, whom I remember vividly. He stood in front of the auditorium—no notes, no papers, nothing written on the board behind him. He spoke of Stalinist Russia during two hour seminars with such intricate knowledge and vivacity that his word as spoken rendered the written superfluous. It was enlivening. I had, concurrently, studied psychology and after I had completed the undergraduate degree, I pursued further studies in psychology in degrees nominated as a "master" of psychology and a "doctor" of philosophy. These courses of study required that I was taught through formal classes, and thereby knew, acronym-reduced techniques of CBT (cognitive-behaviour therapy) and DBT (dialectical-behavioural therapy), undertook psychological work under supervision of a psychologist granted full registration by a governing body regulated by state law, and completed empirical research concerning a psychological topic that could be quantified, subjected to statistics and thereby compared with other such endeavours. It is with a mixture of disbelief and a lack of surprise that I remember that one's own psychotherapy was clearly discouraged. One's own psychoanalysis was not even mentioned. When I began the practicum aspect of my training, I was legally required to work under the title of probationary psychologist, presumably probationary because it was to be observed whether I would execute my work in accordance with prescribed behaviour and technique. What I encountered near the conclusion of the practicum training was a lack of effect with the patients I treated and, floundering in my anxiety, my encounter with history and the word compelled me to ask a colleague, now my wife, for an other place to begin. I was duly handed Freud's *Papers on Technique* (1911–1915), and, two years later, entered a psychoanalysis.

What, then, of this martyr? The etymological root of martyr is the Greek word, *μάρτυς*, which translates as witness. That is, a martyr is one who bears witness by giving a testimony of an experience through the spoken or written word. Testimony is derived from the Latin, "*testis*", the etymological decomposition of which ("te" and "stis") translates literally as "third standing by". Thus, the third in respect to a martyr is speech itself. In my training in psychology, there was an utter avoidance of addressing, through one's own psychoanalysis, the question of testimony concerning the effects produced by one's practice. One's own speech was not privileged. This occurred at a university that was not ignorant of psychoanalysis (in fact, quite the opposite). My castration at the end of my university training thrust upon me whether I considered my practice sufficiently established without being able to form such testimony. In this manner, my practice was predicated solely on the granting of the titles of "bachelor", "master" and "doctor" by an external body, a university, which were thereafter recognised by another external body, a registration board governed by state law. Indeed, I did not consider my practice to be sufficiently established through this mechanism. My psychoanalysis was an opportunity to address this matter.

Lacan's paper, "Variations on the standard treatment" (2007a), interrogates knowledge in psychoanalysis, in particular in relation to training psychoanalysts. Towards the end of this paper, Lacan comments:

> Ignorance must not, in fact, be understood here as an absence of knowledge but, just as much as love and hate, as a passion for being—for it can, like them, be a path by which being forms … The positive fruit of revelation of ignorance is nonknowledge, which is not a negation of knowledge but rather its most elaborate form. (2007a, p. 297)

Ignorance is not to be understood as an absence of knowledge, writes Lacan. Absence requires that this knowledge is known by an other who can bequeath such knowledge. Instead ignorance, Lacan writes, is "a path by which being forms". This path of formation, as opposed to bequeathal, is a psychoanalysis. What is the relation of ignorance to a psychoanalysis? Lacan writes of a "revelation of ignorance": to lift the veil of one's supposed mastery by requesting to speak with a psychoanalyst and by yielding to the analyst's demand to speak under the weight of free-association, discovering castration. This can lead to ignorance. How does this occur? Certainly one never knows what signifiers will visit in the middle of the night. One can only know, in fact, not through remembering but by speaking what one remembers of such nocturnal visits. The castration of speaking thus allows one to be spoken through the signifying chain embedded in free-association, a speaking about which one is, until after the fact, ignorant.

Lacan writes that the positive fruit of such a revelation of ignorance is *nonknowledge*, which he contrasts with a negation of knowledge (let us designate this as non-knowledge[1]). Such non-knowledge can be construed as a position in which knowledge that is not known by oneself is supposed to be known by an other—a psychoanalyst, for instance. In distinction, nonknowledge is a position in which knowledge comes into being through the very act of speaking and the enunciation of signifiers that this permits. It is only through speaking under the weight of free-association in a psychoanalysis that this movement from non-knowledge to nonknowledge can be effected; no amount of formal classes, practicum psychological work or empirical, statistical research can do so. This can only be learned through a psychoanalysis. There is no substitute.[2]

I began my path towards my psychoanalysis by telephoning a psychoanalyst and requesting to speak with him in person. He was the recipient of my demand to alleviate my suffering and such speech demarcated me in a position of non-knowledge. This position persisted until I spoke the associations to my dream of Marat, although I possessed the intellectual knowledge from reading psychoanalytic texts that I was designated in this very position. What of my Marat, matar, martyr? I recall the moment when I rediscovered the painting's name and I was compelled to conclude that I had encountered a signifier. Thereafter I was arrested not only by coming to know my initial position in language of non-knowledge but also by the dislocation of moving to a new position of knowing nonknowledge. This encounter was revealed by free-association that, ironically, has exacted a hefty payment which, once made, cannot be refunded.

Notes

1. I have chosen "non-knowledge" to allow a distinction with the neologism, nonknowledge, as used by the translator, Bruce Fink, in the paper, "Variations on the Standard Treatment" in *Ecrits* (2006). The lack of a hyphen in nonknowledge distinguishes this as an entity which does not exist in opposition to knowledge.

2. Lacan returns to the relation of ignorance to knowledge sixteen years later in Lesson I, 4th November 1971, of his *Seminar XIX, The Knowledge of the Psychoanalyst* (Editions de l'Association Lacanienne Internationale, 2013). Lacan introduces the term "learned ignorance", first proposed by Nicholas of Cusa in his work, *De Docta Ignorantia*, in the fifteenth century. This is an ignorance that is not only learned, with the emphasis on the second syllable, but also learned, with the emphasis on the first syllable. Crucially, Lacan comments: "In order to come to knowledge, I made the remark at an already distant time: that ignorance might be considered in Buddhism as a passion, this is a fact that is justified, with a little meditation. But as meditation is not our strong point, it is only through experience that it can be known." (ibid., p. 15). Lacan uses the French verb, *connaître*, in relation to this "that it can be known", and not savoir. A further digression is required at this point. A second language in which I am familiar, Castellano, has two verbs which English clumsily renders as "to know". "Saber" implies attaining a unit of knowledge relating to facts or procedures via intellectual means: to know the rule of free association, to know the history of psychoanalysis. *"Conocer"* implies to know something by familiarity gained through an encounter: to know Melbourne, to know a friend. The English language, to its detriment, does not impart this distinction with separate verbs. Like Castellano, I understand that the French language imparts a distinction between the use of *savoir* and *connaître* in relation to coming to knowledge through a personal encounter. Importantly, Lacan uses *connaître* in this example, clearly indicating that ignorance is to be learned through an encounter—a psychoanalysis.

PART III

PSYCHOANALYSIS AND THE CHILD

CHAPTER FOURTEEN

In the raw

Michael Currie

In Australian slang there is a saying that captures the delight and revulsion of the homophilia of early male adolescence. Fear of being "caught in the raw" (i.e., being found naked in front of one's school mates) emerges, for example, within the domestic routine in the segregated dormitories at school camp or boarding school. Shared showers, fear of one's bathers slipping off whilst swimming etc.; all lead to the fear of being the object of the ecstatic voyeurism of the adolescent group where the full flesh of the body is revealed. The phrase returns to me to illustrate a similar rawness of speech in the case I am about to discuss, which cannot be divorced from the raw flesh of the speaker. Raw as what is uncooked and indigestible also serves the purpose of my title well.

Charlie was a boy who came to see me in my clinic for children. He was not plagued, as many adult speakers are, by an anxiety of being caught in the raw of speech. Of interest to me is that Charlie seemed to prefer the enigmatic majesty of the raw to common meaning. From Charlie, I heard the raw as constitutive of the voice.

The voice, as partial object, as a member of the catalogue of the object *a* can't be captured, held onto or retained. The drive circles—emerging and returning—to take up its path again or not. As Lacan points out in *Seminar XI* the aim of the drive is not the mark or target (rendered by the French word *but*) rather the aim is the itinerary taken (1979, pp. 178–181). Whilst the drive never hits its mark, does the voice leave a trace in the vicissitudes of the drive? Can the voice influence the realm of eternal lack? Whilst the very existence of psychoanalysis answers yes, such an answer leaves little to work.

Lacan, when he discusses the voice explicitly but enigmatically in *The Third*, produces something that might lead somewhere.

> *Ourdrome* gives me the occasion to put the voice under the rubric of the four objects I have called a; that is to say, to empty it again of the substance that there could be in the noise that it makes; that is, to return to the account of the signifying operation, the one I have specified from the so-called effects of metonymy. In such a way, starting from there, the voice—if I can say so—the voice is free, free to be something other than substance. (1974)

With *ourdrome*, Lacan is punning in French on *disque-ourd-rome*, which is translatable as the record from Rome. The "from Rome" I read as Lacan emphasising the centrality of speech and language and the linguistic structures of metaphor and metonymy he outlined in his first "Rome discourse" in 1953. In my reading of the quoted remarks made twenty years later, Lacan is questioning the centrality of these structures. Rather than the structure itself, the "so-called effects of metonymy" are now the aspects of speech that place the voice under the designating power of the object *a*. The effect of metonymy is to endlessly increase the slipperiness of the meaning of speech; to destabilise the relation of the voice to the substance of what it apparently represents. The sound of speech is not reduced to the symbolic order of meaning via differences. Rather the sound of the voice comes to the fore. Over the time of his treatment, I heard Charlie use sound as a lubricant to create a slipperiness that invented a voice, a voice singularly his own.

When Charlie first came to see me, he was in late primary school. He was aggressive at school, and sad at home. The correlates of his aggressive problems were not hard to find in his history. Recently Charlie's father had slapped him across the mouth with his penis. As he did so, his father told Charlie—*"That's what a real man has"*. The father says in the sound of his penis slapping against his son's cheek: "I have all the enjoyment, and that is what I am interested in." The father, apparently, does not lack.

In one of his first sessions with me Charlie was rambunctious, running around my office, tipping over the toys, barking like a dog and roaring like a lion. He did not want to talk or sit in the chair. After one of his roars I roared back, just like a lion, just like he had roared. I had expected him to receive my roar as something playful, as my joining with him. He stopped. For the first time in the session he directly attended to me. But his sudden stillness and sullenness told me he wasn't playing. He sat in the chair and told me that he did not know if he wanted to come and see me. He had received a roar that left no room for his enjoyment. This was the first shift in his discourse, and it founded the treatment.

In the silence I told him I would be glad to see him again. I told him we were trying to work out whether he wanted to come and see me. I told him I didn't know if he wanted to come back. I took him back to his grandmother.

A colleague said to me: "It is as if you slapped him like his father." This is correct insofar as we are concerned with the use of metaphor to lead us to the truth. After the roar, when I asked Charlie if he wanted to come back, to what was I inviting him? To something quite different to the metaphorical play in which my colleague and I were indulging. Rather the invitation was to a play with the raw of language and the flow of this raw towards the un-representable. Rather than a place of interpretation, of setting limits, or any other therapeutic goal, I propose the function of the treatment in this case was to facilitate this child's engagement with the brilliant, disruptive raw of his own speech.

Charlie accepted my invitation. We moved to a playroom full of toys. The next part of the treatment contained seemingly endless repetitive enactments, session after session of armies of men destroying each other. Cars chased and crashed into each other, wishing for and achieving vengeance and victory. Mass slaughter and chaotic destruction ruled these sessions. Charlie always added a coda of resurrection in the silence after the destruction. The scores of fallen figures on the battlefield rose again. The dead soldier recovered from his wounds. The smashed car worked again.

What was Charlie trying to do in repeatedly playing back and forth over the boundary of death? Rendering an imaginary omnipotence, no doubt, but what else?

Fillupyourpants

In the session that brought a shift from playing god, Charlie started by blowing bubbles with some bubble mixture he had found. Between bubbles he tried a game where he was to guess the number I was thinking. I allowed him to be right the first few times and then he was wrong. He told me *I've used up all my magic thinking.* He then said, "*Fill up, fillip-pee-no* then *fil-up-your-pants*" and laughed. He became chaotic and animated and full of energy in his movements, like he had in the roar session. He blew more bubbles and turned away from me, pulling out the front of his tracksuit pants to catch the bubbles, laughing. "*That's filupyourpants*" he said, laughing again. *Fillupyourpants* bears an unmistakable playing reference to an aspect of the father. As Charlie's omniscience failed him in the number guessing game, he played with a reference to his father. The play, over determined, turns him away from his father's habit of covering lack.

Firstly, Charlie is making a mockery in his linguistic play, saying his father's only interest is in filling up his pants. Through the pleasure that the subject takes in the joke, we know from Freud that the subject takes what has been found within and makes it foreign. *Filupyourpants* as joke, is it Charlie's way of making alien his deep identification with the imaginary father?

Secondly, in the playing metonymy on the reference to his father, he is showing that enjoyment is not only his father's. He questions the all-enjoying omnipotence of the father in the moment of the penis slap.

Charlie went on to fill out his point later in the same session. Charlie caught a bubble in his hand and told me: "I am Michael Currie and I am going to pop this bubble, which is Charlie Y and he will never come back again." Charlie looked at me and said, "Well, should I pop it?"

Y is the surname of Charlie's father, X the surname of Charlie's mother, his full name Charlie X-Y. Charlie's act of bursting the bubble that he calls Charlie Y can be heard as a refusal to accept the inheritance of the complete enjoyment of the father. A bubble is a perfect sphere bounded on all sides. What is within the bubble is complete. Once the bubble is burst what the bubble contains is free to roam, to disperse where it will. The bursting of the bubble is a shift from phallic enjoyment to a beyond. Charlie wants to be done with domination by enjoyment. He bursts the bubble of enjoyment, making it incomplete and unbounded. At the end of a session soon after he told me, when he saw his name on a telephone message on my desk: "You have me there as Charlie X-Y. I don't want to be called Charlie X-Y anymore. Can you change me to Charlie X?"

In the sessions following the *filupyourpants* session, the endless destructive games of war stopped. Charlie started playing with a toy sized boxing ring where two wrestlers battled. Despite the cutting of the father's name, or perhaps because of it, fathers came into Charlie's wrestling play more and more. The moment of death continued to be replayed. As a wrestler/father was mortally wounded, or about to be thrown to his doom by his opponent, the father would enunciate a wish—"I only wanted the best for you"; or "I just wanted to save you"; or "I only wanted to set you free". Commonly the father would also realise his mistake—"If only I had … .!" or "You fiend, you tricked me". Or "I thought you were my brother". Whilst the doomed man was usually resurrected after his death, it was not until after an unfulfilled wish emerged or he had revealed an act in which he had failed. A very different father was emerging who now acknowledges a deficit, a lack, a hole in his omnipotence. The character of death is shifting also. Rather than being like a room in a house where one enters and leaves, death is causing a shortfall to appear within the father. Death had begun to be symbolised on the side of living.

I restricted myself to questioning why the father had to die. Charlie, through the father figure, responded with statements like—"Because there will never be any good in the world whilst he is alive"; or "Because he killed my father/sister/mother". The rivalry of the boxing ring, when questioned, was now returned to a symbolic system. The symbolic system outlined in his play was, to my ears, extremely generic. However, for Charlie this was the seed of a symbolic scheme that would underline his reasons for action within his play.

This brings me to the third function of the utterances that culminated in *filupyourpants*. There is a symbolic meaning in the play on the reference to the father. *Filupyourpants* is suggestive of the enjoyment of the partial objects, the faeces, the erect phallus, and the phrase itself of the enjoyment of the voice. The meaning is the shift from the childish enjoyment of the other objects of peeing and pooing in *fillup—pee—no* (an affirmation and negation in one word) to the enjoyment for the grown man with his erect phallus—*fill-up-your-pants*.

However, *filupyourpants* is formed via homophonic metonymy, where the similarity of the sound and shape of speech allows the play from *fill up* to *fil-lip-pin-no* to *fill-up-your-pants*. The sound that produces the metonymy belongs to the real and produces an enjoyment, freed from the weight of meaning.

This metonymy contains a compressed movement, springing out of the imaginary, pivoting through the symbolic into the real. In following the metonymy Charlie's speech moves to an enjoyment of the sound, beyond the realm of the phallus, of meaning, of what a real man is. The play with words has an object, but the enjoyment that flows from the play is not without an object. It is this enjoyment not without an object that points to a possible shift for Charlie, from the one who is enjoyed by the perverse father to one who enjoys. It is this enjoyment that is freed from representing.

Boy

After many sessions, Charlie decided that he wanted to play outside. He looked for bugs and snails under logs and rocks, and played games of capturing, hiding, and corralling with some snails. He named one of the snails "Boy". Boy and Charlie passed through several adventures, until Charlie threw Boy high in the air yelling "Boy". When the snail crashed onto the concrete he became concerned and upset. He decided to bury "Boy" in the dirt next to the concrete. He asked me to sing some funeral music as he dug a hole, placed the snail inside the hole, covered it over and then placed some strands of grass over the grave.

Charlie went off to play elsewhere and then returned some minutes later, upset once again. "Boy, what have I done?" He turned to me and asked: "Michael do you think Boy is OK? Do you think we can get him up? Can we? Is he OK? Is he dead? I'm going to get him." At this point I said, "No, Charlie. Boy is dead. You cannot dig him up. He is gone and he must stay in the ground." Charlie asked, "Did I kill Boy? Did I Michael?" In the following month, Charlie played a few further sessions outside. He asked if he could dig up Boy to see him. Each time he asked I told him no.

That Charlie was able to put forward these series of questions indicates he had played his way towards them: he was ready for the answer I gave. With the death of Boy Charlie had forsaken the god-play of resurrection. There was no repairing the smashed shell, no reforming the squished, slimy flesh of the snail. He was stuck with a remnant of snail flesh on our side of death. His play had produced a leftover he could not re-use or recycle. For Boy he could only mourn.

In naming "Boy" Charlie lays out an uncertain itinerary. From the object he mourns—a boy whose destiny leans on the perverse father of enjoyment—there emerges another destiny that implies a submission to speech, but not a forsaking of enjoyment. This is the itinerary of the bursting bubble he has begun to show us in his metonymy of *filupyourpants*.

Soon after the snail session Charlie introduced into his play two identical dolls, which he named good Charlie and bad Charlie. In a tantalising taste of what he might show of his future path, the two Charlies fought ferociously. One Charlie was torn apart, and it was unclear which one. Before he left that session, Charlie asked "Will you repair it before I come back again Michael? Will you put Charlie back together?" I left the Charlie doll in bits on my desk for him to find in the next sessions. When he returned he noted the Charlie-in-bits, but never played "good Charlie—bad Charlie" again.

Supernanafrick

In the weeks following the snail session there was another shift in Charlie's discourse. One session within this time of the treatment, Charlie came into my consulting room telling me he felt bad. He returned to his nanna and continued a discussion about how he wanted to go to the park to play with his friends after the session rather than visit his aunt and new-born cousin. Tenacious but polite, dogged but accepting of the protesting utterances of his grandmother he got what he wanted.

He then returned to my consulting room. As he walked there he started saying "It's *Supernanafrick*". He then started skipping and chanting these sounds in a rhythm. Once in my consulting room he continued chanting *supernanafrick* and asked me to chant them in a rhythm.

I asked him what these words meant. Charlie told me he didn't know. He suddenly showed an interest in the doll's house. Animated once again he arranged the furniture and several dolls within the doll's house with a deftness and speed that I have rarely seen in a child. He played out an intricate scene with a crying baby, a comforting nanna, a grandfather, sister and brother accompanied by the *supernanafrick* chant. On a few occasions I ceased chanting *supernanafrick*. When I did so Charlie would stop the action, and say to me, urgently, "keep it going!" He required the chant to support his play. This was the commencement of another shift, where Charlie moved to playing out invented dramas within the dolls' house, which he continued until the end of the treatment.

Supernanafrick heralded the arrival of a power of invention that came to inhabit Charlie. His symbols and objects around him had determined and would continue to determine him. Now, he was able, to some extent, to influence these same symbols and objects. He had begun to apply this influence with *filupyourpants*. The means for influence came from the raw of his speech, where non-sense provided something other than the seemingly unshiftable reality of Oedipus. Charlie's declared name for this invention outside the meanings of history was *supernanafrick*.

Charlie also introduced a new character in this same session: a "hammer of justice" that came to feature in several ways in the closing sessions of the treatment. I hear this hammer as a symbolisation of the jail time of his father, something that is not symbolised within the penis slap.

We can wonder: What does this word *supernanafrick* mean? There are many ways to take it up. The word itself resists reduction to meaning and Charlie himself is on the side of that resistance, declining to give the word a meaning. To assign meaning, say via an interpretation, would be to fill the voice with the weight of representation once again. Rather than drowning in meaning, I want to point to the significance of *supernanafrick* beyond meaning. In asking me to chant the phrase in rhythm Charlie reduces it further to an utterance of noise in time, an utterance of the shape of sound, not meaning. The phrase is a beautifully shaped piece of sound sculpture: *SooouPer nan NA FricK*.

Despite the numerous possibilities of reduction to meaning, it is the non-imitative, non-reproductive aspect of *supernanafrick* which conveys more and more how Charlie has found a way to *frick* which is his own, between the slap of the penis against his face and his nana's moral strictures. The rhythm is an emphatic celebration of the discovery of the enjoyment that is enjoyment in speech itself.

Charlie made use of my invitation to the raw. With *filupyourpants* and *supernanafrick* he used the raw materials of speech as moments of designation where his speech and play were freed from the burden of representing the substance of his history. Such freedom ex-sists: predicated neither on a possible fate nor a past of privation. Such is the power of the raw.

CHAPTER FIFTEEN

Psychoanalysis and the child: history, time, and the transformational formula— an introduction

Michael Gerard Plastow

The following three papers have a number of things in common. Firstly they all arose out of the ongoing seminar Psychoanalysis and the child, conducted by Tine Nørregaard and myself within The Freudian School of Melbourne. Furthermore they are all written versions of seminars that we first presented in Copenhagen, Denmark, in September 2012. The paper "Psychoanalysis of the child: the bastard child of psychoanalysis" was presented to the Danish Association of Psychotherapists and was subsequently presented in March 2013 as a public lecture of The Freudian School of Melbourne. The other two papers were presented together at the weekly seminar of the psychoanalytic school *Freuds Agorá* based in Copenhagen.

Given that these three works arise from the continuity of the work of our own seminar, there are a number of threads that run through them. One of these is an elaboration of the notion of *time* as a temporality outside of history. This is a notion of time that we have worked through Freud's term, the "infantile". As I have noted in the "Psychoanalysis of the child: the bastard child of psychoanalysis" paper, early in his teachings Lacan remarked that, "History is not the past. History is the past in so far as it is historicised in the present" (1991, p. 12). But here we could also put forward that the infantile is not the past either, but rather a temporality that, despite being out of reach, is generally supposed by the subject to have existed in the past. If for Freud this time is one designated by the terms "prehistoric" or the "archaic", with Lacan we can say that the infantile is the exception that grounds the very notion of history.

The paper "Psychoanalysis of the child: the bastard child of psychoanalysis" takes up these questions, not in regard to the clinical history of any one analysand, but in relation to the history of the psychoanalysis of children itself. In doing so, it endeavours to locate a part of the history which is missing from the usual accounts of the history of psychoanalysis of the child. In this manner it gives particular emphasis to the largely forgotten pioneer of this field, Hermine Hug-Hellmuth. I propose in this paper that it was Hermine Hug-Hellmuth, in her challenge to Freud and his analysis of his daughter Anna, who was effectively able to logically establish the field of the psychoanalysis of the child. Hermine Hug-Hellmuth thus provided a basis for separating the psychoanalysis of the child from the raising of children, and thus from the pedagogical bent it has always been prone to taking.

The following two papers, the reader will note, are partly overlapping and interwoven in their themes, and retain in part their character of oral presentations. They address the question of how the subject's history and trajectory become intermeshed and written in what we are describing as a "mapping". However these papers consist of a different type of intermeshing as well. They are an intersection of our seminar Psychoanalysis and the child, and the weekly seminar of *Freuds Agorá*. Thus they are also an encounter of our study the of question of mapping, in part through Freud's case of little Hans, with the Danish group's focus of study at that time on another of Freud's cases, that of the Rat Man. This has led to a hybrid approach to our theme in which little Hans meets the Rat Man. I have endeavoured to capture this cross-fertilisation in my title "The kangaroo rat man", the "kangaroo rat" being a new signifier produced by the meeting of different cultures.

"The kangaroo rat man" examines the way in which Australian indigenous aesthetics of the peoples of the Western desert also participates in a type of mapping in which the actual topography of the land is painted in reference to fragments of stories from what is known as the "dreamtime". As we will see, this dreamtime can also be rendered as the "ancestral present", a time, once again, outside of history. In the transposition of little parts of the stories from the ancestral present onto canvas, the artist as subject literally maps out his place in relation both to traditional culture as well as participating in the marketplace of art.

In this paper as well as the following one by Tine Nørregaard, "The transformational formula of myth", we take up the question of what Lacan refers to as the "transformational formula", unfortunately rendered into a static "transformational form" in the published English-language translation. This transformational formula is precisely what is able to provide an articulation between myth—whether it be a family myth or the mythology of a particular culture—and the fantasm of the singular subject. The transformational formula, like a mathematical formula, thus also affords a transformation, or even a de-formation, from Freud's family romance into Lacan's individual myth of the neurotic. The latter can be read through the terms "poetry" and "truth", the other part of the title of Lacan's lecture which is missing in the English language version. We have rendered the title of the paper more accurately as "The individual myth of the neurotic or poetry and truth in neurosis" (1979, pp. 290–307).

The poetry and truth which are missing, indeed repressed, in the English language version of the paper, come from the title of Goethe's autobiography. Lacan himself no doubt takes the reference to this work from the Rat Man himself; there are several mentions of this work in Freud's history of the case. Interestingly one of these occurred in relation to the Rat Man's rare and extraordinary occasions of masturbation which happened, Freud says, "shortly after his father's death" (1909b, p. 203). It transpired after the Rat Man had read Goethe's *Poetry and Truth from my own Life*, in particular the episode in which the young Goethe had freed himself from the effects of a curse that a jealous mistress had pronounced upon the next woman who should kiss his lips.

Freud pointed out to the Rat Man that his episodes of masturbation always contained two elements: a prohibition, and the defiance of a command. It is no doubt in such moments, moments in which the subject is able to overcome a previously established order, in which an interdiction can be transgressed, that there lies the possibility of grasping a little object: an elusive jouissance. Such moments may be articulated through the fictional form of a new myth, which we may name as a fantasm. But here we must restore the repressed poetry and truth. In doing so, as Tine Nørregaard writes, we move from Freud's form of the novel or Romance, to Lacan with whom truth might be articulated in a poetic form.

CHAPTER SIXTEEN

Psychoanalysis of the child: the bastard child of psychoanalysis

Michael Gerard Plastow

The official version of the history of psychoanalysis of the child often situates its beginnings with little Hans, his father, and of course Freud. And Freud himself named Anna Freud as the pioneer of this field. Melanie Klein and her followers also promote Klein's legitimacy to this crown. Here, however, against such an account of history, we can elaborate what we might refer to as the "illegitimate" beginnings of the field of psychoanalysis with children.

In their writings, both Melanie Klein and Anna Freud give short shrift to the place of another analyst whose writings and work preceded both of them: Hermine Hug-Hellmuth. Here we will give particular prominence to this woman who can be considered the first analyst of children, but whose history is less well known. Hug-Hellmuth's life and work were indeed marked by questions of legitimacy, and very literally the illegitimacy of her half-sister that she never revealed, and that of her half-sister's son Rolf. We can also call into question the legitimacy of her use of her studies of Rolf for a number of her published case studies. Questions, however, were raised concerning the legitimacy of the book she had published anonymously, *A Young Girl's Diary* (2004), endorsed by Freud with a glowing foreword (ibid., pp. 7–8).

However, what I want to come to propose is that the practice of psychoanalysis of the child must necessarily be a bastard child, not the legitimate inheritor of a family legacy. To put this forward, it is not so much in order to correct history, but rather to endeavour to establish a logical beginning for the field of psychoanalysis of the child.

Time and history

In order to do this, we must elucidate the nature of history itself for psychoanalysis. In the first instance, history, for psychoanalysis, is the clinical history that is given by our patients. And since psychoanalysis began with adults, the child first appeared as an historical being: the child in the history of adult patients. Indeed, since most accounts that we have of children come from adults, the "child", as recounted, is most often the effect of the retrospective memories of adults.

In Freud's writings, the child also emerged through his notion of the "infantile", whether it was in his use of the terms "infantile sexuality", 'infantile amnesia' or "infantile neurosis". We can of course differentiate the observable "child" from childhood as retrospectively recounted by Freud's analysands. But the child is in the same position as the adult analysand: there exists both the child in front of us as well as the childhood, or history, recounted by a child. A young analysand, for instance, did a drawing of a series of four penises: "Daddy's penis, Mummy's penis, my penis, and my penis when I was a baby". Here the child differentiates himself from the childhood he supposed himself to have "when I was a baby".

In this manner, the child, as subject and as analysand, is not able to be differentiated from the adult. Both participate in the recounting of a time "when I was a child/baby". So what insists in a history is this *Other* time, a "Once upon a time" we might call it. Thus this mythical time also fills in the gaps of what is missing in the history. This is what we can designate as "the infantile" through Freud. And the mythology that masquerades as the clinical history is already an aetiological formulation by the analysand, something that attempts to give an explanation for that which ultimately cannot be explained. The history, then, is a retrospective attempt to give meaning to the accidents of history, to the gaps in history, that have no meaning *per se*. Freud himself refers to "the distortion and refurbishing to which a person's own past is subjected when it is looked back upon from a later period" (1918b, p. 9).

But the piece that is missing from the history is designated in a number of different ways by Freud, for instance, as "infantile amnesia", "infantile sexuality", the "prehistoric", the "phylogenetic", the "archaic", etc. This does not negate the place of the history but provides a counterpoint to the history by reference to what lies outside of history. Thus David Pereira proposed that Freud allows a place for that which exceeds the history by maintaining the tension "between the historical and the prehistoric, the ontogenetic and the phylogenetic" (1999, p. 63).

One of the implications that follows from this is that we have to pose the following fundamental question: what is history? Lacan remarked that, "History is not the past. History is the past in so far as it is historicised in the present" (1991, p. 12). We take this to include both the clinical history, as we will elaborate upon here, as well as the history of child psychoanalysis itself. Against the illusion of the history as a steady progression of development, what is determining are the "accidental factors", as Freud proposed (1905d, p. 131). The history, nonetheless, is still recounted to us in the guise of a sequence of events, as an historical or chronological account. Any psychoanalysis must constitute a re-writing of this historicisation.

The beginnings of child psychoanalysis

From its very outset, the field of psychoanalysis of the child was an affair of female psychoanalysts, both in regard to those who are better known, such as Melanie Klein and Anna Freud, as well as the analyst to whom we shall give prominence today, Hermine Hug-Hellmuth. We will endeavour to put forward that it was the latter who truly founded the field of psychoanalysis of the child.

Sigmund Freud himself designated psychoanalysis of the child as the sphere of female psychoanalysts. In the thirty-fourth of his *New Introductory Lectures on Psychoanalysis* (1933a) entitled "Explanations, applications and orientations", Freud states the following: "It has automatically happened that child-analysis has become the domain of women analysts, and no doubt this will remain true (ibid., p. 48)." We might hear in this "automatically" something of the "automaton" that Lacan (1979) refers to as the insistence of the signifier. Indeed we could go so far as to say that this "automatically", is also a "symptomatically", a symptom of the origins of the psychoanalysis of children.

In referring to children, Freud places great emphasis, as does his daughter Anna, upon what he refers to as the educational aspects of psychoanalysis. The term that Freud uses in German is *Erziehung*: a term which is translated as "education", but which has a much broader sense than the word education in English and encompasses what we might refer to as "upbringing". Etymologically, "education" derives from the Latin *educere*, literally "to lead out", that is, to lead children, or to bring them up, out of ignorance in which they are born.

Freud is thus also alluding to that other role that is allocated to women as the ones who bring up children, effectively then, to the place of the mother. Here in automatically attributing the field of the psychoanalysis of the child to women, Freud effectively conflates the place of the analyst with that of the parent, and more specifically that of the mother.

We see this same conflation repeated in the common practice of the early analysts of children who analysed their own children and family members. Thus Melanie Klein analysed all of her own children, little Hans was analysed by his father with Freud nominally in the place of supervisor, and Hermine Hug-Hellmuth analysed the dreams, symptoms, and behaviours of her nephew Rolf. And we can add that the foremost of these analyses of one's own child was Freud's analysis of his daughter Anna.

Indeed, it was to Anna that Freud relegated the field of psychoanalysis of children: "I am glad that I am at least able to say that my daughter, Anna Freud, has made this study her life-work and has in that way compensated for my neglect" (Freud, S., 1933a, p. 147). Such a statement articulates the wish that a neglect, a lack on the part of a parent, might be able to be made up for by the child.

The other implication of Freud's comment is that the work of psychoanalysis is able to be passed on through family connections. It is significant that Freud referred to "my daughter", and not "my colleague", "a psychoanalyst" or any other term. Thus the inheritance is, in Freud's own words, bequeathed to Anna Freud on the basis of family relations. We see something similar which besets the Lacanian field through Jacques Lacan having left his intellectual legacy to his daughter Judith and son-in-law Jacques-Alain Miller. This is precisely something we are endeavouring to put into question here: can psychoanalysis be a family affair?

Throughout his lifetime, Freud never diverged from his view that the analysis of one's own child was possible. In 1935 he replied to a letter from Edoardo Weiss who asked Freud about the possibility of analysing his own son. Freud replied with the curious phrase—at least in the translation—"With one's own daughter I succeeded well". He added, "It would not surprise me if you were successful …" (1970, p. 81).

Anna Freud, being analysed by her father, maintained that the child's relations were to the parents who, "are still real and present as love-objects" (1946, p. 84). Hence for her, "the child is not, like the adult, ready to produce a new edition of its love-relationships" (ibid., p. 34), in other words, a transference to the analyst. Strikingly, Anna Freud even put forward that only the child of an analyst could be analysed:

> The analysis of children belongs essentially in the analytical milieu, and must for the present be confined to the children of analysts […]. (Ibid., p. 50)

At that time in Vienna there was a division in that most early analysts were medical practitioners and therefore male, since women were excluded from studying medicine and thus practising as doctors. On the other hand, besides being educators in the home, women were also often educators in their professional lives. Thus women who worked outside of the home were often nurses, child-carers and of course school teachers. But for the psychoanalysis of children there was a difference: training of women in psychoanalysis introduced them to a place previously reserved for men and thus offered the possibility of their emancipation. However such a place also allowed the possibility for some of these women—and this is what interests us here—to assume the position of analyst of their own children. So from the very beginning of the clinical practice of psychoanalysis of the child, the analyst was placed right at the centre of the family drama, not just a symbolic one as proposed by the Oedipus myth, but a real one that was played out between family members.

A field of psychoanalysis of the child?

Is it is possible to say that the child is a separate entity from the adult, for psychoanalysis, or is the child an analysand in the fullest sense that adult analysands are considered to be? Freud, in defence once again of his daughter Anna's approach, wrote to Joan Riviere that, "Ferenczi wittily remarked that, if Mrs. Klein is right, then children really no longer exist" (1992, p. 277). Is there a difference in the child from the adult in respect of psychoanalysis? Can we say that the "child" exists as a theoretical entity for psychoanalysis?

Freud himself initiated the psychoanalytic investigation of children, but upon the basis of supposedly confirming the material that had emerged from the analyses of adults (1905d, p. 132). This was not just any "material", but was specifically that of infantile sexuality. Thus the "observations" of little Hans—of his behaviour, but also of his speech—took place initially to record little Hans' "normal" infantile sexuality. But Freud says at the end of the case history that, "Strictly speaking, I learnt nothing new from this analysis ..." (1909b, p. 146). Here again there was nothing new or different in Hans' analysis from that of adult analysands. The infantile remained, necessarily, at a distance, even the in the analyses of children.

In Hans' analysis it was not the mother in the place of analyst but rather the father. But from Freud's point of view, there was a necessary conflation in Hans' father being in this place:

> It was only because the authority of a father and of a physician were united in a single person, and because in him both affection-ate care and scientific interest were combined, that it was possible in this one instance to apply the method to a use to which it would not otherwise have lent itself. (Ibid., p. 4)

Bergès and Balbo state, in regard to this proposition, that we must give it serious consideration despite its apparently outdated notion of a parent analysing his own child. They emphasise its difference to what they call the "mother-therapies" that proliferate, particularly with very young children and most especially in the case of autistic children (2012, pp. 109–110). It is in these areas that so-called "dyadic" therapies are undertaken, the dyad always consisting of the child and the mother, with the therapist or analyst working through the mother. We must note that in little Hans' case it is a father, and not a mother, analysing his child. Freud's proposition is that the transference of this child with his father is an optimal arrangement. We need, though, to add a caveat to this examination of Freud's statement: this proposition is in the singular and refers not to *the* father in general, but to *a* father, to this particular father, "in this one instance".

Hermine Hug-Hellmuth

Hug-Hellmuth in many ways epitomises the duality that is at the origins of the psychoanalysis of children. She was not a medical doctor, but she was nonetheless one of the very first women to obtain a doctorate degree from the University of Vienna. Her working life seems to have been divided into two quite distinct periods. Up until 1912, the year in which her first psychoanalytic publications on the child appeared—six papers in total in that year alone—she worked as a school teacher. After that time she devoted herself entirely to psychoanalysis. Thus in Hug-Hellmuth's working life there was already a division between education and psychoanalysis.

Her life was marked by a number of scandals and also by many questions of legitimacy. Even the name by which she became known is given differently by different sources. Her father, Knight Hugo Hug von Hugenstein, fathered an illegitimate child seven years prior to the birth of Hermine. This child was initially called Antonia Farmer, but later appeared illegitimately—through a false name and date of birth—in the father's subsequent family as Antoine, now only two years older than Hermine. In 1906, Antoine herself gave birth to an illegitimate son Rudolf Otto Hug, who is commonly known as "Rolf" and who was studied from the perspective of psychoanalysis by Hermine. Indeed, it is curious that we know him by his affectionate name, effectively in this manner perpetuating family relations. Antoine died in 1915 and Rolf, who was troubled from an early age, had subsequent placements in different families and schools that ineluctably broke down.

At one stage Victor Tausk was officially named as his guardian, but Tausk committed suicide not long afterwards. Later Rolf routinely stole from Hermine and tried to get money out of her in different ways. Hermine reported to Isidor Sadger that she was afraid that Rolf would strangle her. In another letter she stated "I will be killed anyway" (Maclean, et al., 1991, p. 42).

In her paper of 1924, "The libidinal structure of family life", Hug-Hellmuth dedicated a section to the illegitimate child. She wrote:

> The illegitimate child soon feels his special position into [which] a cruel society has cast him and his mother. At last when school begins he realizes what it means to not know his father's name when the other children assure him of the humiliating truth that his embarrassed mother could not tell him. The boy's reaction is to unconsciously detest his mother and to secretly see her as a prostitute. Later, in his eyes all other women are prostitutes too. Because of his hatred for women, he will become a "lady killer" for whom all women are available, or he will simply hate women. (1924, p. 270)

In September 1924 Rolf went to Hermine's apartment and awoke her whilst climbing in through an open window. A struggle ensued during which Rolf strangled her. He then took her money and a gold watch. For psychoanalysis this was a great scandal which was covered up in order to avoid consequent bad publicity. The stifling of this history was also in response to an injunction invoked by Hermine Hug-Hellmuth herself before she died, and it is unknown for what reasons she had this injunction made. This perhaps, in part, explains the obscurity into which her history has slumbered. Nonetheless, such injunctions are rarely upheld for such a long time in regards to persons of such historical and theoretical interest. Nonetheless, when MacLean and Rappen were writing their book on Hermine Hug-Hellmuth—which was published in 1991—they wrote to Anna Freud for some information. Anna Freud responded that they should respect the injunction. These authors, however, put forward the view that Anna Freud's motivation for having the injunction upheld was a self-interested one: to illegitimately perpetuate the myth of her primacy as the pioneer of child psychoanalysis.

Psychoanalysis of the child: the bastard child of psychoanalysis

The paper, "On the technique of child-analysis", was read before the Sixth International Psychoanalytical Congress at The Hague in September 1920 before both Sigmund and Anna Freud. The paper begins from the position of the dichotomy between education on the one hand and psychoanalysis on the other, the "*curative* and educative work of analysis" (1921, p. 287). She concludes this work in the following manner:

I consider it impossible for anyone to analyse properly his own child. This is so not only because the child hardly ever reveals its deepest desires and thoughts, conscious or unconscious, to mother and father, but because in this case the analyst is often driven to re-construct too freely, and also because the narcissism of the parents would make it almost unbearable to hear from their own child the psycho-analytic revelations. (Ibid., pp. 304-305)

Hermine Hug-Hellmuth's statement proposes that the field of psychoanalysis of children is struck by this fundamental prohibition: that of the impossibility of being able to analyse one's own child. We can say that the paper, "On the technique of child-analysis" is a type of resolution of the dilemma of the beginnings of the psychoanalysis of the child, the dilemma between education and upbringing on the one hand, and analysis on the other. It is precisely this that allows her to separate out the place of the analyst from that of the parents and educators of the child. I am proposing that it is here that we can locate the establishment of psychoanalysis of the child on a logical footing.

If this is so, what are we then to make of Freud's proposition that it was only because the authority of a father and of a physician were united in a single person that the analysis of little Hans was able to proceed? We can propose, rather, that the unity of the authority of the father (in other words, the Name of the Father), and that of the physician (the transference, or subject supposed of knowledge), is precisely the point of departure of psychoanalysis of the child. This unity then is the situation that exists at the beginning, the birth, of psychoanalysis of the child. And it was precisely at the moments of the dissociation of the paternal authority from the "medical" authority, for instance in Hans' visit to Freud, that the treatment was efficacious (Porge, 2012, p. 120).

The analyst who is confronted with a child is also inevitably confronted by the history of the psychoanalysis of the child. Erik Porge, in his book *Freud-Fließ: Myth and Chimera of Self-Analysis* (1996), puts forward the thesis it is that this conflation between the paternal and medical authorities was not the only one that Freud perpetuated. This conflation is in itself the conflation between the Name of the Father and the subject supposed of knowledge. He proposes that this very same conflation occurred in Freud's transference to Fliess (1996, p. 67). It is a similar conflation, I am proposing here, that is enacted in any parent analysing his or her own child.

We have proposed that this conflation was a necessary one for the establishment of the field of psychoanalysis of the child, as Freud suggests. It is also one that potentially exists at the beginning of each and every analysis, and actually exists when the analysis becomes pedagogical, that is, when it endeavours to teach the child something. Nonetheless it is our task as the inheritors of this legacy to continue to tease apart these two strands that continue to maintain a relation to each other. In other words, if it was necessary for Freud to conflate the paternal and the medical authorities—the Name of the Father with the transference—in the case of little Hans, this foundational position was one that revealed its own impossibility, as articulated by Hermine Hug-Hellmuth. It is highly significant to state that neither Anna Freud nor Melanie Klein were able to recognise, nor to take up, this very impossibility. Thus the seed that was sown by Hermine Hug-Hellmuth was ignored by her immediate successors, and this ignorance was perpetuated by the veil that was cast over Hermine Hug-Hellmuth's life and work.

Sigmund Freud designated his daughter Anna as the legitimate inheritor and pioneer of the field of psychoanalysis of the child. This sort of psychoanalysis of the child is destined to remain a child, to not have an existence in its own right, since it is also determined by the conflation of the Name of the Father with the subject supposed of knowledge. It is only when a child is able to break free from its parental bonds, its "attachment" to the paternal authority, that it might have its own existence. Otherwise psychoanalysis of the child is destined to remain stuck in its conflation with education or upbringing, and ends up being a type of pedagogy. This is the usual fate of all of the erudite fields regarding the child: to literally become a type of ortho-paedics, in the mould of all of the contemporary arrays of developmentalism.

We propose here that it was Hermine Hug-Hellmuth, in her act of defiance of Freud's paternal authority, and her denunciation of the necessary initial step of the analysis of his own child, who was truly able to establish the field of psychoanalysis of the child. Thus any child psychoanalysis worth its weight is an illegitimate child, not the legitimate inheritor of a family legacy. Psychoanalysis of the child is, therefore, the bastard child of psychoanalysis.

CHAPTER SEVENTEEN

The kangaroo rat man

Michael Gerard Plastow

In our seminar Psychoanalysis and the child, we have pursued, particularly in reference to Freud's little Hans, the theme of how the child might map out, through the meanderings of his history, his psychic structure upon the physical topography of the place in which he lives. In order to explicate this case, Freud literally has recourse to production of maps of Hans' phobia and its progression, just as he does in the case history of the Rat Man. Lacan in turn produces more elaborate maps of the trajectories of little Hans' neurosis in Vienna.

Gilles Deleuze also speaks of such mapping in reference to little Hans and the little Richard of Melanie Klein, in his paper "What children say". Then he proposes the following:

> It is in the nature of the libido to haunt both history and geography, to organize the formations of worlds and of constellations of universes, to make continents spring forth, to people them with races, tribes and nations [...]. The libido has no metamorphoses, but rather historical-worldly trajectories. (1993, p. 82–83, my translation)

Here Deleuze links the itineraries of peoples to the mapping of the subject's singular trajectory. In such a mapping, the subject that emerges from the child creates a type of mythological topography of his existence. And the mapping of the history and its topography effects a type of writing: the topographical becomes topological in the writing of the structure of the subject.

In this context I was struck by the form as well as the content of many of the paintings I saw in an exposition at the Ian Potter Gallery at Federation Square in Melbourne: "Living water: Contemporary art of the far Western Desert", which was displayed for most of 2012. Most of the paintings portray a small extract or fragment of the mythology of the particular culture of each of the artists. This mythology often contains reference to both the creation of the landscape, as well as reference to forbidden acts. For instance, a painting by a Pitjantjatjara artist Anmanari Brown entitled *"Kungkarangkalpa"* (Seven Sisters) was accompanied by the following text:

> The Seven Sisters were being chased by a cheeky *kula kula* (larrikin man) called Nyiru. He wanted to take a sister for his wife. A sorcerer, he tried to trick them by turning into *kuniya* (carpet snakes). The sisters did not want him because he was the wrong skin for them to marry. They were frightened, so they hid in the windbreaks and ran away. He chased them right across the desert and into the sky and is still in pursuit. Today, the Seven Sisters can be seen as a constellation of the seven stars, the Pleiades, travelling across the sky.

Here through the story of the *kula kula* wanting to marry one of the sisters, the question of forbidden sexual relations between one skin—or totem—and another, is evoked, and thus, that of incest. Additionally, the text describes a type of story of creation, but strikingly a creation that continues to this day in so far as the sorcerer "is still in pursuit". We are accustomed to hearing this type of mythology described as "Dreaming" or "Dreamtime" but this term is misleading. For instance, in the Pitjantjatjara language this term translates the word *"Tjurkurrpa"* (Ryan & Batty, 2012) in which there is no reference to the notion of dreaming as we understand it in English. Rather, the term refers to a type of timeless time of formative and perpetual creation, as well as to localities on indigenous land where uncreated creation and totemic ancestors, reside. For this reason, Dussart suggests that it is preferable to translate *Tjurkurrpa*, and related terms from other Western Desert languages such as Pintupi and Walpiri, as the "ancestral present" which conveys the fact that it does refer to a time of creation that existed in the past, but which paradoxically continues to exist in the present (Dussart, 2011). It is only in the stories of the present that the past of the ancestors comes alive.

At the same time that I saw "Living water", there was another exposition, entitled: "*Tjukurrtjanu:* Origins of Western Desert art. The term *Tjukurrtjanu* signifies objects "from the *Tjurkurrpa*", little fragments of the *Tjurkurrpa*. Thus it refers to the iconographic language and mythology that is conveyed in this art from the Dreaming. This exhibition focused on the beginnings of what is now known as the indigenous art movement, as it evolved at Papunya during the 1970s. We could say that traditional indigenous aesthetics, conveyed through body paintings, rock paintings, ceremonial songs and dance, and so on, when it remained in its traditional context, became known as "art" when it entered the art market, and was recognised and circulated as such with a defined monetary value.

Prior to this time, in Western hands such indigenous designs were the exclusive domain of ethnography and anthropology, and these objects were to be found in museums, not in art galleries. This is still a contentious issue. When the *Musée du Quai Branly* opened in Paris in 2006, there was a huge debate regarding what had become known as the "primary arts" being displayed as art objects, rather than anthropological artefacts. Indeed, many objects were directly transferred from the anthropological museum (*Musée de l'homme*) in which Claude Lévi-Strauss made his early career, to this new museum in which the focus was shifted towards viewing these objects as art. Lévi-Strauss who, from the beginning of his studies, was interested in the aesthetics of so-called primitive art, had no difficulty with this shift of focus and supported the opening of this new art gallery. Incidentally, the exposition "*Tjukurrtjanu:* Origins of Western Desert art" was on display at the *Musée du Quai Branly* until the 20th January 2013.

At times indigenous paintings and expositions have had to be removed as they have been considered to be "dangerous" for those members of the culture for whom they are not intended—such as uninitiated males, or members of a different "skin"—or when they have transgressed the rights of the owners of the stories that they convey. The book *Nomads of the Australian Desert* published by Charles Mountford in 1976 was obliged, in the same year, to be removed from circulation as it was found by the Northern Territory Supreme Court to be in breach of confidence of the Pitjantjatjara people who had provided the author with information and allowed him to take photographs in relation to totemic and sacred matters. Thus we see that there are fundamental prohibitions, both in the content matter of indigenous aesthetics, as well as through the limits upon circulation of the stories. Here we have a prohibition, such as those Levi-Strauss wrote of in *The Elementary Structures of Kinship* (1969). The prohibition is indicative of the interdictions that exist within the society from which the objects came, as indeed they are foundational to that culture.

It was common for groups of men to be involved in the painting at the beginnings of the indigenous art movement at Papunya in central Australia, in part through the encouragement of the teacher Geoffrey Bardon. And often these men, whilst they painted, would tell the mythical stories that were depicted on canvas, lowering their voices for parts that were particularly secret. This was the case in paintings associated with the Kuninka (native cat) and its site Yawalyurru, the name of which was often whispered, even in private. This could lead to misunderstandings. A type of painting keenly sought after by collectors is the so-called "kangaroo rat" series by Pintupi artist Anatjari Tjakamarra. According to Myers, "the kangaroo rat—whatever that might be—is not really one of Anatjari's Dreamings". He asks, "What did Anatjari—whose English was limited—really say to Bardon?" (2011, p. 37). Thus through a misinterpretation or a mis-hearing we have the invention of a new signifier, the 'kangaroo rat', a creature that is inexistent in the Pintupi *Tjurkurrpa*, but nonetheless has an existence in the art market.

This painting movement began in a town with a mix of different Western Desert peoples. And whilst the paintings conveyed elements of the culture of each of the artists, they also marked the particular place of each artist within his culture. Hence each artist has a name, a given name, and the second name of each is that of his or her skin. Dussart describes the way in which, at the beginnings of indigenous art on canvas, the works were not the work of one individual, as we usually consider the artist to be:

> Paintings on canvas, far from being the solitary act of an isolated painter, was at its outset the gesture of collaboration between painters and their families, and between the owners and the guardians

of the myths. Often the canvases carried the name of one or two people in order to satisfy a need to create an authentic artistic individuality, a typically Western value. But the paintings were the product of many brushes and of complex negotiations between family and painters. (2011, p. 142, author translation)

The birth of this art movement is also a type of birth of a new subject, in the subject of each painter or writer. The indigenous art movement began with artists painting "stories", or myths, but in a partial way as generally these stories are only allowed limited circulation, for instance amongst initiated males. As we have already noted, to circulate beyond this is perceived not only as prohibited but also as dangerous for those for whom they are not intended. The creation of the painting that conveys a certain story is also at the same time, therefore, the partial suppression, or repression, of that story, and a retelling of it in a new way. In addition, certain artists, whilst taking their support from traditional values tied to the "ancestral present", used painting for different purposes. Here Dussart speaks of painters from the Walpiri language group:

Certain younger painters began to change the modalities in which they managed their identities. Whilst taking their support from Walpiri values tied to the Ancestral Present, they endeavoured to escape from the gerontocratic tyranny of mythical and ritual knowledge. (2011, p. 44)

Thus the painting usually marks the place of the artist in reference to his culture. Deleuze cites Barbara Glowczewski in speaking of the writing of the aesthetics of the itineraries of indigenous Australians:

Thus the Australian aborigines combine nomadic itineraries and the dream voyages that together compose "an intermeshing of travels", "in an immense cut-out of space and of time that has to be read like a map". (1993, p. 83)

A painting by both Tim Leura Tjapaltjarri and Clifford Possum, "Spirit dreaming through Napperby country" (1980) depicts the itinerary of a subject in reference to the mythological history of his people. That is, the painting is at once a reference to the Other of a cultural story, but literally portrays the place of the artist within that culture. Kean states in regard to the work of Tim Leura Tjapaltjarri, that:

> His paintings work as a visual metaphor, in which iconographic elements that represent the certainty of the Dreaming are enlivened by ephemeral washes and over-dotting, capturing the ongoing influence of the ancestors on the contemporary landscape. (2011a, p. 182)

In a number of the papers published in the book that was produced of the exhibition (Ryan & Batty, 2011), some of the authors refer to elements of the iconography of the paintings as "signifiers", but we might rather consider them as letters, the concrete support of the signifiers by which a (version of the) story is retold. We are proposing that these letters form a type of writing of a map of the place of the subject in relation to the Other, thus delineating the structure of the subject.

The evolution of indigenous painting also occurred as an effect of the medium that was used. For our purposes, it is interesting to consider that the making of the painting into a type of map occurred in the mid and late 1970s as an effect of the difficulty of handling large canvases, the size being used to emphasise the number of participants involved in the ceremony:

> Larger canvases [...] were placed flat on the ground, generally in the direction of the land to be depicted, and the artist moved around the painting, at times sitting on the flat canvas and painting from a bird's-eye view. This change in painting method fundamentally altered the artist's conceptual relationship to the work, taking it from a cerebral re-creation to being a map, where the Cardinal points north, east, south and west were kept consistent throughout the painting's creation. (2011b, p. 51)

Lacan's lecture, "The Individual myth of the neurotic or poetry and truth in neurosis" was published in English, in the version transcribed by Jean-Alain Miller, as "The neurotic's individual myth" (1979), stripped of its reference to Goethe's autobiography. Moreover, the possessive in the published title in English conveys a fundamental misunderstanding: Lacan demonstrates how the subject is possessed by the myth, not the other way around. Lacan is primarily working the myth through the question of the signifier and the manner in which the signifier establishes a structure for the subject through the Other of the family. This also, of course, echoes Freud's establishment of a structure of obsessional neurosis through the case of the Rat Man.

However, through Goethe's *Poetry and Truth*, Lacan introduces the question of truth, a dimension which is explicitly missing from Lévi-Strauss, as Erik Porge points out (2005, p. 48). Nevertheless, we do find in Lévi-Strauss the articulation of culture—which we can also refer to as *myth* at a societal level—and family myth, in how it is taken up by the family, with nature:

> [...] the prohibition of incest is at once on the threshold of culture, in culture, and in one sense, as we shall try to show, culture itself. (1969, p. 12)

Here we are taking "nature", as being opposed to "culture", that is, we are taking nature in the sense of the real: all of that which cannot be circumscribed by language and images. And we could say that Lévi-Strauss' articulation does in fact, at least at a societal level, approach a type of truth, that is, a position taken up in regard to the real.

Truth, with Lacan, is expressed in an aesthetic or poetic modality, which we can also nominate as "style". It is true that poetical form, including that of Lacan's own writing, evokes something of truth, of the relation to the object. This is something very particular to Lacan since with Freud, truth, in one way, is articulated through a romance, a family romance for example, that is, through a novel, whereas with Lacan it is explicitly articulated through poetic form. With Lacan then it is the form rather than the content that is able to animate the object.

Whilst the family myth is structuring for the subject, Lacan notes that, "there is always an extremely clear-cut discordance between what is perceived by the subject on the plane of the real and the symbolic function" (my translation).[1] Lacan says that the Oedipus complex has its value in this gap, and we could say that it is precisely through this gap that the object falls. This is where we find a window onto the real, but mediated by the fantasm, as the "transformational formula" that Lacan refers to in his paper. We could say that the "discursive formula"—misleadingly translated as "discursive form" in the published English translation (Lacan, 1979, p. 406)—is the symbolic aspect of the fantasm.

The fantasm as *transformational formula* provides some articulation of the subject's immersion in history with the real.

We have articulated what we refer to as "time" with history, in so far as time refers to a type of temporality outside of historical time, a type of ancestral present. Thus time as we are conceptualising it is what lacks in history and pertains therefore to something of structure. Giorgio Agamben, who also works the question of history in relation to myth from Lévi-Strauss, proposes that, "while rites transform events into structures, play transforms structures into events" (1993, p. 82). Thus it is the play of the child, or the play of the signifier, that histori-cises structure in a psychoanalytic session, and thereby the place of the object. In this way the structure of the subject can be made into something that can be worked with in analysis.

Lévi-Strauss gave a tribute to Wagner as the "undeniable originator of the structural analysis of myth", in quoting the following from the opera *Parsifal*:

> *Du siehst, mein Sohn/zum Raum wird hier die Zeit.*
> "You see my son/here time turns into space",

[...] as, "the most profound definition of myth" (2010, p. 282). This *time turning into space* is precisely what we are referring to as the "transfor-mational formula".

Lacan makes some striking observations of Freud's case history of the Rat Man. One of these is his commentary upon the Rat Man's dream regarding Freud's daughter. Here Freud recounts the dream:

> He dreamt that *he saw my daughter in front of him; she had two patches of dung instead of eyes*. No one who understands the language of dreams will find much difficulty in translating this one: it declared that *he was marrying my daughter not for her "beaux yeux" but for her money*. (1909d, p. 199)

Despite Freud's comments about the Rat Man's anal drive, he does not make more of these anal objects in front of the Rat Man's eyes. For Lacan, these patches of dung are spectacles, the Rat Man's lost pince-nez, in other words they are signifiers. And of course it is precisely the pair of spectacles that is the object that animates the Rat Man's case history and bring him to see Freud, the spectacles as a lost object, imbued with all the complicated conditions for their retrieval attributed to them by the Rat Man. Here the family history and mythology, in particular that of the father's gambling debt and the inability to repay it, is activated in the Rat Man's neurosis and his transference to Freud.

I was also interested to see Freud's reference in the Rat Man case to Ibsen's play *Little Eyolf*. This Eyolf, a young child, functions in the play as a sort of mythical creature, perhaps related by way of the signifier to another mythical being, the elf. In Ibsen, Little Eyolf, like the Rat Man's spectacles, is the object that animates the play. Little Eyolf is the little *a*, an object that disappears at the end of act one, after which the adults are left to pick up the pieces. Freud makes the following comment in a footnote:

> Ibsen's Rat-Wife must certainly be derived from the legendary Pied Piper of Hamelin, who first enticed away the rats into the water, and then, by the same means, lured the children out of the town, never to return. So too, Little Eyolf threw himself into the water under the spell of the Rat-Wife. In legends generally the rat appears not so much as a disgusting creature but as something uncanny— as a chthonic animal, one might almost say; and it is used to represent the souls of the dead. (Ibid., p. 214)

Thus giving us the confirmation of the status of the rat and of Little Eyolf who was lured into the water like a rat, as something uncanny or *Unheimlich*, as a little fragment of the real.

In reference to Goethe's autobiography, Lacan speaks of a quatuor, or a foursome, with a splitting of both the subject and of his object. Lacan attributes this quaternary structure to the Oedipus complex. Such a quatuor is also striking in Ibsen's play which Lacan could just as easily have utilized for "The individual myth of the neurotic". This play, additionally, dramatically and poetically denotes the place of the little *a*. In *Little Eyolf*, moreover, we have many splittings, or pairings, of the three remaining characters in the play: Allmers and Rita his wife, Allmers and Asta his sister, then the revealing of the fact that Asta was *not* his sister and thus opening the possibility of being his lover; and Borgheim, his counterpart, and no doubt his rival in love for Asta. The question of incest, and thus of prohibition, is not far away in regard to the love between Allmers and Asta. There are two Eyolfs as well, as this was also the name reserved for Allmers' younger brother who was never conceived, and thus the nickname given to Asta, his younger half-sister/not-sister.

Ibsen's play creates another type of mythology, such as that with which we began today, a mythology that is able to transform structures into events, into events that are effectively fictional, but necessary for the production of a truth. We have spoken today of this mythology by reference to the mythology depicted in Western Desert art, by that of the family myth, and indeed by that of any clinical history. Lacan's insistence is not on the content of the history, but rather on its form. For this reason he insists on the title of Goethe's autobiography, *Poetry and Truth*. It is the form, the poetic form of the mythology, and not its content or meaning, that gives access to a truth. Dussart, whom we have cited earlier in reference to indigenous art, notes that:

> The transformations of mythical knowledge and of its representa-tion (and even lack of representation) on canvas are intimately tied to the development of neocolonial policies in regard to indigenous Australians and the manner in which these policies have been experienced and have been transformed by the Aborigines them-selves. (2011, p. 145, my translation)

It is in such a transformation through a work of art, or through a poem or play, that might be able to produce a little truth. And it is through the articulation, in psychoanalysis, of the free association of the analy-sand, that something uncanny may be produced in the unfurling of a structure. At the same time this transformation is struck by a fundamen-tal prohibition, a prohibition that effects a limit to what is knowable, to what is able to be said or represented. What precipitates out of this formula is a little object, an uncanny little object, a little *Tjukurrtjanu*, a little Eyolf, or a little *a*.

Note

1. Lacan, J. *Le mythe individuel du névrosé ou poésie et vérité dans la névrose*. Accessible at: http://www.ecole-lacanienne.net/pastoutlacan50.php (*cf.* published translation: "There is always an extremely obvious dis-crepancy between the symbolic function and what is perceived by the subject in the sphere of experience".)

CHAPTER EIGHTEEN

The transformational formula of myth

Tine Nørregaard

W hen studying the function of myth in the case of little Hans in his seminar on The Object Relation (1994), Lacan defines Hans's walks with his father in Vienna as a "ceremony of already travelled itineraries" (1994, p. 249). On these walks, through the Other of language, Hans familiarises himself with the others in his world, re-encountering and re-locating the signifier of the phallus in different places, like in the giraffes at the zoo, the ones he again later draws and crumbles in play. However, it is also in this familiar space that Hans encounters the Other as un-familiar, which his phobic symptom is an expression of. The mapping of these places along Hans's trajectory functions as ceremonies or rites which structure his own myth, and offer him a passage at the crossroads of his family structure. Such a mapping may be seen as a means of transforming time into space. This is a way of giving an account of what Freud calls the accidental factors of one's history (1905d, p. 130). It is these accidental factors that also determine what is outside of time, one's prehistory, which we have referred to as the infantile, the lack that is marked by infantile amnesia, the real. In the case of little Hans Lacan draws on the actual image of the cartography of the map of Vienna, to see how the phobic symptom may function as an entrance to the phantasm for the boy.

Freud describes the trajectory of Hans' phobia, from the encounter with the sexual enjoyment of his own body, to the investigation he embarks on concerning the size of the "widdler", the one of the little sister, the one of the mother, the one of the giraffe, and the one of the horse. This trajectory becomes a "because of the horse", (*wegen des Pferdes*) (1909b), which ties the Other of his sexual enjoyment to an image, a marker in space, the "anxiety-horse". It is the horse which he comes across on his walks, the one who has a similar "widdler" to the giraffe, and a larger one than his mother, but it is also the horse that falls from the heavy weight of the cart it pulls. The cart is heavy, like his mother's body, full with the pregnancy of the little sister, but also with the weight of the family travelling to Gmunden, to where the father leaves the boy in the closeness of his mother's bed. We may read the structure of the Oedipus myth through the itinerary that is mapped by these "others", who are situated in different ways as objects, people, places, and symbols in the world of the subject.

In his paper "What children say" Gilles Deleuze refers to Melanie Klein's case of Richard, a boy who made a cartography of his world, centred around the names of leaders and countries from World War II: England, Churchill, Germany, and Hitler (1997). According to Deleuze this is a mapping of the libido's trajectory through the milieu that makes up the child's world:

> It is the libido's business to haunt history and geography, to organise formations of world and constellations of universes, to make continents drift and to populate them with races, tribes and nations. (1997)

In the case of little Hans, Deleuze proposes that this mapping is a structuring of the affects that is created through a "becoming" of the child as subject, and with the naming of places and objects in the following way:

> A list of constellation of affects, an intensive map, is a becoming: Little Hans does not form an unconscious representation of the father with the horse, but is drawn into a becoming-horse to which his parents are opposed [...]. The image is not only a trajectory, but also a becoming. Becoming is what subtends the trajectory, just as intensive forces subtend motor forces. Hans' becoming-horse refers to a trajectory, from the apartment house to the warehouse.

The passage alongside the warehouse, or even the visit to the henhouse, may be customary trajectories, but they are not innocent promenades. We see clearly why the real and the imaginary were led to exceed themselves, or even to interchange with each other: a becoming that turns the most negligible of trajectories, or even a fixed immobility, into a voyage; and it is the trajectory that turns the imaginary into a becoming. (Ibid.)

We see that the anxiety horse in this sense is the "becoming—horse", the signifying element that enables Hans to move around in his world. For Lacan phobia has the function of substituting the object of anxiety with a signifier that is frightening (1968–1969). The imaginary is transcended through the symbolic inscription of this signifying function. Through this symbolic inscription, through language, the boy's own myth may be mapped in a space of different locations and objects, which also mark the distance and closeness of his relationship with the mother and the father. However, we see that in this case, there is a difficulty with the function of the symbolic with regard to a father who is not able to intervene in the close relationship of the son and the mother. This father situates himself on the same level as his son in the family drama, not unlike Oedipus who finds himself at the same level of his father, the fellow man he kills.

It is Freud's construction in the session with the boy and the father, which makes the myth efficacious for Hans. In this construction, Freud evokes the symbolic father beyond the actual father, that is through his masculine traits, which he jokingly refers to by asking whether Hans's "horse wears glasses or has a moustache" (1909b, p. 42). We see then that the *wegen des Pferdes* becomes *because of the father* through the paternal function, which intervenes as a prohibition in the boy's close orbit with the mother.

In his seminar *The Object Relation* Lacan puts forward that myth displays truth through the structure of fiction, but that this structure is not open to any modifications (1994, p. 253). Several myths may in this way be read together according to the consistency of their structure. Myths form part of discourse, as attempts to provide answers to essential questions concerning the origins of man, and the social bond which differentiates man from nature. For the child, the small circle of the family appears as the first others, to whom the questions of sex and death are addressed. In the case of little Hans the birth of a little sister opens the question of sexuality, and how Hans himself is part of this riddle through his own sex, that is, whether this sex appears as a natural given or not. In this respect myths are the stuff of the infantile sexual theories, which Lacan also refers to as "mythical infantile creations" (ibid., p. 255).

Particular elements in myth can be taken as analogous and comparable even though they are far from being identical. Lacan reads Freud's two big myths Oedipus and *Totem and Taboo* in this way. The myth of Oedipus already existed as an epic story of the riddle of the Sphinx, which Freud made use of to display something of each subject's relationship with sexuality in a particular history; whereas the myth of *Totem and Taboo* is Freud's own construction of a myth that is beyond any particular history. For Lacan it is precisely the elements of murder and incest which transform the positions of the mother, father, and the brothers in these two myths. This occurs through the consistency of the prohibition that is related to both these elements. The act of murder in one generation is transformed into a law that is regulated through the prohibition of incest in the next generation. We can say then that the elements of the myths may be read in a similar manner to the way Lacan makes use of Edgar Allan Poe's story of "The purloined letter", where the letter transforms the meaning of the relationship between the characters in the story. It is the contingency between the elements of the myth or several myths, which is central to how it can be read as a universal structure.

In *The Structural Study of Myth* Claude Lévi-Strauss states that: "Myth is language, to be known, myth has to be told; it is part of human speech" (1955, p. 430). He rejects any understanding of the myth as an interpretation of the meaning. This also includes Jung's understanding of the myth as an archetype, which according to Lévi-Strauss reduces myth to "idle play or to a coarse kind of speculation" (ibid., p. 429). Lévi-Strauss calls the symbolic elements of the myth "mythemes", and it is through their structure that prior myths are handed down and transformed; the meaning of the particular myth bears solely upon its contingent relation with other myths.

In Freud's late work on *Moses and Monotheism* he traces the significance of two different accounts of the history of Moses (1939a [1937–1939]). In the first account Moses is assumed to come from a royal family in Egypt, and in the second account, which is told according to the bible, Moses is assumed to come from a family amongst the Jewish people. Even though these two accounts occur at different times in history, and the elements appear to be contradicting a historical reality, Freud takes them as analogous accounts, which together display an element of truth about the figure of Moses. Freud hereby constructs the idea from two different myths that the man Moses was an Egyptian. He proposes that these two myths display a central structure of the fiction of a *family romance*, which he describes in the following way:

> When a people's imagination attaches the myth of birth which we are discussing to an outstanding figure, it is intending in that way to recognise him as a hero and to announce that he has fulfilled the regular pattern of a hero's life. In fact, however, the source of the whole poetic fiction is what is known as a child's "family romance", in which the son reacts to a change in his emotional relation to his parents and in particular to his father. (1939a, p. 249)

So, we see that Freud, by taking two different accounts as one, also reads the myths according to their structure, rather than their content. However, while Lacan reads the structure of myth according to way that the contradictory elements are transformed through a consistency in language, Freud stresses the myth according to its structure of a poetic fiction, which is based on the narrative of a family romance.

In his paper "Family romances" (1909c) we see that Freud situates this fiction as a fantasy that is constructed when the child attempts to liberate himself from his parents. Both the family romance and the infantile sexual theories appear as fantasy formations at the time of the child's encounter with the riddle of sexuality. However, while the infantile sexual theories appear as hypotheses spurred on by the lack that the phallus introduces regarding the body, the family romance is a fantasy that is created as a response to a lack that is experienced in relation to the actual parents. In this way, it is the construction of a fiction which portrays the ideal of the parents, like the figures of heroes in a novel. It is an imaginary fantasy which sustains an ideal family structure. For Freud this idea of a romance in lyrical form, and as a romantic longing, was something he pursued in relation to daydreaming and the creative writing of Goethe. We could say then that Freud's poetic fiction, based on the family romance, sustains a reading of myth through the structure of a novella or a "roman".

In the paper "The neurotic's individual myth" (1979), Lacan continues this discussion of myth, this time in Freud's case of the Ratman and in Goethe's writing. Here he places emphasis on the individual or the particular myth of the neurotic, a formation that becomes the individual phantasm. We see that Lacan, as different to Freud, underlines the individual rather than the family in what defines the myth of the neurotic. Further, Lacan also proposes that truth is only able to be expressed in a mythical mode, which shares a similar style to that of a poetic writing; something which Michael Plastow has already pointed to as missing from the title of the English translation of the paper. This proposition of the relationship between the phantasm and the writing of poetry is very different to the relationship that Freud proposes between fantasy and a novella, a *roman*.

The term "individual myth" is the same one Lévi-Strauss uses in his paper "The effectiveness of symbols" (1963), first published in 1949. In our seminar we have pointed out that according to the original title of this paper, *L'efficacité symbolique*, it is "the effectiveness of the symbolic", and not symbolism, that is at stake here. In this paper, Lévi-Strauss compares the structure of myth in shamanism and psychoanalysis. In the first case, the sick person receives a "social myth" from the shaman, who speaks it to enable a cure, and in the latter case, it is the "individual myth" that is constructed by the analysand from the elements of his own past (ibid., p. 199). Lévi-Strauss underlines that in native texts myth is displayed as a medium, a set of symbols that make up part of a coherent system, on which the conception of the universe is construed. According to Lévi-Strauss: "the myth *form* takes precedence over the *content* of the narrative" (1963, p. 104). We may in this way understand the structure of myth as something that appears through language, through the symbolic, and that the ability for each one to make use of the individual myth in social discourse, is pending on the effectiveness of this symbolic. As Lévi-Strauss proposes: "It is the effectiveness of the symbolic which guarantees the harmonious parallel development of myth and action" (1963, p. 201).

Lacan, in his paper, also raises the question of how effective the symbolic is in the case of the Ratman. It is a question of how the individual myth is able to function as a pathway for the Ratman's own trajectory at the crossroad of the family myth. The individual myth is shaped by the subject's debt to a prehistory, but this debt can weigh more or less according to how the elements of the family mythology appear in the phantasm. We see here how Lacan also makes use of the structure that is made of the conception of the universe, in his terms "the constellation", when referring to the prehistory of each subject:

> The constellation—why not? in the sense astrologers use it—the original constellation that presided over the birth of the subject, over his destiny and I would say this prehistory, specifically the fundamental family relationships which structured his parents union, happens to have a very precise relation, perhaps definable by a transformational formula, with what appears to be the most contingent, the most phantasmatic, the most paradoxically morbid in his case, that is, the last state of development of his great obsessive fear, the imaginary scenario he arrives at as a resolution of the anxiety associated with the precipitations of the outbreak. (1979, p. 409)

The particular status of the individual myth is the manifestation of what is *most phantasmatic* which appears in a scenario that resembles a little play or a chronicle. Rather than relying on the content of this phantasmatic scenario, Lacan like Lévi Strauss proposes that the individual myth functions as a "transformational formula" which allows a contradiction to be overcome. The contradiction may be seen in what both Lacan and Freud refer to as the most paradoxical element in this case; the sexual enjoyment or jouissance at play in the Ratman's obsessional symptoms.

In reading the case history of the Ratman again I found it interesting that Freud himself also uses the word "formula" to describe the structure of the Ratman's defensive obsessional ideas that occur when he tries to ward off the fantasy scenario of the rat punishment:

> He broke off his story in order to assure me that these thoughts were entirely foreign and repugnant to him, and to tell me that everything which had followed in their train had passed through his mind with the most extraordinary rapidity. Simultaneously with the idea there always appeared a 'sanction,' that is to say, the defensive measure which he was obliged to adopt in order to prevent the phantasy from being fulfilled. When the captain had spoken of his ghastly punishment, he went on, and these ideas had come into his head, by employing his usual formulas (a "but" accompanied by a

gesture of repudiation, and the phrase "whatever are you thinking of?") he had just succeeded in warding off both of them. (1909b, p. 166)

The German term is *Formeln*, which is something much more akin to a mathematical writing similar to how Freud writes the formula of sperm in the dream of Irma's injection. In a letter to Abraham in 1907 I found a reference to a similar concept, the "form-giving factor", which Freud uses to describe how the associations of infantile sexuality become traumas *nachträglich*, as the thought processes that are barred by repression. He states the following to Abraham:

> For you, as for me, the compelling thing is that these traumas become the form-giving factor in the symptomatology of neurosis. There is one consideration that I must not withhold from you that is certainly valid in the case of hysteria—I do not know whether it also applies to dementia praecox. The hysteric later moves very far away from infantile autoeroticism, he exaggerates his object-cathexis (in this he is the counterpart of the fully demented case, who in our assumption, reverts back to auto-eroticism) He accordingly fantasises his need of objects back into his childhood and clothes his autoerotic childhood in fantasies of love and seduction. (2002, p. 2)

We can see the central aspect of this "form-giving factor" in the construction of fantasy, that is what gives form by way of "clothing" the objects of the auto-erotic childhood. Also here, we note that it is the form rather than the content of the fantasies that is central. Perhaps we can see the map that Freud draws in the Ratman's case as such an attempt to give form to the fantasy scenario of the rat punishment and the contradiction at play concerning his utterance "but, whatever are you thinking of?" The map displays an itinerary of the Ratman's individual myth, in the sense that a trajectory can be traced between the different localities and people who play a part in the economy of his debt, and how this is played out. We can see this map then as an expression of the formula in which the objects have been clothed and provide form to the phantasm. If we follow Lacan, this "form-giving factor" and the formula are both aspects similar to the transformational formula, which enables a pathway from the family myth to the individual myth of the phantasm.

It is through the maps, which occur in both these case stories, that we are able give form to the anchoring points in space, of what we may describe as the libidinal economy of little Hans and the Ratman. The transformational formula is the structure of the myth that allows a transformation of time into space. This is the transformation of time as ones prehistory, the constellation that presides over ones birth, marked by the elements that structured the parents' union, a time lost, inaccessible, barred by repression. The mapping in space is a way of tracing a trajectory of the subject's libido, as Deleuze refers to it, that is also a way of dealing with the lack concerning time as real. This prehistorical time is only able to be accounted for through the fragments of "the accidental factors" that appear in the telling of one's own family history. This is the loss that each subject accounts for through the crossing points of the individual myth with the family myth.

Lacan takes this aspect of the transformational formula of myth from Lévi-Strauss, who speaks of the power of myth to re-construe previously existing elements into a new form. This permits an evolution of mythology that takes into account current circumstances in which society finds itself.

Returning to Lacan's paper, we can discern the way in which he works with this idea of the myth as the transformational formula, when he takes the contradictory elements at play in Freud's case in the following manner:

> The conflict rich woman/poor woman was reproduced exactly in the subject's life when his father urged him to marry a rich woman, and it was then that the neurosis proper had its onset. (1979, p. 140)

It is the Ratman's obsessional neurosis and his phantasmatic relation to the object of desire which is revealed by the contradiction implied in the conflict, as well as in his transference to Freud. Here, like in the case of little Hans, there is a difficulty with the effectiveness of the symbolic with regard to the position of the father. Lacan sees this difficulty with the symbolic father as the most "paradoxically morbid" element in this case, which the Ratman gives expression to at the beginning of the treatment: "Thoughts about my father's death occupied my mind from a very early age and for a long period of time, and greatly depressed me" (1909b, p. 161).

The presence of death is so intense in the Ratman's account, that it takes Freud by surprise to find out that his father had in reality already died years earlier. Freud sees this part played by death as a difficulty with a "father complex". It is a dead father who keeps reappearing in the form of a ghost, the one which haunts him as jouissance. It is a ghost that appears both as the fear inhibiting his sexual relationships with women, and as an image that is invoked with his masturbatory fantasies in front of the mirror (ibid., pp. 202–203). So, this father, even though long dead, is kept alive as an ego ideal, which in the individual phantasm keeps a measure with the family myth, through the circulation of the debt that the Ratman cannot pay.

With Deleuze, we could say that it is the becoming-debt, which functions as a signifier that the Ratman can move around with in the structure of the individual myth. However, it is at the same time this element that displays a difficulty with how the symbolic is functioning for him, that is a difficulty at the point of the pathway from the family myth. Lacan relates this as a difficulty with the Name of the Father for the Ratman (1979, p. 422). It is a difficulty which, according to Lacan, is marked by the value given to the debt as elements of the family legend. This is recounted by the Ratman in the stories of a debt, which the father never paid to an unknown friend, and in the reference to the unclear status of the poor woman, who the father knew prior to the marriage. These measures of a family debt are constantly re-valued and re-evoked through the destructive elements of guilt and punishment in the Ratman's jouissance. Lacan points out that the father in the Ratman's account is constantly idealised and devalued, through the references that he makes to fellow men, like the friend of high opinion, to whom he confesses his "criminal impulses", and the captain who had told him of the cruel rat punishment. In these accounts the place of the father is assigned to an imaginary fraternal position, rather than a symbolic one (ibid., p. 423).

For Lacan "myth and fantasy reunite here" (ibid., p. 415). This is the particular aspect of the neurotic's individual myth, which in another moment, manifests itself as the phantasm within the transference to the analyst. As he states: "Myth is what provides a discursive formula for something that cannot be transmitted through the definition of truth" (ibid., p. 406).

We find the transformational formula at this point of the structure of the individual myth, which enables the ties with the family myth to become discursive. The phantasm is at the same time discursive and acts as a transformational formula, in so far as it provides a possibility for the subject to articulate something of the truth of his individual myth beyond the family myth, and which also situates him in the social bond of discourse. The articulation of the discursive formula, as we have put forward with Lévi-Strauss, relies upon "the effectiveness of the symbolic to guarantee the harmonious parallel development of myth and action". This is a paradigm that gives expression to the function of the symbolic, by tying the imaginary and the real through the individual phantasm. This occurs through the transformation between the two myths: the family myth and the individual myth.

We could also see this discursive formula as an articulation that occurs in the mapping of the subject's trajectory in space. We started off with the map of Vienna in the case of little Hans, which marks the possibility of the symbolic of his Oedipus myth in being able to tie the imaginary and the real at the crossroads of the boy's family constellations. Similarly, in the case of the Ratman, Freud draws a map with a trajectory that outlines the obsessional scenario of a debt to be paid. In the analysis the map may function as the possibility of marking the transformational formula of the Ratman's individual myth with the family myth. This passage of the transformational formula of the individual myth may occur at the points, where the symbolic, in being anchored with the real and the imaginary, can make it possible to carry the weight of the family heritage. It is in the writing of the formula of the debt/death of the father in the analysis that the individual phantasm of the Ratman also becomes a discursive formula.

PART IV

PSYCHOANALYSIS AND ART

CHAPTER NINETEEN

From erotic initiation to death*

Oscar Zentner

For man, unless there is castration,
that is to say, something that says no to the phallic function,
there is no possibility that he will enjoy the body of a woman,
in other words, to make love.

—*Jacques Lacan, Encore*, 20th February 1973

Nagal Kafu says in reference to kanraku (pleasure) that nothing is more pathetic
Than a woman that one has had after a successful attempt at having her
[…]. For this reason the principal dominion of coquetry is the relational continuation,
that is to say: the preservation of the possibility as possibility, which is the secret
of kanruku (pleasure).

—*Kuki Shuzo*, Reflections on Japanese Taste—the Structure of Iki

*This essay was published in *Me Cayó el veinte,* Revista de Psychoanalysis, école lacani-enne de psychoanalyse, 26, Mexico, 2012.

What you desired is not mortal.

—*Ovid*, Metamorphosis

You have not seen anything in Hiroshima. Nothing.
I have seen everything, everything.

—*Marguerite Duras*, Hiroshima Mon Amour (1958)

First things, first

I never affirmed, and still less wrote, that Lacan was infallible. What I affirmed instead and I keep maintaining, was the extreme subtlety with which he was able to extract the essential from the debris of common places.

He himself did not hesitate to point out to Freud's delusional thought, more delusional (*délirant*) than any of his own. This compliment in reverse, was indeed his way of proposing his own delusional (*délirant*),[1] out of the square, ways for new openings in the rarefied domain of psychoanalysis.

As when in his seminar *Anxiety*, in the session of 3rd July 1963, he stated:

> [...] any irreplaceable German could find his replacement in the
> first Japanese from around the corner. (1962–1963)

He was referring to *Hiroshima Mon Amour*, in which the mastery of Duras combines the transience,[2] of love, of the memory of a forbidden and lost love, between the heroine and a soldier of the *Wehrmacht*, killed shortly before liberation, who is finally remembered and forgotten in the same act in Japan—*juste après* Hiroshima—between Nevers and Hiroshima, in the encounter with a new love, which dissolves the old one by fusing both into one where life flows inexorably into *Lethe*.

The irony of Lacan, a Japanese replacement of a German, went further since that phrase was a condensation of one consequence of WWI, whereby Japan effectively replaced the German possessions in China.

Then, history in bits and pieces

In 1886, Japan coming out of a self-imposed isolation and modernising itself, reaches industrial and military capacities comparable to the western countries.[3] This was shown in a series of military triumphs over China and Russia with everlasting consequences, of a change without return that culminated with the reorganisation of Japanese society and the slow decadence and eventual disappearance of the Samurai class.

In conjunction with the above, there was an elevation of the army to a similar rank occupied before the *Meiji restitution*, by the Samurai class in the times of the Tokugawa Shogun,[4] which lasted for a little more than two centuries. This Shogun was replaced by the Meiji restitution (Enlightened Rule) under the Emperor Mutsuhito (1867–1912). It is during this period that Japan's modernisation took place, a modernisation that continued from 1912 until 1926, the Taisho period (Great Righteousness) under Emperor Yoshihito. This period finished with his death and the assumption of his son Emperor Hirohito (1926–1989) inaugurating the Showa period (Illustrated Peace).

The epoch that comprised the Taisho period, from approximately 1920 including the Showa until 1930 approximately, was known under the very revealing name of: *Ero, Guro,* and *Nansensu,* which could be translated as: erotism, eccentricity, and non-sense. These words, as a matter of fact, translate very well the full acceptance and almost unconditional imitation of ideas and Western values, until the great earthquake of Tokyo in 1923.

A popular belief existed in Japan regarding the cause of earthquakes; this belief was that they were caused by the movement of a huge carp fish underneath Japan. The devastating 1923 earthquake was interpreted by popular imagination as signal of the mistake, almost a sinful one, of abandoning traditional Japanese values.

The outstanding Japanese writer, Junichiro Tanizaki, to take an illustrious one amongst many, exemplified this through his own rejection of his previous blind acceptance of Western values. The rejection and return to traditional values can be read without much effort in between the lines of his magnificent *In Praise of Shadows* (1977).[5]

In counter distinction to *the Ero, Guro,* and *Nansensu* of the twenties, the period from 1931 to 1941, known as the valley of darkness (*kurai tanima*), was precisely characterised by the rejection of Western values, together with a re-affirmation of an ethic of self-sacrifice, similar to the *bushido ethics, the way of the warrior,* of the Samurais.

Coincidently—even if for contradictory reasons—together with the militarisation of Japan, there were two opposite outlooks, one of admiration and another one of rejection of the West, while Japan at the same time attempted to reach the same level of Western powers, primarily those of England and the United States. The way to achieve it was by trying to reproduce, in the fashion of European countries, the construction of its own empire in Asia, which included the Protectorate of Korea, the successive and partial domination of China and the incorporation of great part of Manchuria, under the creation of a puppet regime and Kingdom, *The Manchukuo*.

It is around these years that within the Japanese army two factions are formed, both nationalistic and anti-communist. One of them will become known as the *Seinen shōko undō* (Young Officers) and it is this group that constitutes the *Kodo–ha* (School of the Imperial Way) faction that was discreetly approved by prince Chichibu, brother of the Emperor Hirohito. This faction wanted re-distribution of wealth, suppression of the *Zaibatsu* (big business), and to eventually attack the Soviet Union.

The other faction, *Tosei-ha* (Control School), did not have any interest in the re-distribution of wealth and/or the suppression of the Zaibatsu. Its military objectives were to attack Northern China and from 1941 to attack Australia and British, Dutch, French, North-American, and Russian possessions in Asia.

Both factions, the *Kodo-ha* and the *Tosei-ha* respected the *Kokutai* (national polity), which conceptualised the Japanese nation as a single family, with absolute submission to the Emperor, a representative of the Japanese spirit and head of that family. The *Seinen shōko undō* (Young Officers) of the faction *Kodo-ha,* had been strongly influenced by the teachings of the ultra-nationalist and fascist ideologue Kitta Ikki (2006) with his proposition of returning economical and political power to the Emperor and his people.

The army was alerted to this faction through its intelligence services, so much so, that when they were made aware of the imminence of a *coup d' état* to be carried out by the minority *Kodo-ha* faction, they decided, as a way of stopping the *coup*, to move them to Manchuria, but when receiving the orders, the *Kodo-ha* faction decided to bring forward the *coup* (*Ni ni roku*) to 26th February 1936. They attempted the *Showa Restauration* through the *Ni ni roku*, emulating those who almost seventy years before carried out the *Meiji Restauration*. The *Ni ni roku* was carried out by a group of close to one thousand four hundred soldiers. They succeeded in occupying governmental offices and killed a few important officials from the government. This insurrection lasted a few days until the Emperor declared them rebels, and gave orders of reprisal.

On 25th November 1970, Kimitake Hiraoka, known as Yukio Mishima, emulated the same rebels of the attempted *coup d'état* of 26th February 1936 with his small semi-military group *Tate no kai* (Shield Society). They also had the sympathy of (right wing) politicians and some military figures. Commanding this group he took the Office of General Kanetoshi Mashita, commander of the Eastern Army in Ichigawa, Tokyo, and from the terrace spoke to the troops about the Bushido, the spirit of Japan and of the *Osei fukko* (restoration of Imperial rule).[6]

But his attempt to provoke a rebellion of the soldiers was met with indifference, and in that way he failed as the *Ni ni roku* of 1936 failed. Perceiving his complete failure he shouted one last time *Tenño Heika Banzai* (Long live the Emperor) and began the rigorous ritual of his *Seppuku*.

We will recall in passing, that Mishima had written, represented, or/ and alluded to his own heroic death by *Seppuku*, in theatric and cinematic representations, in his admired novel *Confessions of a Mask,* and in the 1936 *Coup d'état* novel *Patriotism*. The latter, was an exaltation of purity, idealism, and the spirit of Japan and with its title *Patriotism,* Mishima gave account of a prevalent sentiment in many Japanese people after World War Two, who ascribed a supposed purity and glory to those who attempted that failed *Coup*—a sentiment that still lingers until present day.

The name of patriots was given at the time of the events by the same High Command, who following orders from Hirohito, repressed them, while at the same time did not fail to recognise shared values, values put into play five years later in 1941 as Japan enters the war.

This very incomplete contextualisation is the atmosphere of this singular and extreme history that we are opening.

All the way to Masaki Tea house

Three months after the failed *coup d'état*, on the 19th May 1936 also in Tokyo, in the *heya* (room) of the *Masaki Ochaya* (Masaki Tea House), a singular drama takes place, a drama that has neither political nor social dimensions. It is far apart from what took place three months earlier, and yet in the four walls of that *heya* the reaffirmation of mores that rejected the Western and Christian values is expressed, if not *de jure* then *de facto*, in a passage to the act.

Christianity was introduced to Japan through the Jesuits in 1549, one hundred years after it was introduced to South America, until they were expelled from Japan in 1614.

This is not the place, nor do I have the inclination to even outline a scheme of the transformation that the introduction of the Judeo-Christian religion, with the idea of a single God, the Original Sin, and consequent guilt, meant for the prevalent Buddhism[7] and Shintoism.

I invite you reader, because even when I am not your scribe I acknowledge that it is for you that I write, to take any story or novel of Tanizaki, Natsume, Akugatawa, Kawabata, Mishima, or Inou to name only some of them, to compare it with Shuzako Endo's novel *Silence*. You would then be able to verify for yourself the distance and difference of *mores* implied by the entrance of Christianity in Japan.

Let us return then to the Tea House *Masaki* on 19th May 1936. It will be on the futon of its small room that Abe Sada and Kichi Ishida, while making love, will begin to experiment sexually. This is, of course, hardly surprising or strange among lovers and in the midst of the lovemaking Kichi tells Abe in passing that he heard how asphyxia increases sexual enjoyment. From that moment on a shared desire to experiment with this "technique of the body" that I call *sex-mortal* is awoken in both. This game of two that they begin is increasingly driven towards a fate sealed in a swirling trip of no return.[8]

> Initiation is that of which we have the debris, under the name of occultism, which simply proves that the only thing that at the end is still of interest to us about initiation. Therefore, I do not know why I would not give to initiation, known since antiquity, some hierarchy. [...] something of the order of initiation is bound to what [...] Mauss called "the techniques of the body"; that is to say that what we have and what concerns us of this discourse, as much analytic as scientific, of the university, of the master and whatever else you want [...] is that initiation presents itself [...] always as an approximation; an approximation which is not effectuated if not by all classes of detours, slowness, as an approximation to something [...] which strictly speaking is of the order of Jouissance. I want to say that it is not unthinkable that the "body in as much as we believe it to be alive",[9] would be something much more difficult than the knowledge of the anatomist-physiologists. Perhaps there is a science of Jouissance, if such expression is possible. Initiation

cannot be described in any other way. But unfortunately there are no traces anywhere of initiation. (Lacan, 1973–1974)[10]

This is why we could say that it is from this "technique of the body" of: "I asphyxiate you and you asphyxiate me",[11] when the *Corrida* is unleashed—in a quasi-bullfight initiation—to which both abandoned themselves and in that subtle and inexorable *Corrida* things start to take place, among others, that Abe Sada interchanges with Ishida Kichi, the position he occupied at the beginning of the *affaire*,[12] while at the same time, in a *crescendo* without return they are taken to the *arena* of the futon, in which the *act-art* of asphyxiation passes literally from the hands of Kichi, who in his active passivity,[13] gives himself to the hands of Abe. Surpassing the *tantric* techniques a climax is reached as Abe strangles Kichi, her employer and lover, with her *Obi*.[14] Kichi's attitude on this point meets Lacan's deafening silence; we will refer to it later in greater detail.

Kichi Ishida not only does not resist or defend himself as Abe's declarations showed;[15] but moreover, as I said before, he seemed to have been an active participant through his passivity, suggesting an end-game[16] of two: that I call *sexmortal*.[17]

> [...] I put into doubt that (love) is ever a passion [...] But if knowledge, including the unconscious one, is what is invented to supply what perhaps only is *the mystery of two* [my emphasis] [...] to say that something is passionate implies to speak of it, *as a game where it is because of the rules that one is active* [my emphasis] [...] therefore, if I maintained my formula that love is passionate, it is as strictly truthful. Yes, [...] strictly true, is never true, but only by half, as the truth can only ever be half-said. [...] All half said, to say a half-truth, has death as its principle. [...] the truth [...] is what in summary makes the body to go towards Jouissance and that which forces it, is nothing other than the principle [...] so then sex is very specifically linked to the death of the body. (Lacan, 1973–1974)[18]

It is not difficult, I think, to find the resonance of the above words in connection to initiation, Jouissance and the death of the body with what took place in Tokyo, that 19th May 1936; as it is not difficult either to find the same resonances in Nagisha's film titled in Japanese: *Ai no Korida*, literally: *The Corrida of love*. And it is not a small detail that the

Japanese title passed to the West as: *In the Realm of the Senses,* erasing in this way not only the trace of the bullfight reference (*La corrida del amor,* as one says: *bullfight!*), but furthermore death as the outcome: the *sexmortal* (our neologism condensing the meaning that for the speaking being, there is no sexuality without death).

I do not know the reasons that Lacan had for not mentioning the change of title; moreover when we know that he knew sufficient Japanese, in any case, much more than the one who is writing here. I do not know the reasons for not having questioned the change in the title of the film, but if I am not wrong, I think I found traces of the possible reasons. Where? In Lacan himself, and three years prior to the viewing of the film, in the session of 18th December 1973, in which although implicit, the Biblical reference is strong, knowledge is always carnal knowledge, gifting us together with the happening of Adam in his encounter with Eve. Eve, as Lacan reminds us, means "the mother of the living", in Hebrew. Then:

> Love, if it is effectively the metaphor of something, is about try-
> ing to find out what it refers to. We should start from, as I said
> before, what takes place. It refers [...] to the metaphor of knowl-
> edge, before anything else, it refers to a happening. To those things
> that take place, let us say, *when a man meets a woman* [our emphasis].
> And why not? Because in general it is the fish that one attempts to
> drown; when I said when a man encounters a woman, *I am modest,*
> *I am saying that I do not pretend to talk about what takes place when*
> *a woman meets a man* [...] *because my experience is limited,* [...] [our
> emphasis]. (1973–1974)[19]

Lacan on 15th March 1976 in the company of Jacques Aubert, among others, watched in a private screening Nagisha's film *In the Realm of the Senses.*[20] We know this because he speaks about it the following day in his seminar during the session of 16th March 1976. He characterises the film as belonging to female erotism. He remarks as well how much he was surprised by the film and asks himself why the woman after killing the man, and not before, cuts his penis and he answers: "[...] because the fantasy of the woman is not (a fantasy) of castration."

Although this is apparently the case, I think that there are sufficient merits, and I will show them, to re-open the question. Effectively, Lacan does not authorise himself to say or to know on 16th March: "*What happens when a woman encounters a man* [our emphasis] [...] *because the experience of Lacan was limited* [...]", wasn't it? This is despite what is said in Nagisha's Film *Ai no Korida* (*The Corrida of Love*) as well as in Abe's declarations in 1936 to the police, which to our astonishment seem to say exactly the same thing as in the film. But the fact remains that Abe Sada displays her encounter with Kichi as "meeting a man", and with her "passage to the act" she shows what Lacan did not want or could not say[21] in the session of the seminar.

The fact that Lacan did not remember or allude to the same thing that he described in his seminar *Les non-dupes errent* three years before, could be seen as a matter of indifference or dispute, except that during the commentary of the film in his seminar,[22] not remembering or even alluding to it seems to be the trace of something elided; because what he said about the film, let us face it, was very little indeed.

It might be, and this is my proposition, that while referring to the film with too much irony, saying that he would not have wanted to give bad ideas, something other is elided, something he already stated that we found in the seminar *Encore* (1972–1973), four years prior to the seminar *Le sinthôme* (1975–1976) and one year before the seminar *Les non-dupes errent* (1973–1974). It is in *Encore* where he says exactly the same that Abe Sada will "tell him" on the 15th March when "she shoots" him unexpectedly at close range from the screen with *his*, Lacan's, own message in an inverted form,[23] comparable to the manner described by Freud in "The uncanny" (*DasUnheimliche*).

What Lacan says is that for a man the woman is a *sinthôme*,[24] and for a woman (the encounter with a) man is a ravage. This is exactly what Abe "tells" him from the screen. In her declaration to the police she remarked: [...] although she had sex with many men, she never lost herself, the exception was her encounter with Kichi.

If we return once more to the session of 16th March 1976 of *Le sinthôme*, in which Lacan says: "[...] the fantasy of that woman, is not (a fantasy) of castration, [...]" and he goes on to speak of the *sinus cavernosa* and blood, all of this seems as if Lacan is embarking on an exercise to disguise something. Moreover, in the end he finishes by acknowledging that he does not know much about it. All in all, one cannot help but thinking of Borges' story *Guayaquil* with his withering words: *trop meublé*, and why? If not, because these were traces not to follow, traces that potentially had the possibility of erasing the clues he gave himself prior to the seminar *Le sinthôme* and the viewing of the film.

Nagisha confronts and insinuates in *Ai no Korida* (*The Corrida of Love*), a rare combination of a magisterial narration of Japan at the door step of the WWII and a crime of passion taking place in 1936. All of this in a given moment of the film is metaphorised and condensed in a narrow street where the Imperial Forces marching abroad towards the reinforcement of the troops abroad faced Kichi walking in the opposite direction. Yet both are unavoidably going towards their destruction, the former publically and the latter in the anonymity of the game of two.[25]

Sorting it out

I went to Japan more than ten years ago with expectations awoken by my increasing interest in its literature and history and as result of questioning what happens with love and with tenderness when a subject is taken by a limitless passion in which life lacks all meaning if the loved one is not all the time at her or his side. In the limitless erotism of Abe and Kichi I found traces of my incomplete question. In principle, the sexuality outlined in this historical event exceeds the sex-psychoanalytic *status quo,* through an erotism that proves Psychopathology's classification for what it is: a Procust's bed. From this perspective Japan rewarded me in excess, and it is because of this reward that perhaps in this moment you have this writing in your hands.

Once the Japanese name of the film is recuperated: *Ai no Korida* (*The Corrida of Love*), startling things become evident; the subject is taken in and by language, and in consequence of this he is inexorably carried as in the case of initiation to *run*[26] *contranatura* (2003). And furthermore the subject's sexuality and erotism know nothing of a sex called masculine or feminine; as such we are lead to underscore something avoided for a long time: seemingly, that the subject could only make love with her or his unconscious, or in other words that psychoanalysis contrary to the wide spread moralistic fear rather than being *Pan sexual*, brings to the fore that there is no sexual relation (*il n'y a pas de rapport sexuel*) (Lacan, 1969–1970).

> [...] it is surprising that the number is already given in language as what is transmitted in it of the Real. Why not to admit that the sexual peace of the animal [...] is due to the fact that it is not hooked to its language? [...] but who knows what to do with a body of a speaking being (*parlêtre*) more than embracing it more or less tightly, a bit silly for "fucking", anyone knows how to do it better,

I said anyone [...] what language could do better is to show itself to be at the service of the death drive. This is an idea of Freud, a genial idea that is confirmed with the following: language becomes effective when it becomes writing. (Lacan, 1980, p. 106)

Lacan's phrase mentioned earlier in this text: "it is clear that the fantasy of the woman (the Japanese), is not a fantasy of castration", is an affirmation that invites us before taking it automatically, to compare it with the session of 24th June 1964 seminar *The Four Fundamental Concepts of Psychoanalysis* (1979 [1964]), in which he stated:

I love you, but because I love in you something more than you, the object *a*, I mutilate you.

Mutilate? Is that what the Japanese woman does to her *partenaire*? Lacan differentiated in psychoanalysis the Real, the Imaginary and the Symbolic in which "castration" permits the access to desire. Another seems to be the function of *mutilation*, which, as in the film, seemingly is a beyond jouissance.

Concerning Kichi's fantasy, Lacan is tellingly silent; after all, it is not difficult to see Kichi's giving into a growing passivity obedient to the quasi-pedagogical erotic initiation he received. This is why the original Japanese title of the film is of utmost importance. It shows the way the director of the film, Nagisha, metaphorises in crescendo with the highly ritualistic *Corrida* (Bullfighting) Kichi's outcome. After all both, Kichi as much as the bull in the ring, go through a ritual *against nature* to confront their death. Needless to say, that apart from the Japanese title, there is nothing at all in the film about bullfighting.

Abe Sada's erotism was on the opposite extreme of life and desire, as we will see the difference by comparing Lacan's formulation in *The sinthome*:

[...] it is clear that the fantasy of the woman (the Japanese), is not a fantasy of castration [...].

With the formulation of the seminar *L' angoisse*:

In any case, it is inasmuch that she wants my jouissance, that is to say to enjoy me, that she provokes my angst, and this is so [...] [because] there is no desire, if not by implicating castration. [...]

It is inasmuch as it is about jouissance, that what she wants is my
being, that the woman cannot reach it, if not by castrating me [...].
(1962–1963)[27]

The *Corrida* that took place in Japan, unleashed a beyond castration (-φ)
and desire; that is to say that Abe Sada's fantasy of mutilation resulted
in Kichi's *Aphanisis* (Zentner, 1979) and *a-ization,* as demonstrated by
strangling her lover and cutting off his penis and scrotum.

I take up again Lacan's formula from the session of 13th March 1963,
from *L'angoisse,* but beware, I have changed it completely in order to
include Sada's "passage to the act". Lacan's original:

It is inasmuch as it is about jouissance, that is to say that what she
wants is my being, that the woman cannot reach it, if not by castrating me.

My modification: It is inasmuch as it is about [and beyond] jouissance,
that is to say that what [for what] she wants is [not enough] my being,
that the woman cannot reach it, if not [any longer] by castrating me, [but
by mutilating me with my subsequent aphanisis].

Of course, this is not what Lacan said or proposed, this is my proposition, debatable as it may be.

When I went to Japan it was already too late to see it but the Museum
of Medical Pathology in Tokyo University used to have in display[28]
those objects *a* of Abe Sada's erotism: the penis and scrotum of Kichi
Ishida, until they disappeared mysteriously, as did Abe Sada.

After strangling Kichi with her peach *obi* and cutting off his penis and
scrotum, Abe wrote using his blood on the sheets and on his leg: *Sada,
Kichi together,* and before leaving she engraved her name with a knife in
Kichi's left arm. She explained this to her interrogator by saying:

Writing on the sheets and on his leg I felt that he was a part of
me, and engraving my name with the knife on his arm I felt that I
became part of him. (Johnston, 2005)[29]

If mourning is to lose someone who is the support of castration, could
we include the above within the parameters of mourning? Or in
Ishida's case, more than being Abe's support, was he a supplement for

castration? I quote, once again: "[...] that which is invented to *substitute* something is, perhaps, only the mystery of two [...]"[30] (my emphasis).

Catastrophe, ravage, have only been given one meaning in this text, the same one given and perhaps forgotten, by Lacan, to specify "what takes place when a woman meets the man". To which, I add, not as a complement but as a supplement.

One of the Abe Sada's interrogators describes her behaviour as follows:

> The woman by name Abe Sada, doubtlessly had a very straightforward manner. The questioning was simple. She said with much fervour: "I am mortified to have caused so many problems", but one could clearly see a deep satisfaction for having been able to take absolute control over the man she loved. There wasn't, however, anything inside of her that made her seem like a criminal. She was a woman in the prime of her life, a woman in the *elegant, old Edo style, who was sexy in a different way, a way one does not typically think of a geisha or a restaurant waitress* [our emphasis]. [...] At the time people were saying that she cut it off Ishida because of its larger than average size [...] which was not the case [...]. She told me, "Size doesn't make a man in bed. *Technique* [our emphasis] and his desire to please me was what I liked about Ishida. (Johnston, 2005, p. 124)

In 2009 I heard Jean Allouch in a seminar in Buenos Aires mention the *Iki*, a concept that awoke my interest and drove me to read Kuki Shuzo's *Reflexions on Japanese Taste—the Structure of Iki*, This book opened doors to other reading and interests such as his and his father's mentor, Okakuro Kakuzo,[31] and Kakuzo's teacher, Ernst Fenollosa (2007).

In December 1926, Kuki Shuzo finished his first draft of the script on the *Iki* in Paris, The book was then published in Japan in 1930. However, defining what *Iki* is, is a complicated matter.

Attempting to do justice to the book *Reflections on Japanese taste—The Structure of Iki* or even its concept, is beyond the reach of this essay. Suffice to note, that among others things, Kuki Shuzo attempted to define Japanese aesthetics, using Heidegger's hermeneutics.

Kuki Shuzo considered *Iki* as something particular to the Japanese, and if at moments conceding that the West could have something alike, he always came back to suggest that similarity was not sameness. *Iki* was for Kuki Shuzo something not only Japanese, moreover proper of the Edo area, different from the *Sui* that was equivalent, not the same and proper of Kyoto.

Kuki Shuzo, as well as that particular generation of cultivated Japanese who have become acquainted with and enthusiastic about with the West, began to withdraw and to re-valorise their own proper culture, so much so, that for Kuki the *Iki* was the separating line between the West and the Orient.

Iki, this aesthetic of pretence and concealment, of dynamic quietness, applied both to men and women, was very different from *dandyism.* The latter applied only to men and did not exclude homosexuality. *Iki* instead included both sexes at once but excluded homosexuality. This "know how to do", as I said before, was different in Edo (Tokyo) from Kyoto, and was very well captured by Borges in his travels to Japan between 1979 and 1983, who in an *Iki way,* captured it, in one sentence without naming it:

> [...] from a writing that exercises *insinuation* [our emphasis] and it
> is at the same time ignorant of the hyperbole. (Gasio, 1988)

But you reader, having always the advantage of the last word, could exercise your right by questioning everything I have put forward so far, by simply wondering: what of the order of Japanese aesthetics, or for that matter any aesthetics, could keep correlation with the gruesome crime described above?

Touché, certainly the scales seem to lean on your side, and you still have ammunition, since *Iki* is always a calculated resignation which does not shy away from being brave and detached, a kind of intent of intended indifference, in which the understated elegance of the gesture is of equal value to the action of the gesture, a displayed sophistication which, if shown, would need to be modest and at the same time convey absolute risk, including one's life. If these were to be your objections, I should say that you are right, that from this perspective Abe was, if anything, completely unrestrained and yet there is at least one element in the confessions of Abe Sada which make me reconsider agreeing with you. I repeat, the element I am referring to is of great value as it came first hand from one of the interrogators, who reflected upon his interviews with her:

She was a woman in the pinnacle of her life, a woman in the old, elegant
Edo style, sensual in a very different fashion from that one which it is gen-
erally ascribed to a geisha or a restaurant waitress [...]. (Johnston, 2005)

Yet in actual fact she was a geisha who, having failed as such, followed the
trodden path of the unsuccessful geishas, to become a prostitute in different brothels and cities until she escaped, overcoming extreme adversity.
She then became a lover and kept woman of a politician, who offered her
a different life and wanted her to learn how to run a restaurant to acquire
skills to break off with the circle of prostitution that comes with not having formal skills and needing to work. Following the good intentions of
her lover's advice: to start as a waitress so as to eventually learn how to
run a restaurant, she went on to learn how to be a waitress, and it is this,
that takes her to the fateful restaurant owned by Kichi.

In Abe Sada, there was something more than what was obscured by
the sensationalism of the time, as her subtlety in her attention to some
elegant details, like the description of the way she put her *obi* around
Kichi's neck, and the colour of the *obi*. Thus a reason for me to consider
that she carried with her, perhaps in a dreamlike state, the *Iki* of an
already dying epoch.

Another element that comes together with the above mentioned
impressions of the interrogator is the politician who fell in love with
her, and who clearly was educated and of a certain class, who might
have been able to distinguish in her the same qualities the interrogator
found.

Let us re-trace briefly Nagisha's film narration of Abe Sada's ravage, along with her own declarations. We can say with confidence that
because of the strictness of the film, its power is shaped by the loyal
description of what took place.

On 8th May 1936, Abe and Kichi, already lovers, separated due to
the lack of money and commitments on Kichi's side, which prevented
them from continuing to meet in Tea houses (*Ochaya*). This separation
did not come about without numerous scenes of wailing and making
love. From then onwards, Abe could not stop thinking about Kichi.
They were separated for three days and on 11th May, Abe, inspired by
a scene in a play she had seen the previous day, bought a large knife in
a hardware shop. That night they met again and Abe declared to the
interrogator that Kichi told her:

I am so enamoured that I will always come back, [...] I thought it would be impossible for him to be home for three days and not to have sex with his wife and this made me jealous [...]. So after we had sex I pinched and hit and bit him all over his body in a really violent way. [...] he only asked me to forgive him, saying that since we had parted he had been consumed by jealousy [...] I continued to torture him and he said "Don't kill me." [...] In any case, on the evening of the eleventh I was so happy that I felt as though I were seeing the man of my dreams [...] I could hardly speak and we spent the whole night without any sleep, just crying and teasing the entire time. [...] From early in the morning until 11 pm, on the fifteenth I was out with professor Omiya (the politician). Except for the time when Ishida (Kichi) went to have a haircut on the evening of the sixteenth, until I killed him on the evening of the eighteenth we spent the entire time with each other naked in bed. (Johnston, 2005, p. 195)

There was no reason for him to think of committing suicide [...]. I decided that there was nothing I could do but to kill him and make him mine forever. [...] After a while Ishida was sound asleep so I took my peach-coloured obi that was next to his pillow with my right hand and pulled the end of it under his neck with my left hand, wrapping it twice around his neck, adjusting the ends, and pulling on them. He opened his eyes and said "Okayo." His body raised up a little and moved as though he was going to give me a hug. I put my face against his chest and cried "Forgive me", [...]. After I had killed Ishida I felt totally at ease [...] while I was playing with Ishida's penis I thought of cutting it off and taking it with me [...]. (Johnston, 2005, p. 199)

Abe wrapped Ishida's penis and testicles, but a lot of blood was flowing out of the wound. This was the same blood of course with which she will write on Ishida's left thigh and on the bedding "*Sada, Kichi together*".

After the many interrogations she was under, I underscore this one:

When I had choked him the previous night I had not decided for certain if I wanted to kill him [...]. While having sex with him and choking him at the same time, I adored him. [...] so much I adored him that I wanted to kill him [...]. Finally, I would like to say [...] if you investigate my past […] I have had sex with men to the point that I almost *forget myself. But I have never actually forgotten myself* and have always kept time and place clearly in mind. […] *It was only with Ishida that* (in contrast) I allowed things to *get out of control* […] (he) swallowed me up *body and soul* […] there are women who fall hopelessly in love with a man […] when an incident like mine happens, it isn't only because a woman is (only) *crazy* about sex. (Johnston, 2005, pp. 207–208) (my emphasis)

I specifically highlight this because it is an extraordinary description of what Lacan said about the outcome that follows a woman meeting *a man.* The outcome is "a catastrophe, a ravage". Taking up Abe's words, that the woman does what she did not only because of her craving crazily for sex, with the final moments of the *Corrida,* where he submits to her, for a beyond jouissance, and as proof of the importance of the Japanese's name of Nagisha's film, beyond a shadow of doubt, Abe Sada like the bullfighter who cuts the bull's ear after the killing, took with her Ishida's penis and scrotum, keeping them wrapped under her kimono, for almost two days, until she was detained by the police.

These object(s) *a* close to her body showed jouissance as a deadly successful metaphor, that is to say obtainable and mortal, in contrast to Ovid's *What you Desired is not Mortal,* quoted at the beginning, which implies desire as being always in the metonymic horizon, that is potentially possible and as such on the side of life.

As you perhaps already noticed I did not use even once the word *masochism* because, whatever *masochism* might be, it is always on the side of desire and life, and what took place on the 19th May 1936 in Tokyo, is beyond life and desire. Kichi Ishida, accepting the rule of "fucking" continuously, as demanded by Abe, situated himself in an initiation, which would take him to the footsteps of a trip of no return.

Abe Sada after killing Ishida and carrying with her his penis and scrotum, had sex with professor Omiya, who did not know or even suspect what had taken place a few hours before. While they were making love in the futon, he commented that she had a strange smell, proving in this way, unwittingly that the objects *a* for one (Abe Sada), could smell rotten for others (Omiya).

After I compared the material I read with that of the film *Ai no Korida,* I was startled to notice its fidelity shown all the way through the smallest of details. There is little doubt that Nagisha read all the available police and court case records of 1936. And as is known, Nagisha interviewed Abe (with a shaved head) for the last time in 1969 in the Buddhist Convent of Kansai.

In his "Homage rendered by Jacques Lacan to the castrating woman", Jean Allouch expresses at the end of his paper a statement in reference to *In the Realm of the Senses*. He states: "The same phallus, but flaccid, an object petit *a* which in possessing it makes her mad."

Allouch's statement invites us to slow down, and to open two questions. The first question: That phrase: "an object petit *a* which in possessing it makes her mad"—does it allude to a "before" or to an "after"? As I stated above, what is shown to us through Abe Sada is a lack of mourning and this is more complicated than it appears. Based on her declarations, her "madness" cannot be said in terms of "before" (when she was "mad" with jealousy) or "after" (when she cuts Ishida's penis and scrotum).

The second question: Could a subject ever possess the object petit *a*? This second question is a weightier one and as such will be treated in another writing.

Abe had threatened to kill Ishida if he dared make love with his wife. While Ishida was alive, she needed to have him, inside of her, literally, all the time and expresses jealousy at the thought of someone else having Ishida's penis and scrotum. Her "madness" was present before and after. She herself confirms this statement when coming back to "sanity" and explaining why she mutilated Ishida's body:

> I cut Ishida's penis and testicles, because it was what I loved the most of him, and I couldn't bear the idea of his wife, when washing his body, having them in her hands [...]. (Johnston, 2005, p. 201)

Then, we agreed with Allouch, that it is the "same phallus, but flaccid, an object *a*", and we point out that although mad, certainly not psychotic, neither before nor after.

In reality, the path I take now is a different one as a consequence of having read Abe's declarations and the memoirs of the judge[32] in charge of her case, Hosoya Keijiro,[33] which were read to me by a Japanese[34] acquaintance, and as a result of these readings I favour and choose a direction that goes, so to speak, from Shakespeare to Freud or Lacan, rather than from Freud or Lacan to Shakespeare.

I persevere in this way to exercise, *extramuros,* what I understand *Iki* to be: that constantly sliding and fugacious, yet supreme path (Zentner, 2007) of "being able not to", giving then place to a certain suspension, to some reserve, allowing that which took place to show itself in act, thus avoiding to fall in the seductive traps of psychological explanations.[35]

"… because it is not that"

The psychological, or for that matter, psychoanalytic explanation, always acts as a palliative to anaesthetise the angst provoked by the confrontation to what in this case took place, the act which in fact not only exceeds, but moreover excludes us.[36]

Abe Sada, from the perspective of "I ask you to refuse what I offer you, because it is not that" (1971–1972),[37] could not reject the offer of complete submission of Kichi Ishida. Abe was only able to confirm this: that in her persistence of wanting to take with her the penis and testicles of Kichi Ishida, "they were not that".

At the end, and when it was already too late, she was able to realise that "those objects were not that", and in the same line others, like the Museum of Medical Pathology of Tokyo University, also did not know that Kichi Ishida's penis and testicles, "were not that".

Notes

1. *Delire,* from Latin, means to sow out of the furrow.
2. Sigmund Freud, "On Transience".
3. Alluded to in Giacomo Puccini's opera *Madame Butterfly,* partially based on the novel *Madame Chrysantheme* by Pierre Loti.
4. Apparently Mishima was related via his grandmother with the clan Samurai of the Tokugawa.
5. Junichiro Tanizaki published his book in 1933 and it was translated and published in English by Leete's Island Books, in 1977.
6. Influenced by the *Shimpuren Rebellion* conducted by Saigo Takamori, and the legend of his *sepukku.*
7. Buddhism was partially replaced perhaps as an indirect result of the expulsion of the Jesuits, by Confucianism, with its implication of a submission to a central power, in this case the *Tokugawa Shogunate.*
8. With the exception of Ulysses, (in regard to *Lethe*) *Lethe* like the *Rubicon* is crossed only once.

9. As corroborated by Abe Sada declarations after having killed Kichi Ishida.

10. Jacques Lacan, *les non-dupes errent* (1973–1974), session of 20th November 1973, available at: www.ecole-lacanienne.net/seminaireXXI.php (my translation).

11. In a sleeping city in Tasmania, some twenty years ago a doctor killed her lover by accident, playing the same sexual game.

12. The passage from *Erastes* to *Eromenos* is not rigid, it is highly labile, circumstantial and singular.

13. As stated by Abe, in her ample and very credible declarations to the police, showing that after failing as a Geisha, she became a prostitute, until her encounter with the politician Omiya, who made her a kept woman, offering as well to come out of that life, until the catastrophe of her encounter with Kichi Ishida, her employer and lover.

14. Sash, with which the kimono is closed and when knotted at the front, indicates the profession of prostitute, otherwise is knotted behind.

15. Her detailed declarations, saving the obvious distance, calls to mind the degree of care and ritual with which the "Tea Ceremony" is executed.

16. Although less metaphorical yet more lethal than Samuel Beckett's *Endgame*.

17. With this neologism I am underlying the unavoidable intermixing of the S with sex and mortality.

18. Jacques Lacan, *Les non-dupes errent* (1973–1974), session of 12th March 1974.

19. Jacques Lacan, *Les non-dupes errent* (1973–1974), session of 28th December 1973.

20. The title of the film is similar to Roland Barthes' book *The Realm of Signs*.

21. As when Mario Vargas Llosa, author of *The City and the Dogs*, is told by Roger Callois: "You have not understood (your own) novel, think it over!" El Pais Newspaper, Madrid 20th June 2012.

22. Lacan stated somewhere that the seminar was *his analysis*. Did he mean as a means of obtaining more than what he obtained with his ex-analyst Lowenstein? If that was the case, apparently he was not mistaken.

23. As you might remember to receive your own discourse in an inverted form was something that Levi-Strauss' wife, Monique gave Lacan as a "gift". But Abe Sada was not Monique.

24. Jacques Lacan, session of 17th February 1976, *Le sinthôme* (1975–1976b).

25. See above footnotes 19 and 20.

26. Very much in two senses, as *Corrida*, which literally means the run of the bull in the ring and the confrontation with the bullfighter.

27. Jacques Lacan, session of 13th March 1963, *L'angoisse* (1962–1963).

28. Perhaps as artistically arranged as Zurburán's painting of the breasts and eyes of St. Agatha, floating in a washbowl.

29. Notes from the police interrogation of Abe Sada, published in Japanese newspapers at the time. In: Johnston, W. (2005) *Geisha, Harlot, Strangler, Star: A woman, sex and morality in modern Japan. Asia perspectives: History, Society and Culture* (1955). New York: Columbia University Press .

30. Jacques Lacan, session of 12th March 1974, *Les non dupes errent.*

31. Okakuro Kakuzo, *The Book of Tea.* This aesthete, was asked by Kuki Shuzo's father to travel back from the USA, with his wife who had a psychotic incident, thereafter they become lovers, and the influence of Okakuro Kakuzo on Kuki Shuzo was fundamental.

32. I am in possession of the book *Dotera Saiban,* thanks to Mr. Miyakawa Katsutoshi, Director of the Information and Cultural Centre of the Embassy of Japan, Canberra, Australia.

33. Hosoya Keijiro, Dotera Saiban, Moriwaki Bunko, Tokyo, 1956.

34. This took me to pay close attention to the teachings left by James Joyce with his irony and attack on Gogarty, whom he described with these implacable words: "To be a surgeon amongst the literati and a literati amongst the surgeons."

35. Pitifully, William Johnson's very important book cannot avoid, at times, falling into making use of a certain psychoanalytic-psychology.

36. I silently paid homage here, to the French film director Claude Lanzmann, to whom I had the opportunity to listen in his abysmal, deafening silence with which he answered the immense angst of his audience, asking him explanations about the film he had shown on the extermination camp at Birkenau. Thus in a practically complete silence he left me with an invaluable lesson: there are things that can only be shown, but neither demonstrated nor explained (the latter two belong to psychology and possibly to some kinds of psychoanalytic practice.) In fact to explain these things, to give sense to them, is to assimilate them with what it is already known. This of course, is to try to erase the non-sense of the real.

37. Jacques Lacan, lesson of 8th February 1972, seminar ... *Ou pire,* (1971–1972).

CHAPTER TWENTY

No light, but rather darkness visible

Rodney Kleiman

Some years ago whilst travelling, not aimlessly but with a long ago departed freedom, in the Dordogne region of France, there was realised a proximity to the site of the famous Paleolithic cave paintings at Lascaux. I say famous now, not because I was at all aware of them at that earlier time. Having driven out of our way to this place my excitement was somewhat tempered by the discovery that the original caves were now closed to the public. Even tourist brochures have fine print to confound the lazy. A cave closure dictated, ostensibly, as a consequence of the scientific concerns for preservation due to the potential corrosive eroding effects of raised carbon dioxide levels: the many breathless exhalations of visitors in the 1960s, or one suspects, a touch of that potent Gauloise/Gitane atmospheric mixture, so redolent of European monuments. The potent acid threatened the survival of the ancient cave paintings. So the original caverns were sealed and preserved, to exist evermore in the quiet company of various technological devices and equipment, only to be entered by appropriately monitored scientific parties and the occasional dignitary and his girlfriend.

Lascaux Deux (Two) awaited us. Not the sequel to Lascaux one, a la Hollywood, not a sequel but an exact reproduction. It's rare that a copy has quite the provenance of the original. No one more than glances at the copies of Michelangelo's David in the square whilst waiting for tickets in a long Florentine queue. A wait which is worth the time due to the extraordinary impact of the original. And Lascaux Two, the copy? In this case I was pleasantly surprised to find the experience of viewing these very, very old master's paintings, no less real, no less intense. In fact, grasping at clichés, it was quite awe inspiring to venture under the ground to confront an exact replica of the cave. Or better to be confronted by it. If the authorities were somewhat wiser they would only have a sign at the exit announcing the fact that this was not the real thing preferably in very small print and I'm sure that others and I would leave none the wiser.

But neither the question of replication nor the status of the copy, nor French technical expertise is my focus here. These pictures, these writings on the wall were painted some 16,000 years ago, by the savage hand of hirsute Magdalenians. And rediscovered by some slightly less hirsute teenagers in 1940 whilst rescuing their dog from a hole, also a common pastime. Some 2,000 images of animals, all sorts of animals: huge bulls, horses, bison, cows, stags, cats, and bears, even a rhinoceros. Europe was somewhat different in those times.

They were originally thought by some to be fakes given the apparent complexity and draughtsmanship. These and other similar works, threw the proverbial spanner into the art world because they denied the apparent progression of art, the gradual accretion of knowledge within the studio, of perspective, of the means of production, of the sense of movement. No one had thought that Paleolithic man could represent with such a modern trained eye, even using the curve of the rock, this natural canvas to emphasise a three dimensionality.

It's nothing but beautiful that's indubitable. But more than that, it's art, undeniably art. As ill-defined as that statement is. Art defined thus, "It's not simply decorative." It's not just an adornment on the walls. It means something. Even if we don't know what it means, it means something. It represents something. And it represents something beyond what is apparently represented. It's not just the animals that are represented. But amazing as this artistic proficiency is, I am not going to dwell on that either. My question concerns motivation. My question concerns therefore the particularity of motivation peculiar to the interests of a psychoanalyst, the unconscious. The unconscious, that which drives our desires including the desire of the artist.

Why were these painting created? This question produces a plexus of supposition to follow. It's important to know, surprisingly, that these caves were not inhabited. These artists were semi-cave dwellers, setting up camp at the entrances, but these caves were not dwellings. It's not because being at a loose end during the evening, with little good to watch on television that men began to doodle on the walls. To paint these pictures, by the light of flickering animal fat lamps, required a somewhat hazardous underground journey, leaving the natural comfort of the sunlight and for many hours toiling in an unlit darkness. A true blackness which we of the light bulb have long forgotten. Elaborate scaffolds set up to produce monstrous paintings. How monstrous they must have seemed to the viewers, when later these animals sprang from the walls reanimated by the flickering torch light. These were art galleries added to over thousands of years. They were places to go to view art and chosen because they protected the art from the elements but also emphasised the figures by virtue of the surrounding darkness. There is thus clearly no motivation except the requirement to create. A requirement, which is of the most imperious kind. Simply irresistible. It wouldn't otherwise appear to be so inviting to venture into the darkness. This was not a refuge but a risk.

Many theories have been put forward to explain the motivation. None have stuck. They had no religious significance for nothing speaks of ceremony or religious musings. Neither to furnish control over the harsh environment and assist the hunt; nor to have a ready supply of food, inedible but digestible. Inadequate explanations all.

These are not paintings of the artists themselves; there are no self-portraits. There are no human figures but almost exclusively figures of animals. Animals: objects slated by desire. Sources of food, clothing, light. But the source too of anxiety, fearful creatures. Not less so when leaping out of the darkness. Who eats may themselves be eaten. He who eats is never alone, the monster says.

What led to the painting? What led to the viewing by others of these flickering images, here in the art gallery of its time?

What this art portrays is that some force has driven man, driven him with the same intensity as it does today, driven him without knowing why, to represent something. What led him to the art of darkness? The unconscious? Can you imagine the musings of a Stone Age man? No. But these works were not caused by mere musings any more than today's art is an amusement.

Imagine a time before the artificial. Before the steel and the right angle and the concrete, a natural time. Before paradise lost. Before man's first disobedience, and the fruit of that forbidden tree, whose mortal taste brought death into the world, and all our woe, with the loss of Eden.

We can't imagine it.

These people of the Palaeolithic did not choose. They had no choice but to represent by writing on the wall. Long before writing on the page existed. What is astounding is that in spite of all the thousands of years of subsequent developments and the appealing illusion that we have entered a future more knowing than our ancestors, it is clearly but an illusion that we are so "of the future". These colourful tales of the past demonstrate that something functioned, has always functioned, to compel man unknowingly into the darkness to create an image. We could no more say why now than we ever could give some absolute final reason for this compulsion. Which is why we talk endlessly about it.

These Cavemen had fallen prey, not to their carnivorous companions but to the forbidden fruit; words, words which bring knowledge. The knowledge of mortality and sexuality, of sin and desire. Words which bring the question of meaning but not the answer. Language is not the why, it's not the cause, but it is the force which compels creation. Words create effects. Art is one effect. The unconscious another.

What is the relevance of this excursion to psychoanalysis? Is it not the same force which drives one onto a couch to explore that art which is analysis? It is a dark art which rests on meaning but never produces the absolute meaning. It paints a picture of those terrifying desirable objects on the walls of your little room, the objects catalogued in your gallery of fear. Why do people venture into the darkness of the soul? Not out of choice but driven by the force of desire.

For me, the paintings of Lascaux are incontrovertible proof of the essence of man.

They speak of a timeless insistence, an absolute requirement for that which does not develop gradually by learning, of that which is only apparently rediscovered by each with reference to history, of that which grasps one where it hurts, of the compulsion to attempt to represent the invisible essence of our anxiety.

These pictures are anti-developmental, timeless, mythically determined, concerned with the limits of man's attempt at representation of the object as cause of desire. As such they are as psychoanalysis, which shares these characteristics. Timeless. Mythical and anti-developmental, transmissible beyond and despite a teaching, working with the semblance of the object cause of desire. They play with man's enjoyment of the terrifying, the ineffable, and the ephemeral. They decry the apparent historical developments of mankind by showing the presence of art and its relation to desire and jouissance, long before a word of it was writ in the manner we now speak of writing. Before the philosophers, before the historians, before the art schools, before the university. Before the analysts. Prior to all that we call civilisation, cultural heights, the modern, the postmodern, the artificial, the technological, the multimedia and the globalised. Before all that. Eons ago. An unspeakable truth beckoned the artist amongst us. And created an audience.

From out of the caves this force has been civilised, illuminated now under glass on the spot lit white walls of our galleries, typed neatly on our parchments and carved onto David's marble thigh. A slingshot fit for us, Goliaths atop our intelligent perch.

Here in the darkness dwells absolute proof of the insistence of meaning, thus of language. These paintings, prehistoric, are proof of man's fall from Eden. Art coincides with the fall into meaning and leaves no natural state to which to return. Here is some proof that his true motivation is unconscious.

Psychoanalysis originates from a recognition of the drive consequent from desire. But the analyst is not an artist. The artist produces a work to grab the public gaze. That was the status even in the caves of Lascaux. The artist makes visible the truth in its universal form. Art generates a general interest even when manifested as rejection or aversion. Analysis, quite differently produces a particular reading of one person's subjection and relationship to the truth. Thus both art and analysis originate as human endeavours from the consequence of language imposing itself on man and the possibility linked with the limits of knowledge. But the method is very different. Analysis produces a singular fact, whilst Art is that which can be displayed to disturb and enthrall the many. One reason why art will survive but psychoanalysis may not.

When paradise was lost, when man began to speak, art was born. Some 200 centuries later Freud discovered the truth that had always given art its impact. Man, not Satan, but man, dwells in the blind poet Milton's hell:

> As one great furnace flamed, yet from those flames
> No light, but rather darkness visible
> Served only to discover sights of woe
> Regions of sorrow, doleful shades, where peace
> And rest can never dwell.

Life is hellish, horrible, ever monstrous and through art, as a consequence, quite beautiful.

CHAPTER TWENTY-ONE

Snapped by the image: the inverted art of the photograph and the artifice of psychoanalysis

Peter Gunn

A minute in the world's life passes! To paint it in reality! And forget everything for that. To become that minute, be the sensitive plate …

—*Cézanne*

In his early paper "Screen memories" (1899a) Freud's interlocutor (who we know to be none other than Freud himself) talks about some memories which have persisted from childhood, memories which Freud characterises as being ultra clear (ibid., 313). The interlocutor speaks of his memories as being made up of pictures. Indeed, as he begins to recount one memory it is as if he were describing what he sees when standing in front of a picture:

I see a rectangular, rather steeply sloping piece of meadow-land, green and thickly-grown; in the green there are a great number of yellow flowers—evidently common dandelions. At the top of the meadow there is a cottage and in front of the cottage two women are standing chatting busily, a peasant-woman with a handkerchief on her head and a children's nurse. Three children are playing in the grass. One of them is myself (between the ages of two and three); the two others are my boy cousin [...] and his sister [...]. We are picking the yellow flowers and each of us is holding a bunch we have already picked. (1899a, p. 311)

Suddenly however this seemingly innocent and rather static tableau seems to burst into life:

The little girl has the best bunch; and, as though by mutual agreement, we—the two boys—fall on her and snatch away her flowers. She runs up the meadow in tears and as a consolation the peasant-woman gives her a big piece of black bread. Hardly have we seen this than we throw the flowers away, hurry to the cottage and ask to be given some bread too. And we are in fact given some; the peasant-woman cuts the loaf with a long knife. In my memory the bread tastes quite delicious. (Ibid., p. 311)

At this point, Freud's interlocutor tells us, the scene breaks off.

To those of us who listen, the coming to life of the tableau in this last description lends the whole picture a rather different character. But the interlocutor seems not to recognise this. As a memory it is a matter of indifference to him, seeming both innocent and superfluous. He cannot understand why it should have left such an unforgettable impression. As he remembers them, the events do not account for this impact.

But in regard to the picture there is something which strikes him; something is not quite right. There is distortion, distortion which lends the whole picture a strange, hallucinatory quality:

The yellow of the flowers is a disproportionately prominent element in the situation as a whole, and the nice taste of the bread seems to me exaggerated in an almost hallucinatory fashion. (Ibid., p. 312)

Rather reluctantly, these words, "yellow", and "bread", which are also elements in the picture, lead our interlocutor to a different kind of picture. This too involves pictorial distortion, but coupled now to sexual impropriety:

I cannot help being reminded of some pictures that I once saw in a burlesque exhibition. Certain portions of these pictures, and of course the most inappropriate ones, instead of being painted, were built up in three dimensions—for instance the ladies' bustles. (Ibid., p. 312)

Coming back to those words, those elements which are not quite right in the original picture, he is lead, and again rather reluctantly, to two memories from when he was seventeen, memories to which he is not at all indifferent. These relate to two experiences with young women. Indeed he admits that one of these was the occasion of his first encounter with love, an encounter, he admits, which excited him powerfully. It is by this device that he is brought to imagining the sexual enjoyment he might have had with these women.

Now it is for these latter imaginings, these pictures, these phantasies, as Freud calls them, that the first memory functions as a screen or cover. Such screen memories, he says, owe their "value as a memory not to [their] own content but to the relation existing between that content and some other, that has been suppressed" (ibid., p. 320).

In its function for phantasy therefore the screen memory has the status of fiction. But it is no less genuine for that. Its value lies in fact; it lies, that is, precisely in not being a memory. It is a picture, and it is this only inasmuch as it functions as a device; it is, we can say after Lacan, a signifying construction, one by which that other scene which is called the phantasy is built.

It is clear then that if it is to have this function neither can such a picture be inert. This is, as we have seen, a picture which must come alive, and alive, furthermore, in a manner which is at once peculiar and suggestive. What is animated is not the content, that is, the events of the memory, but rather certain elements of the picture. It is these elements which, in turn, lend animation to the picture as a whole.

Let us then take a closer look at this troublesome animation. A clue to its mechanism is given by the interlocutor's association to the bustles in the burlesque pictures. To quote him again, "instead of being painted they are built up in three dimensions".

The dimension in which the anomalous bustles in these burlesque pictures are built up is the one which lies in front of the pictures; that is, it lies in the direction of the one who is viewing the pictures, pictures which, otherwise, are two-dimensional. It is by the device of the bustles that, in being looked at, these pictures burst out to implicate the one who looks in their own looking. The viewer is thus caught in a position similar to the voyeur in the moment that he is caught out looking through the peep-hole or the bedroom window.

Now, oddly enough, it was the use of just such devices, windows and peep-holes, as well as mirrors, which led to the development of the picture which we now find so familiar, the picture, that is, in which three dimensions are represented within two. It was these devices which Renaissance artists and architects used to assist them with per-spectival representation.[1]

But if the elaboration of Renaissance perspective prescribed the position of the eye of the enquirer at the window or the peep-hole, this remained a device to which the eye of the artist was not subordinated. As a consequence, neither can the viewer of the paintings of this period expect to get off scot-free. As Merleau-Ponty comments, beneath such mechanical tricks artists recognised "the metamorphosis of seeing and seen which defines both our flesh and the painter's vocation" (1964, pp. 68–69).

Renaissance perspective *was*, nevertheless, associated with the development of science, specifically, the science of optics. A variety of formalised procedures were devised for obtaining perspectival repre-sentations. These too were constructions, constructions *more geometrico*, in the manner of the geometers. They were intended, as one commenta-tor puts it, to provide a "practical means for securing a rigorous two-way, or reciprocal, metrical relationship between the shapes of objects as definitely located in [three-dimensional] space and their pictorial representations [on a two-dimensional plane]" (Irvins, Jr., 1973, p. 9).

Now this aspiration to capture the world in a frame, and, thereby, to tame the object, is, as Merleau-Ponty has also commented, one which found its ideal in philosophy in the guise of the Cartesian subject (1964, p. 169). And by its alliance to the mechanical device of the camera it would therefore seem reasonable to propose that, rather than the paint-ing, in the domain of the artefact it is the photograph which is best qualified to represent this ideal.

Certainly the camera, particularly in its modern, easy-to-use form, has come to be thought of as what one art historian has called a "natural machine" (Joel Snyder, 1980, p. 510). Unlike the painter, it is supposed that the photographer does not interfere in the process of representation. When the shutter is released the light which passes through the lens simply imprints an image of the world onto the sensitive panel. On this view, it would seem, the camera does indeed frame the world according to a model in thought, the model being a bio-mechanical one; the camera models what we suppose happens when we open our eyes to let light to impinge on our retina. Art does not come into it; the camera simply "snaps", that is, "photo-copies", the world.

Let us consider then that kind of photograph which we might suppose to be the darling child of this Cartesian lineage: the snapshot. Of all photography the snapshot would seem to be the most automatic. No consideration need be given to matters of technical realisation or artistic fashioning. When he presses the button of his little apparatus the snapshot photographer aims simply to reproduce scenes of pleasant and innocuous domesticity, without fuss, objectively; we might even say, object-lessly.

But, as Freud's burlesque pictures show, it is the very precision of the framing which can give the game away. With the right framing even the snapshot can stir up trouble.

We can see this in what the photographer Henri Cartier-Bresson famously labelled "the decisive moment". This was the title of the English version of the book, published in 1952, which probably did most to make Cartier-Bresson's name. It comes from an epigram attributed to the seventeenth century Archbishop of Paris, Cardinal de Rietz: "There is nothing in this world that does not have a decisive moment." Cartier-Bresson had his own definition of the decisive moment in photography: "The simultaneous recognition in a fraction of a second of the significance of an event as well as of a precise organization of forms" (quoted in Cookman, 2008, p. 60).

In an interview he gave to *Le Monde* in 1974 Cartier-Bresson emphasised the importance of form. Indeed, the title the newspaper gave to the interview was, "None may *enter* here who is not a geometer" (ibid., p. 69). This is of course the injunction which was supposedly inscribed over the entrance to Plato's academy. But in invoking it in the interview Cartier-Bresson made a mistake: he attributed it to an author from the Renaissance.

As is often the case, this mistake is one which we can put to use. We can use it to re-frame Cartier-Bresson's definition. We can say that this moment is one which is recognised in an instant, suddenly, and, apparently entirely intuitively, as decisive. Despite appearances however, this recognition does not in fact arise intuitively; that is, it does not arise autonomously. It depends on the subject position given by the conjugation with form, form which, in turn, is given by the same science which informed the investigations of the artists of the Renaissance.

It is this science which, once again, provides the device of representation, the framing apparatus. The alliance of the eye and camera of this photographer is itself an apparatus, one constructed in the manner of the geometers, or, to use Cartier-Bresson's phrase, by means of a precise organisation of form. It is only by such precise organisation that the moment can be captured, albeit that it is only in being seen that it can, retrospectively, be granted significance, significance which we can then call decisive.

With this reading of Cartier-Bresson's decisive moment we can I think legitimately turn Cardinal de Rietz' axiom on its head. It now reads, "There is nothing in a decisive moment other than what fabricates this world as representation." Indeed, it is for Cartier-Bresson precisely this quality of fabrication which distinguishes the snapshot as a work of art. To quote him, "A work of art is a unity of means aimed at an effect. Artists are not penitents, reciting their sins, they are fabricators who work toward a purpose. [...] it is necessary to learn how to fabricate" (quoted in Cookman, 2008, p. 63).

The fabrication involved in the snapshot is not however mechanical basket-weaving; it has something about it which is both arresting and for which one might be arrested; snap-shot: something snaps, there is a shot. This is an act then, one which causes a break, a traumatic intrusion. And if the necessity of fabrication undergirding this act is not circumscribed by the box of the confessional, there is an animation here which has something of the sinful enjoyment of the sexual. Cartier-Bresson indicates this in the interview with *Le Monde* when he speaks of his act as a lover might of an illicit encounter: "I'm a bag of nerves waiting for the moment, and it wells up and up and it explodes, it's a physical joy, dance, time and space all combined. Yes! Yes! Yes! Like the ending of James Joyce's *Ulysses*. Seeing is everything" (quoted in Jeannery, 2006, p. 15)."

But it is not only the shooting which has this illicit character, what is shot has it as well. This is captured in the French title of Cartier-Bresson's 1952 book: *Images à la sauvette*. This can, I believe, be translated as "Images on the run", but also as "Surreptitious images". Once again there is a strong smell of the enjoyment of the sexually illicit. Indeed Cartier-Bresson spoke of wanting to catch life in the raw, *in flagrante delicto*: "The photographer (too bad if he's behaving badly) should take life by surprise, fresh out of bed" (ibid., p. 14)."

But, and again despite an apparent similarity, we have a departure here from the position of the voyeur with his device. Cartier-Bresson's snap-shot does not recede into the shadows in order to maintain the perspective of the window as a frame for the sins of the day (or the night); it is not there to be a reproduction of what Every-One, that is, the [big] Other, supposedly enjoys there. It functions rather in the same way as the cracking branches in the famous scene which Sartre paints in *Being and Nothingness* to illustrate his account of the existence of others (1966, p. 347). The snap-shot is the sudden intrusion of a little something lying outside the frame that I look through; it is, to use Lacan's formulation, the gaze from the field of the Other (1979 [1964], p. 84). This gaze does not comprehend every-one but only, and very precisely, me.

By an imperative which couples geometric precision to flagrant salaciousness, the snap-shot shows up the window in its failure as frame; it does so by showing that it is precisely the structure of the window which is the mechanism of representation. The window now turns back to me; it shows me up, finds me out in the enjoyment of looking from my hiding place. And what it finds there is subjective disparity, that corrupting effect which representation itself carries but which can also be a cover.

The built-up bustles of the burlesque pictures function in the same way. It is into the perspectival representation of the picture frame that they intrude to disturb Freud's interlocutor. If they have tremendous presence on the screen it is because they break it; they burst into that other, illegitimate space between the picture frame and the viewer. In so doing they throw into relief the frame of representation by which the picture constitutes the interlocutor as subject in the phantasy. In other words, the bustles throw him. To use one of Freud's terms, we could say that the bustles designate the picture as *Vorstellungsrepresentanz*. They make of the picture a snap-shot which presents the subject, but in fading, in being that signifier which, as Lacan says, represents the subject for another signifier.

Now, as you may have gathered, this paper has really been about psychoanalysis all along. In saying this I am acknowledging that, as with any artist, the photographer of the decisive moment has his own reasons. But by it is by reason of his artifice in presenting a framing which gives the lie to what is framed that the photographer bears a resemblance to the position which the psychoanalyst takes up. And so, to conclude, let us come out in the open and declare our reasons.

A felicitous phrase of Mariá Inés Rotmiler de Zentner gives us the opening. She speaks of the "aperture to the subject" in the session (1990, p. 86). In such a privileged moment the subject appears, fleetingly, by means of a mistake. This is a presentation, necessarily by indirection, the subject being divided. What it reveals is the signifier which re-presents the subject, not as such, but for another signifier.

This too is a decisive moment. And Cartier-Bresson's descriptions of his own encounter with this moment, this time, have a logic which has its relevance for psychoanalysis. If this is the time of the subject, it is time out of joint. Akin to the moment of sexual orgasm, time here is conjoined to space and thus dis-placed. In other words, it is in this time that the subject is thrown, thrown in that it emerges from, but in deformation of, the familiar, reciprocal perspective of the Cartesian model, whether that model be constructed from a point of homogeneous space or a point in chronological time. The subject, on the contrary, emerges uncontained, florid. In recognising this it can, in psychoanalysis, be called jouissance (de Zentner, 1996, p. 50).

As with the snapshot however the subject of psychoanalysis does not make an autonomous entrance. Its time is, as Rotmiler de Zentner puts it, the transference in act (ibid.). The possibility of this time is tied therefore to the precise signifying construction of the phantasy which insists in the transference. Functioning as *semblant* of object *a*, that is, the object as such, the object in its insistent otherness, this time is the transference which the analyst both foments and stands back from. In order therefore to allow space for that rupture which is the decisive moment the impossible art of the analyst is to be a chimera, that one which marries the body of flagrant salaciousness to the head of signifying precision.

Note

1. On the subject of Renaissance perspective see, e.g., Hubert Damisch, *The Origin of Perspective*, The MIT Press, Cambridge Mass., 1994; James Elkins, *The Poetics of Perspective*, Cornell University Press, Ithaca, 1994; William M. Ivins, Jr., *On the Rationalization of Sight*, De Capo Press, New York, 1973; Erwin Panofsky, *Perspective as Symbolic Form*, Zone Books, New York, 1997.

CHAPTER TWENTY-TWO

The pearl of analysis

Michael Currie

In *An Autobiographical Study*, Freud wrote that a psychoanalytic reading of art is of "[…] the drive impulses at work in it—that is to say that part of (the artist) which he shared with all men" (1925d [1924], p. 65). As attested by the numerous psychoanalytic studies of artworks following Freud's study of Leonardo (1910c, p. 59), such an endeavour quickly loses its potency, ready to find confirmation of Freudian themes predictable before any work is done. Further, Freud sees the psychoanalytic reading of art as different to "[…] the perceptual pleasure of formal beauty […] what I have called an incentive bonus" (1925d, p. 65). For Freud, the aesthetics of art is a lure. The enjoyment of the art is irrelevant once the psychoanalytic study of the object commences. For the followers of Freud art was used to constrict and confirm the findings of psychoanalysis.

I propose that the object of art can be taken up in a way that expands and loosens the relation of psychoanalysis with its own history. Following Lacan, there is an aspect of the drive which gives rise to what is most particular in all men. Here the enjoyment of formal beauty is based on an enigma: "Why does this work move me so?" The enjoyment is crucial (not just a lure) insofar as it is tied to an obscurity of meaning. In other words, the object that psychoanalysis elicits in art maintains an impossibility in regard to meaning, but not in regard to enjoyment. *"Wo es war, soll ich warden"* (Freud's: "Where it was, so the I shall be" (1933a, p. 80)), can be taken as an aesthetic imperative, where the synchronic structure of the enigma of beauty is dia-chronically re-encountered. "Where it was ...", then leads to a fidelity to what summons the unreal and alien.

I wish to use a painting by Giambattista Tiepolo, *The Banquet of Cleopatra* as an illustration of my proposal.[1] Tiepolo's painting captures a moment at the end of days of feasting in Alexandria where Mark Antony had been particularly gluttonous. Cleopatra and Antony sit opposite each other, with Cleopatra's arm outstretched, a pearl earring dangling from her hand above a wineglass of vinegar.

Cleopatra wagered she could prepare a meal worth more than 80,000 pounds of gold. After serving a meagre meal to Mark Antony, she ordered a second course—a single glass of vinegar. She detached one of the pearls from her earrings, reputedly the largest pearls in the world, and dropped the pearl into the glass of vinegar. The pearl dissolved and Cleopatra drank it down.

I am not alone in liking this painting. Touted as one of the gallery's most popular works, it is caressed by the look of hundreds of patrons daily. That the painting is emblematic of the vicissitudes of love and desire is evidenced by the line of paramours who have sought it out as a setting for the proposal of marriage (Murray, 2011, p. 62). Lovers have used the painting to gesture to the specifics of their own love whilst proposing the general frame of marriage. Beyond its function as a backdrop to the proposal of a legal pairing, Cleopatra's drink contains an enigma that is the elixir of psychoanalysis. What does Cleopatra's destruction and consumption of a priceless good bring forth in Antony?

The enigma is further elicited by the provenance of the painting. The painting, completed in 1744, is based on an anecdote of Pliny the elder, a Roman historian (Secundus, 1847, pp. 155–157). Pliny's retelling of the story has a moral aim, to illustrate the Asiatic vice of luxury in contrast to the apparent virtue of Roman moderation. The painting itself was commissioned for Augustus the third of Dresden, in an attempt to enhance his collection, add to the prestige of his court, and emphasise his own Roman heritage declared in his royal name. The message in the painting shifts from that of the anecdote, becoming not a moral comment on luxury, but an illustration of royal power. The painting's power is such that it fostered a fable that it was acquired by Catherine the Great at an auction conducted by conquering armies following the flight of Augustus III from his estate in Dresden. In fact it was Catherine's son, Paul I who acquired the painting, resulting in a one-hundred-year stay in the Hermitage. The resonances across the centuries of the power and intrigue of a queen ruling over a great empire have been received most strongly by men who owned, studied or viewed the painting. However, in 1925, the painting was placed for international sale by another group of men, to raise money by the People's Commissariat of Foreign Trade of the USSR. In short, the painting was seen as surplus for its depiction of decadence. The painting was offered to London's National Gallery and was rejected due to politics of governments and acquisition committees. In London lurked a fear that expenditure of public funds on such a painting would offend public opinion in a time of economic hardship. The Soviets accepted the National Gallery of Victoria's offer of 30,000 pounds for what was by then a piece of international detritus on the condition that payment be made in cash in small notes. The exchange occurred near Trafalgar Square: a suitcase of cash given to the Soviets, and the painting then sent to Melbourne, an apparent surplus to public utility.[2]

London's National Gallery eventually acquired another version of *The Banquet of Cleopatra*, painted a year later by Tiepolo. In that version, with its huge expanse of sky, the perspective from below, not above, the figures of Antony and Cleopatra smaller, and the pearl not assuming the centrality in perspective that it does in the Melbourne Tiepolo, the enigma as given in the Melbourne version is diminished in London. Viewing London's version *in situ*, with the image of the Melbourne version in mind (now so familiar to me), it is possible, despite the incredible riches on display in London's gallery, to render the presence of its absence there.

The partial object is a remainder which escapes the play of libido between *i(a)* and *i'(a)*.[3] The fate of *The Banquet of Cleopatra and Antony* seems to echo its status as a painting with strongly moral reverberations. The painting has been tossed between various owners because of how these moral reverberations capture, enhance, and metaphorise the status of the owner of the painting. Here we have a preliminary, imaginary reading of the painting that imparts the name "Cleopatra's Antony" to the scene. In such a reading, as Shakespeare notes in the first scene of his play, Antony is transformed from "a pillar of the

world" into "a strumpet's fool". Yet there is an object in the painting
that escapes the play of libido.

We can take Cleopatra to represent the work of analysis—the grasping of that which is beyond the good of value—and Mark Antony to
represent the analysand. Cleopatra's act, in destroying a priceless good,
catapults her beyond need, wealth, and price into the arena of psychoanalysis. Cleopatra says to Mark Antony in drinking the pearl—"I am
the feast of a very different order. You may only have this feast with me,
Cleopatra, regardless of how powerful you are, how many men you
command, how much tribute you collect in gold and the outcome of
your rivalries in Rome."

Cleopatra's drink aims at something other than the quenching of
thirst or the sating of hunger. The aim is to satisfy something other than
the fullness of the mouth. This is the other feast, the feast that causes
desire. It is here, beyond pleasure and sexual satisfaction, that Lacan's
object a, cause of desire dwells, where the mouth attains a satisfaction
without being full, where the drive attains satisfaction without attaining its aim, where pleasure is separated from desire.

In Shakespeare's play, the place of Cleopatra for Antony, the place
beyond the feast of food (which is only referred to obliquely by
Shakespeare) is described by one of Antony's lieutenants, Enobarbus:

> Age cannot wither her, nor custom stale
> Her infinite variety. Other women cloy
> The appetites they feed, but she makes hungry
> Where most she satisfies;[4]

Cleopatra is not reducible to the normal vicissitudes of love and sexual
desire, which rise and fall and come and go according to their satisfaction. Once conquered the longing leaves. Cleopatra occupies a different
place. The pearl-drinking makes a thirst at the scene of satisfaction.

The vanishing point of the painting leads all perspective to a point
proximate to Cleopatra's upheld hand from which dangles the pearl.
The vanishing point, the point of the nothing in the painting, is the
point where in the moment after the scene in the painting, Cleopatra
will drink down her priceless drink. The picture is a powerful symbolisation of Cleopatra stepping into the place of the nothing for Antony
via an act which places her beyond value.

Cleopatra's clothes, chair and palace are all decorated with images
of the Sphinx, the mythical Egyptian riddler of man. We can take the

image of the Sphinx as an approximation of the agalma that Antony loves in Cleopatra. She is not just another Roman possession, but one who questions his soldier's desire to conquer. All this shows the place Cleopatra occupies for Antony: she opens the nothing, in consuming the drink beyond value, where she is enigmatic and riddling. It is articulations in this place beyond the good, beyond the cure that the desire of the analyst aims. We favour Egypt over Rome, despite the existence of Rome.

As well as Pliny's account, Tiepolo's inspiration for the painting was probably also drawn from Plutarch's *Life of Antony*. Shakespeare's play is more or less based on Plutarch's work. The scene of Tiepolo's painting can be inserted into a series of events within the semi-mythologised liaison between Antony and Cleopatra. According to Plutarch, the moment depicted in the painting occurred at a similar time to the formation of an association between Cleopatra and Antony—"the association of inimitable livers".[5] We can take the drinking of the pearl as the founding act of such an association. We can also take this as an outcome of analysis, the production of a life lived without imitation.

We know from Plutarch/Shakespeare that Mark Antony was previously a beloved, pursued and seduced by Cleopatra. She sailed her barge down the river Cyndus to meet with Antony. Shakespeare describes her as:

> O'erpicturing that Venus where we see
> The fancy outwork nature.

Cleopatra, in the position of lover, attempts to seduce Antony, one of the three "pillars of the world"—the Roman triumvirate which ruled over the empire, Antony being assigned the Eastern third.

The moment of Tiepolo's painting depicts the tipping point where fancy does indeed outwork nature. Mark Antony's response to Cleopatra's drink is to transform Cleopatra from his lover—the Venus as she first appeared to him—to his beloved. Antony himself undergoes a transformation from beloved to lover, with a corresponding loss.

What a metaphor for analysis! We can imagine Antony's loss in the shift from beloved to lover. He comes to Egypt, a ruler of the world, master of himself and his legions of soldiers. Cleopatra's pearl-drink opens a place where he does not rule as master. He is inexorably drawn to this place, as Plutarch's biography and Shakespeare's play relate.

There is Cleopatra, in front of Mark Antony, inimitable, but just as he imagined her to be. He can have her, on the basis of his imaginings that are linked to his loss. What this loss might be is given in his favourite pastime with Cleopatra, related by Shakespeare—Plutarch: To go onto the streets of Alexandria at night in the guise of a commoner "tippling with slaves" and to "stand the buffet with knaves that smells of sweat …".[6] This is a veritable enactment of abandoning the place of mastery so he may find something beyond mastery with Cleopatra. What he finds is not the object given or brought, but found in the random and chance encounters on the street with the commoner. Not an object desired and known in advance, but causing desire in the moment of its (re)finding. We are in the inimitable company not of $i(a)$, but a. Here is the instrument, Lacan calls it an apparatus in *Seminar XI*, that lies at the heart of analysis, in that it will always be what it is, a piece of algebraic notation designed to denote identity, the object a.

Cleopatra's act depicted in the painting constitutes an object by designating it. The hidden cost of the designation is that the act of consuming the pearl designates nothing at all. So whilst we can find the non-representing a in the painting, the painting itself, being an image, can be taken as a metaphor for an analysis. The painting is a metaphor for an analysis in that it adds a creative spark at the lifeless point in Lacan's theory where there is no metaphor. With the object a as designating, not representing, the aim of each analysis in practice is to animate this apparently lifeless apparatus. We could say that in writing this paper, my discussion of the painting performed precisely this function.

Notes

1. The painting hangs in the National Gallery of Victoria and can be viewed at: http://www.ngv.vic.gov.au/col/work/4409
2. Anderson, J. Tiepolo's *Cleopatra*. Macmillan, Melbourne, 2003.
3. Compare Lacan's discussion from Seminar VIII, 21st June 1961 with his later assertions in Seminar X, 9th June 1963.
4. Shakespeare, W. *Antony and Cleopatra*, II, 2, 240–3.
5. "They had a sort of company, to which they gave a particular name, calling it that of the Inimitable Livers. The members entertained one another daily in turn, with all extravagance of expenditure beyond measure or belief." Plutarch, *Life of Antony*, trans. John Dryden.
6. Shakespeare, W. *Antony and Cleopatra*, I, 4, 19–21.

CHAPTER TWENTY-THREE

The medieval voice

Helen Dell

"Medievalism" is sometimes called the afterlife of the medieval. I understand it as a coverall term for a variety of post-medieval notions about what is called the Middle Ages. Almost anything can pass as medieval in the modern imagination. This multiplicity is driven by the signifier itself. The terminology of periodisation has left the Middle Age with a title but with no proper name of its own. It is retrospectively identified only as what is neither modern nor ancient. Despite the capital letters proclaiming its status it is an empty, ahistorical space framed between one age and another, more geographical than temporal. As such it has a kind of presence which is nonetheless negative, like "The little man who wasn't there" (1955, p. 429) of the poem. I call this ahistorical space the "medieval" (the scare quotes are an indication of the status of the medieval as fantasy. Having said that I shall now drop them!). What follows is my reading of the medieval fantasy as it relates to music and the singing voice. One voice in particular—the countertenor.

The medieval in fantasy may have a dormant, even a deathly aspect, framed between the death of the Classical Age and the rebirth of the Renaissance, which the term "dark age" captures nicely. It may be imagined as a time of unspeakable brutality as in its famous use in Quentin

Tarantino's Pulp Fiction: "I'ma getting medieval on your ass—with a pair of pliers and a blowtorch." But the frame provided by its nameless placement in the middle can also lend the medieval a mysterious luminosity which speaks to nostalgic urges. What is framed gains intensity; it becomes numinous, sublime. This Middle Age may present itself as a lost and longed-for paradisal home. Medievalism abounds with nostalgic fantasies of a harmonious time or place at peace and in tune with nature or, for others, in tune with God's will—either way a time when something worked.

The term medieval carries a bewildering diversity of meaning and valence. It is possible, however, to identify certain broad categories of medievalism. These categories are organised around sites of tension and anxiety. The medieval of medievalism, however it is conceived, is generally presented as monolithic. It is either stable or unstable, rational or sensual, Apollonian or Dionysian, spiritual or bodily, sacred or profane, orderly or chaotic, native or foreign, civilised or barbarous, dark or light. But these categories are also unstable and subject to reversal, although the urge to cling to a monolithic Middle Age generally disallows the simultaneous acknowledgement of conflicting accounts. Whatever the account it insists on its correctness, refusing contradiction and ambiguity. One account will repress or dominate the other or they are dealt with by being allocated to different parties according to an overarching moral grid, as it is often presented in medievalist fantasy fiction and film: order against chaos, light against dark. Fantasy aspires to the reasonable. We fight for our fantasies and for the logic of either/ or to which they cling. As Lacan wrote in his *Seminar XXV* (1977–1978), *The Moment to Conclude*:

> I would like to point out to you that what is called "the reasonable" is a fantasy; it is quite manifest at the beginning of science. Euclidian geometry has all the characteristics of fantasy. A fantasy is not a dream, it is an aspiration. (ibid., p. 1)

Fantasy aspires to cage reality and disregards any straggling pieces which do not fit the cage. It is "ready to wear" (*le prêt à porter le fantasm*) as Lacan observed, not tailor made. "[T]he whole of human reality" he argued:

> [...] is nothing other than a montage of the symbolic and the imaginary [...] the desire, at the centre of this apparatus, of this frame

that we call reality, is [...] what covers [...] the real, which is never
more than glimpsed. Glimpsed when the mask, which is that of
fantasy, vacillates. (2002, p. 6)

Reality is not stable. It wavers or vacillates and when reality vacillates
it becomes harder not to glimpse the real. A recent TV miniseries (2012)
captures the instability of the medieval reality, protesting, in its title,
that the "Dark Ages [was really] an Age of Light". The Middle Ages
maintains a perpetual but hidden oscillation between opposing versions of reality. The medieval fantasy is profoundly conflicted and the
pain of that conflict is evident in the urgency of attempts to resolve it
one way or the other. Its aspiration to the reasonable is what gives it
away as fantasy. Many academic arguments have this hidden side of a
fantasy struggling to maintain the desired reality and shut out the real.

I see the medieval as a fantasy of origin. As *pre*-modern it is what
we were before. It is what we moderns must reject in order to be modern but we may mourn for what we have lost in the process, perhaps
Johan Huizinga's medieval "child-life" of wild vitality and spontaneity
(*Waning of the Middle Ages*, 1924, p. 3) from which we emerge to be adult.
Alternatively, it might be a "fatherly" Middle Age for a modern child
who has strayed—a golden age of reason, stability and order laid down
by the (church) fathers and, above them all, the Father. Our understanding of this Middle Age and our attitudes and responses to it are riven by
ambivalence and by a suppressed ambiguity which is never resolved.

The music we call medieval reflects the same patterns. A similar
struggle is played out in studies, performances, and recordings of medieval music and in the responses of listeners. Although the discipline of
study challenges notions of a monolithic Middle Age scholars are not
immune to the lure of the medieval. If my own path is any guide fantasy
is often the driver of study to begin with and that initial predilection is
never entirely erased. In musical fantasy the medieval Age of Light is
sometimes heard as an Age of Consonance based on Pythagorean theory. Author Jamie James, in *The Music of the Spheres*, speaks longingly
of an age of sublime order and harmony, lasting in human history until
"the Industrial Revolution and its companion in the arts, the Romantic
movement":

Picture to yourself, if you can, a universe in which everything
makes sense. A serene order presides over the earth around you,
and the heavens above revolve in sublime harmony. Everything

you can see and hear and know is an aspect of the ultimate truth: the noble simplicity of a geometric theorem, the predictability of the movements of heavenly bodies, the harmonious beauty of a well-proportioned fugue—all are reflections of the essential perfection of the universe. And here on earth, too, no less than in the heavens and in the world of ideas, order prevails: every creature from the oyster to the emperor has its place, preordained and eternal. (1993, p. 3)

Not many today would identify as Pythagoreans but the longing for an orderly and harmonious universe has not declined. It is an aspect of the aspiration to the reasonable, an attempt at conflict resolution.

The concept of the harmony of the spheres is based on mathematical relations between musical frequencies. Put simply, there is said to be in music,

[...] a natural hierarchy, reflected in the harmony of the scale, that is based on the simple progression of numbers from unity to complexity. From the perfect consonances of the unison and its octave (expressed as 1:1 and 1:2) we pass to the ratios of 2:3, the musical interval of the fifth, which functions musically as the opposite pole of the harmonic spectrum in its role as the dominant degree of the scale, and is the next most consonant, and fundamental interval; and its inverse, the fourth, or subdominant, with a ratio of 3:4.[1]

Based on these mathematics all creation is understood as deriving from simple relationships between the first four integers. Everything springs from numbers. That fundamental harmony orders the universe and everything in it and has ramifications for every aspect of human life: bodily, emotional, ethical, and spiritual. It also has ramifications for sounding medieval music and how the post-medieval world has understood it.

A history of western medieval music usually begins with a reference to the legendary figure of Pythagoras (sixth century BC) and his discovery of the harmony of the spheres. This is the account of the legend by Iamblichus, Pythagoras' "biographer" (AD c. 259–325):

[A]s he was walking near a brazier's shop, he heard from a certain divine casualty [causality?] the hammers beating out a piece

of iron on an anvil, and producing sounds that accorded with each
other, one combination only excepted. But he recognized in those
sounds, the diapason [octave], the diapente [fifth], and the diatessaron [fourth], harmony. He saw, however, that the sound which
was between the diatessaron and the diapente was by itself dissonant, yet, nevertheless, gave completion to that which was the
greater sound among them. (1818, p. 62)

In other words the fourth and the fifth intervals together make up an
octave (for instance CGC). In this arrangement they are consonant,
although when played simultaneously at the interval of a second (for
instance FG), they are dissonant. This mathematical circumstance
became the guarantee for a fantasy of universal harmony which can
incorporate dissonance without harm to itself.

St. Augustine (354–430), a father figure for medieval thought whose
Christianised Pythagorian theory the Christian Middle Ages could
accept, gave support to the claims of number over sounding music,
for instance in the title of the final chapter of his *De musica*, Book VI,
"The ascent from rhythm in sense to the immortal rhythm which is in
truth" (1949, p. 85). In this divine harmony even evil (dissonance) has
a part to sing, without becoming less evil in itself. Augustine wrote in
On Order: "Within order, evil contributes to the beauty of the universe"
(2007, p. 63).

Augustine's understanding of Pythagorean theory was mediated by
his knowledge of Neoplatonist writers like Plotinus (AD 205–269/270),
for whom it was the joint efforts of all, good and evil, which make the
universe good:

> The Universe is good [...] when everyone throws in his own voice
> towards a total harmony, singing out a life—thin, harsh, imperfect
> though it be [...] what is evil in the single soul will stand a good
> thing in the universal system [...] and still remains the weak and
> wrong tone it is. (1986, p. 21)

Boethius (c 480–524) another influential figure, bequeathed to his
medieval heirs a three-tiered hierarchy of music: *musica instrumentalis*
(human-made, sounding music, lowliest of the three), *musica humana*
(the music of the human body and soul, keeping each in health and in
harmony with the other), and, lastly, above and governing all, *musica*

mundana, the divine, unheard music of the universe (1989, pp. 9–10). That subordination of sounding music to the mathematical music of the universe, I believe, has profoundly influenced modern approaches to the study and performance of medieval music.

Universal harmony speaks to a yearning for the resolution of contradiction. Harmony tunes the apparent chaos of human experience into a meaningful design, worked by the divine hand. As Boethius expounded in the theory of *musica humana*: "[W]hat unites the incorporeal nature of reason with the body if not a certain harmony and, as it were, a careful tuning of low and high pitches as though producing one consonance" (1989, p. 10). Through *harmonia* difference is resolved into consonance and individual evil into universal good. Consonance, with its logic of complementarity, is a version of the sexual relation, one which has proved so enduringly attractive that it is central to modern fantasies about the medieval world and its music. This is a universe in which, as James maintained, 'everything makes sense [and] every creature [...] has its place, preordained and eternal (1993, p. 3).

In this harmonious arrangement the figure of the medieval countertenor strikes for some a dissonant note. He represents an ambiguity which cannot be easily resolved, perhaps because he himself is perceived as already ambiguous, like his ancestor the castrato. The countertenor, perceived as a man who sounds almost but not quite like a woman (or a castrato) may be, for fantasy, both a man and a woman and neither a man nor a woman. Femininity and castration are both associatively linked to the countertenor as they are linked to each other. Like the castrato in Balzac's *Sarrasine* as Roland Barthes read him, the countertenor is "the blind and mobile flaw in this [symbolic] field; he moves back and forth between active and passive; castrated, he castrates" (1974, p. 36). Barthes' Zambinella, in his alternation, cannot be squarely categorised as both sexes or as neither. He throws the sexual and thus the symbolic relation into doubt. The countertenor's ambiguity cannot be easily absorbed into consonance as one voice among the many, because he is not one. Like the little man who wasn't there he cannot be dislodged. He sticks between the teeth and cannot be either spat out or swallowed.

In the 1980s the countertenor became entangled in a musicological argument over authentic performance practice for medieval music which still lingers in a modified form.[2] On the side of the "authenticists" there was an insistence that the modern performance of medieval music should be strictly based on evidence derived from medieval sources. Christopher Page, then director of the Gothic Voices ensemble, put this succinctly in a 1993 essay:

> This approach gives primacy to facts, to evidence and to sources, so that the line between knowledge and speculation remains clear: it values imagination but tends to marginalise whatever seems fanciful or eccentric. (1993, p. 459)

For Page the evidence suggested that much medieval music, monophonic and polyphonic, had been sung without instrumental accompaniment. He founded Gothic Voices to put this theory into practice. Since many like-minded musicologists and historians are also musicians and directors, this theory has resulted in numerous "authentic" performances and recordings. The Gothic Voices recordings were much loved and consequently extremely influential in promulgating Page's ideas. He also enjoyed the support of what Daniel Leech-Wilkinson has called "the *a cappella* group", a group of influential scholars and reviewers (2001, 132). "Authentic" performances became the norm in England. Some recordings in the early days of the movement even boasted their authenticity with a label on the cover like the label on organically grown vegetables.

On the basis of rather sparse and equivocal documentary evidence the countertenor was banned from the performance of medieval music by some musicologists and directors. Some of this evidence came from prohibitions of falsetto (countertenor) singing issued by churchmen, like this one in a Ghilbertine statute from 1134:

> It befits men to sing with a manly voice, and not in a womanish manner or [...] with "false voices", as if imitating the wantonness of minstrels. And therefore we have stipulated that a medium is to be used in the chant. (Page, 1981, p. 71)

Page was cautious about how to translate this passage: "virilis" might not mean "manly", he suggested, "in more femineo" might refer not to the pitch but to the manner of singing. But his final argument rested on the prohibition itself:

> [N]obody would be prepared to assert [that the medieval countertenor did not exist] in view of the fragmentary evidence at our disposal. Yet even if it can be demonstrated that one medieval use of fausetum undoubtedly does mean falsetto, we must keep a very open mind about the liturgical use of a voice which evoked disgust amongst at least some medieval churchmen. (Ibid., p. 72)

It is hard to understand, however, why such prohibitions would be in place if the offence were not occurring. Underneath the neutral academic tone there is more here than can be accounted for by evidence. That word "disgust", attributed to medieval churchmen, stands out. The authenticity argument was, I believe, driven by an anxiety not entirely historical. This anxiety stemmed from the fantasy of the medieval past as a true home from which the modern world has strayed. Stripping back any later accretions (excretions) from the music of the Middle Ages was part and parcel of a nostalgic quest for the medieval as pure origin. Everything added on was waste matter—shit. The voice in particular must be purified to sing something approaching, as near as possible, a silent music. To this end, vibrato, the beat of the body in the voice, even timbre, the idiosyncratic tang of the voice created by the body's shapes and functions, were suppressed by many performers, particularly among the English ensembles. In my reading the countertenor voice with its connotations of sexual ambiguity and of a mysterious and forbidden sexual knowledge, power and enjoyment created a disturbance for the fantasy of the pure medieval. He was judged and pronounced guilty of inauthenticity. Banishing the countertenor became, I believe, an attempt to banish ambiguity and with it the body in the voice. The lure of purity is precisely that it banishes ambiguity.

Christopher Page, set out in his 1993 essay a list of performance practices which, some English reviewers claimed, should be avoided in the performance of medieval music on the basis of the evidence. The list reflects his own ideal in a negative form. This ideal is what is left when all inauthenticity has been removed. He based it on the Middle English word, "clanness" (cleanness), which "blurs the edges of earthly things with a nimbus of heaven [...] and yet it can make what is celestial seem clearer to human sense" (ibid., p. 466). The list included: the use of too many instrumental colours; strings of short pieces "each characterised by a different instrumentation to give [...] novelty and variety"; "doubling or replacing voices with instruments"; "the 'Arab' hypothesis which looks to certain non-western traditions"; "extending pieces [...] with swathes of improvisatory instrumental material"; "'over interpretation' " (ibid., p. 469).

For Page and others like him such strategies added up to a kind of tawdry flamboyance, a preference for theatricality over the simple, unvarnished truth of evidence—"cleanness". It was an argument of exclusion based on an ideal of purity, a stripping back of unauthorised enjoyments. Enjoyment was not an acceptable argument for performance practice.[3]

On the other side of the argument the countertenor was welcomed in performance despite his somewhat dubious claims to historical authenticity, although this side too claimed a kind of authenticity backed up by different arguments. These stressed the influence on European music from its Middle Eastern and North African neighbours, that is, what Page called the "Arab" hypothesis. Falsetto singing, along with a raft of exciting and alien instruments and an improvisatory style, was supposedly imported into Europe via the crusades and the Moorish invasion of Spain.[4] These were performances which tended towards excess rather than purity, the exotic rather than the native. The ambiguity of the countertenor voice evoked fantasies of the mysterious East. Medievalism and Orientalism have proved a potent blend for an exotic fantasy of the Middle Age.[5] "The past is a foreign country", as David Lowenthal wrote, and this approach in performance allowed a very foreign fantasy with sometimes an exciting spice of Eastern barbarity.

That transposition to the East functioned as code for another transposition, this time sexual, to the realms of ambiguity. One instance of this in performance was countertenor Richard Levitt's remarkable interpretation of Peire Vidal's "Baron de mon covit" on Studio der Frühen Musik's *Chanson der Troubadours* (1970). In one strophe Levitt leaps up and down the octave between alto and baritone registers, as if to enact his capacity, like the "true love" of Feste's song from *Twelfth Night*, to "sing both high and low". That is, I think, to perform sexually as a man or a woman, or as an active or passive partner. I saw another performance in which a medieval dialogue between a man and a woman was sung by a countertenor who alternated between the man's part in baritone and the woman's in alto.

In *The Object Relation* Lacan spoke of such a magical alternation with reference to fetishism, a term he associates with *fée* (fairy; féerie is enchantment). He is relating the story of Jacques Cazotte's novel, *Le diable amoureux*. The devil, here a "fetish character" for Lacan,

> [...] becomes [for the narrator] a ravishing young man, and then a ravishing young girl, these two moreover never ceasing right until the end to mingle in a perfect ambiguity, and to become for a time [...] the surprising source of every felicity, [...] of the strictly speaking magical satisfaction of everything which he may wish for. (1956–1957, p. 92)

This was the place in fantasy of the castrato (and by association the countertenor) for men and for women.[6] We can imagine him saying: "I can be whatever you want". There is something here too of what does not want to be known, but it is of a different kind. The magical cornucopia of sexual delights relies not on a suppression of ambiguity but on a disavowal of lack. Unlike the purist fantasy which takes refuge in the logic of the symbolic, insisting that something either is or is not, this fantasy refuses the lack implicit in either/or. It bears a fetishistic relation to the symbolic.

Perhaps the foreignness of the Oriental fantasy places it far enough away to be entertained with impunity. Perhaps, like the holiday romance, it can be left behind where it belongs when one returns home. That foreignness could stand for "a bit on the side" which does not trouble the main game, an unthreatening, ancillary enjoyment. But I am not sure it is so easily contained since its lure is precisely its polymorphous, *un*contained enjoyment. It flouts the ideal of purity and the dream of consonance. If fantasy aspires to the reasonable is this then not a fantasy? I think it has the flavour of fantasy, at least insofar as it provides something to keep the real at bay. This perfect ambiguity is also not the real—the real does not comply with human inclinations. Perhaps the fantasist knows what he refuses to know, and that symbolic "knowing" spares him.[7] Like little Hans he both sees and does not see.[8] Lacan calls it a game of hide and seek. Perhaps, in the present context, there is enough of the game to defuse the terror. Certainly there seems less agony involved in allowing the countertenor than in denying him. The music at least is more playful and light-hearted, less reverent. It does not bear the weight of the demand for authenticity.[9]

There is an ambiguity which is more difficult to contain. For those who rejected him at least, the countertenor became an emblem of inauthenticity. I believe his presence placed a painful pressure on the medieval fantasy of purity. He represents its underbelly, its obscene mirror image—what *must* be scrubbed clean but never can be. His body is inescapable in its uncontainable, unclean ambiguity. This ambiguity is not a dissonance tamed by its opposition to consonance and subsumed under it. In this sense dissonance is not in opposition to consonance. That could be tolerated and absorbed, as Plotinus demonstrated. In this more profound sense dissonance is what cannot be contained within an opposition. As everything that cannot be resolved—the leftovers, the waste matter—dissonance throws the illusion of opposition and thus of complementarity and harmony into disarray and something unspeakable is glimpsed.

Julia Kristeva observed: "It is [...] not lack of cleanliness or health that causes abjection but what disturbs identity, system, order" (1982, p. 4). But it is horror of the abject, the disturbance to order, that constitutes the body as unclean—the waste matter of the soul. The uncleanness of the singing body was at times so disturbing to the fathers of the church and their medieval heirs, that it was only grudgingly tolerated because less rational souls were drawn, by the sounding music of voices, *numerus sonorus*, to the unheard, numerical music of the universe, composed by God. For instance, Augustine wrote in *On Order*:

> Reason [for whom number is divine] grievously tolerated that the splendour and purity of number should be somewhat clouded by the material sound of voices (*Et iam tolerabat aegerrime splendorem illoru atque serenitatem corporea vocum materia decolorari*). (2007, p. 105)

The anonymous ninth-century author of the "Scholica enchiriadis" wrote:

> Notes pass away quickly; numbers, however, though stained by the corporeal matter of voices and moving things (*corporea vocum et motuum materia decolorantur*), remain. (2001, p. 4)

It is the same root in both works, the verb *"decolorare"*, to discolour or stain, though differently translated. The singing body stains the splendour and purity of divine number. We have inherited that fascinated horror of the stain in the voice and both the fascination and the horror return when the medieval and its music are evoked.

Notes

1. "On the Pythagorean Tradition http://www.fiddletree.com/reflections/on_the_pythagorean_traditi.htm

2. Daniel Leech-Wilkinson has written an excellent account of some aspects of this argument in *The Modern Invention of Medieval Music: Scholarship, Ideology, Performance*. Cambridge: Cambridge University Press, 2002. The countertenor was incidental to the authenticity debates but as a figure of ambiguity he struck at the heart of the fantasy.

3. Page's arguments were (and are) more complex and varied than I can do justice to here. And he was often right. Some recordings of the kind he critiqued did drown the music in an overblown medievalism which obscured its own splendours.

4. See for instance Peter Giles' *The History and Technique of the Counter-tenor: A Study of the Male High Voice Family*. Aldershot, Hants, England: Scolar Press; Brookfield, Vt.: Ashgate, c1994.

5. For a perceptive account of the way the two have become entwined in the modern Western imagination see John Ganim's *Medievalism and Orientalism: Three Essays on Literature, Architecture and Cultural Identity*. New York: Palgrave Macmillan, 2005.

6. The castrato whose potency miraculously escaped the blade was a popular, if almost mythical figure.

7. The purists, on the other hand, never seem to be certain enough of what they know.

8. When Hans sees his little sister Anna in the bath he says: "Her widdler's still quite small [...]. When she grows up it'll get bigger all right." Freud, Sigmund. *Case Histories I: Dora and Little Han'*. A. & J. Strachey (Trans.). This volume Angela Richards (Ed.). Harmondsworth, Middlesex, England: Penguin, 1977, p. 175).

9. For some at least of those who accept the countertenor the agony seems to be more in the effort of denying their interest in his sexuality. Negation is strenuous. I'm thinking of listener comments such as these on a YouTube recording of Andreas Scholl's Habañera from Carmen: "Who cares gay or not, his voice is crystal clear and arias are there to sing [...]. Why travesty??? Music does not have gender, and this aria is written for high voice, so what is the problem?", and "why all these comments? if you are gay you can sing better maybe???or if you are married to a woman your voice sounds better??? Stupid discussions". http://www.youtube.com/watch?v=tzi_M-Vl_38&feature=kp

REFERENCES

Agamben, G. (1993). In playland: reflections on history and play. In: *Infancy and History: on the destruction of experience*. Heron, L. (Trans.). London: Verso, p. 82.

Allouch, J. (1995). *Erotique du deuil au temps de la mort sèche*, Paris: Epel—passage translated into English in *Erotics of mourning at the time of dry death*. In: *Invention in the Real: Papers of the Freudian School of Melbourne, volume 24*, London: Karnac, 2012.

Allouch, J. (2007). *Lacan Love—Melbourne seminars and other works*. Carolyn Henshaw (Trans.). Rotmiler, M. -I. & Zentner, O. (Eds.) Australia: Lituraterre.

American Psychiatric Association. Diagnostic and Statistical Manual of Mental Disorders, 5th edition, DSM-5. (2013) Arlington, VA: American Psychiatric Association.

Anderson, J. (2003). *Tiepolo's Cleopatra*. Melbourne: Macmillan.

Aristotle (1998). *The Nicomachean Ethics*. David Ross (Trans.). Oxford: Oxford University Press, p. 92.

Augustine (2007). *On Order*. Silvano Borruso (Trans.). South Bend, Indiana: St. Augustine's Press.

Bergès, J. & Balbo, G. (2012). The treatment setting: demand, transference and the contract with the parents and for their child. In: *Intervention in the Real: Papers of the Freudian School of Melbourne volume 24*. London: Karnac, pp. 109–110.

Barthes, R. (1974). *S/Z: An Essay*. Richard Miller (Trans.). New York: Hill and Wang, p. 36.

Bataille, G. (1991a). *The Accursed Share, Volume 1, Consumption*. Robert Hurley (Trans.). New York: Zone Books.

Bataille, G. (1991b). *The Accursed Share. An Essay on General Economy. Vol. II. The History of Eroticism*. Robert Hurley (Trans.). Zone Books, New York, p. 32.

Boethius, A. M. S. (1989). *Fundamentals of Music*. Calvin M. Bower (Trans.). New Haven, CT: Yale University Press.

Boulez, P. (1984). Sonate que me veux-tu? In: *Points de repère*. Paris: Bourgois, 1964.

Bremmer, J. (1987). *The Early Greek Concept of the Soul*. Princeton: Princeton University Press. p. 17.

Canguilhem, G. (1991). Essay on some problems concerning the normal and the pathological. In: *The Normal and the Pathological*. C. R. Fawcett & R. S. Cohen (Trans.). New York: Zone Books.

Collingwood, R. G. (1982). *An Autobiography*. Oxford: Clarendon Press, reprinted 2002, pp. 31–43. Translated into French by Guy Le Gaufey, *Toute histoire est histoire d'une pensée*, Paris, Epel, 2010.

Cookman, C. (2008) Henri Cartier-Bresson reinterprets his career. *History of Photography, 32, 1, Spring 2008*: 60.

Damisch, H. (1994). *The Origin of Perspective*. Cambridge, MA: MIT Press.

Davidson, A. I. (2001). *The Emergence of Sexuality*. Massachusetts: Harvard University Press.

Deleuze, G. (1993). Ce que les enfants dissent. In: *Critique et clinique*. Paris: Minuit, pp. 82–83.

Deleuze, G. (1994). *Difference and Repetition*. Paul Patton (Trans.). New York: Columbia University Press, p. 27.

Deleuze, G. (1995). Letter to a Harsh Critic. In: *Negotiations, 1972–1990*. Martin Joughin (Trans.). New York: Columbia University Press, p. 8.

Deleuze, G. (1997). What children say. In: *Essays Critical and Clinical*. Minnesota: University of Minnesota Press, p. 61.

Deleuze, G. (2004). Deleuze and Guattari fight back. In: *Desert Islands and Other Texts, 1953–1974*. Michael Taormina (Trans.). Cambridge Mass: Semiotext(e), MIT, p. 218.

Deleuze, G. (2006). *Nietzsche and Philosophy*. Hugh Tomlinson (Trans.). Columbia: Columbia University Press, p. 17.

Deleuze, G. & Guattari, F. (1972). *Anti-Oedipus. Capitalism and Schizophrenia*. Robert Hurley, Mark Seem, & Helen R. Lane (Trans.). New York: Penguin, p. 53.

Department of Health and Ageing (2007). *National Mental Health Report 2007: Summary of Twelve Years of Reform in Australia's Mental Health Services under the National Mental Health Strategy 1993–2005*. Canberra, Australia: Department of Human Services.

De Saussure, F. (1966). *Course in General Linguistics*. W. Baskin (Trans.). Toronto: McGraw-Hill, p. 94.

de Zentner, M. I. R. (1990). The Times of the Analysis. *PFSM, 11*: 86.

de Zentner, M. I. R. (1996). The Follies of Time. *PFSM 17*: 150.

Didi-Huberman, G. (2004). *The Invention of Hysteria*. Massachusetts: MIT Press, p. 77.

Dussart, F. (2011). De la terre à la toile: peintures acryliques de l'Australie central. In: *La Fabrique des images: Visions du monde et formes de la représentation*. Descola, P. (Ed.). Paris: Musée du Quai Branly, pp. 137–145.

Elkins, J. (1994). *The Poetics of Perspective*. Ithaca: Cornell University Press.

Ellmann, Richard (1983). *James Joyce: New and Revised Edition*. Oxford: Oxford University Press.

Falzeder, E. (Ed.) (2002). *The Complete Correspondence of Sigmund Freud and Karl Abraham. 1907–1925. Completed Edition*. London: Karnac.

Fenollosa, E. (2007). *Epochs of Chinese and Japanese Art—An Outline History of East Asiatic Design, Vol I & II* (1912). Berkeley, Cal.: Stone Bridge Classics.

Foucault, M. (1977). Confessions of the flesh. In: *Power/Knowledge—Selected interviews and other writings, 1972–1977*. New York: Pantheon Books.

Foucault, M. (1990 [1976]). *The History of Sexuality, Volume 1*. R. Hurley (Trans.). London: Penguin, pp. 59–60.

Foucault, M. (1998). Preface to the *History of Sexuality, Volume 2*. In: *Essential Works of Foucault 1954–1984, Volume 1*. P. Rabinow (Ed.). Melbourne: Penguin Books, pp. 199–222.

Foucault, M. (2001). *Fearless Speech*. J. Pearson (Ed.). Los Angeles: Semiotext(e), pp. 14–15.

Foucault, M. (2007). For an ethics of discomfort. In: *The Politics of Truth*. S. Lotringer (Ed.), L. Hotchroth & C. Porter (Trans.). Los Angeles: Semiotext(e), p. 124.

Freud, A. (1946). *The psycho-analytical treatment of children*. London: Imago, p. 34.

Freud, S. (1888d), Hysteria. *S.E., 1*. London: Hogarth.

Freud, S. (1895b [1894]). On the grounds for detaching a particular syndrome from neurasthenia under the description of anxiety-neurosis. *S.E., 3*. London: Hogarth.

Freud, S. (1895d), *Studies on Hysteria. S.E., 2*. London: Hogarth.

Freud, S. (1898a), Sexuality in the aetiology of the neuroses. *S.E., 3*. London: Hogarth.

Freud, S. (1899a), Screen memories. *S.E., 3*. London: Hogarth.

Freud, S. (1905d). *Three Essays on the Theory of Sexuality. S.E., 7*. London: Hogarth.

Freud, S. (1909b). Analysis of a phobia in a five-year-old boy, *S.E., 10*. London: Hogarth, p. 84.

Freud, S. (1909d). Notes upon a case of obsessional neurosis. *S.E., 10*, pp. 151–318. London: Hogarth.

Freud, S. (1909c [1908]). Family romances. S.E., 9, pp. 235–242. London: Hogarth.

Freud, S. (1910c). Leonardo da Vinci and a memory of his childhood. *S.E., 11*. London: Hogarth.

Freud, S. (1911–1915 [1914]). *Papers on technique. S.E., 12*. London: Hogarth.

Freud, S. (1913j). The claims of psychoanalysis to scientific interest. *S.E., 13*. London: Hogarth.

Freud, S. (1914c). On narcissism: an introduction. *S.E., 14*. London: Hogarth.

Freud, S. (1918b [1914]). History of an infantile neurosis. *S.E., 17*. London: Hogarth.

Freud, S. (1923b). *The Ego and the Id, S.E., 19*. London: Hogarth.

Freud, S. (1925d [1924]). An autobiographical study, *S.E., 20*. London: Hogarth.

Freud, S. (1925h). Negation. *S.E., 19*. London: Hogarth.

Freud, S. (1933a [1932]). Anxiety and instinctual life. In: *New Introductory Lectures on Psychoanalysis. S.E., 22*. London: Hogarth.

Freud, S. (1933a [1932]). Explanations, applications and orientations. In: *New Introductory Lectures on Psychoanalysis. S.E., 22*. London: Hogarth, p. 148.

Freud, S. (1937c). Analysis terminable and interminable. *S.E., 23*. London: Hogarth.

Freud, S. (1937d). Constructions in analysis. *S.E., 23*. London: Hogarth.

Freud, S. (1939a). *Moses and Monotheism: Three Essays. S.E., 23*. London: Hogarth.

Freud, S. (1985) *The Complete Letters of Sigmund Freud to Wilhelm Fliess 1887–1904*. Translated and Edited Jeffrey Moussaieff Masson (Ed. & Trans.). Massachusetts: Belknap, Harvard University Press, p. 403.

Freud, S. (2004). Preface. In: Anonymous (2004). *A Young Girl's Diary*, Fairfield IA: 1st World Library, pp. 7–8.

Ganim, J. (2005). *Medievalism and Orientalism: Three Essays on Literature, Architecture and Cultural Identity*. New York: Palgrave Macmillan.

Gasio, G. (1988). *Borges in Japan and Japan in Borges*. Buenos Aires: Editorial Eudeba.

Giles, P. (1994). *The History and Technique of the Counter-tenor: A Study of the Male High Voice Family*. Aldershot UK: Scolar Press; Brookfield, Vt.: Ashgate.

Godwin, J. (1986). *Music, Mysticism and Magic: A Sourcebook*, London: Arcana.

Guillaumont, A., Puech, H. -C., Quispel G., Till, W., & Abd al-Masih, Y. (Trans. & Eds.). (1959). *The Gospel according to Thomas*. New York: Harper & Brothers.

Heidegger, M. (1982). A dialogue on language. In: *On The Way To Language*. P. D. Hertz (Trans.). New York: Harper Collins. p. 52.

Heidegger, M. (2000). The fundamental question of metaphysics. In: *Introduction to Metaphysics*. G. Fried & R. Polt (Trans.). London: Yale University Press.

Heidegger, M. (2002). *The Essence of Truth*. Ted Sadler (Trans.). London: Continuum.

Harari, R. (2002). *How James Joyce Made his Name*. New York: Other Press, p. 169.

Holsinger, B. (2001). *Music, Body, and Desire in Medieval Culture: Hildegard of Bingen to Chaucer*. Stanford, California: Stanford University Press, p. 4.

Hug-Hellmuth, H. (1921). On the technique of child-analysis. *International Journal of Psychoanalysis, 2*: 287–305.

Hughes, A. (1992). Letters from Sigmund Freud to Joan Riviere (1921–1939). *International Review of Psycho-Analysis, 19*: 265–284.

Hug-Hellmuth, H. (1924). The libidinal structure of family life. In: George MacLean, & Ullrich Rappen (1991) *Hermine Hug-Hellmuth: Her Life and Work*. New York: Routledge, p. 270.

Huizinga, J. (1924). *Waning of the Middle Ages*. New York: Dover Publications, p. 3.

Huysman, J. -K. (2003). *Against Nature*. London: Penguin.

Ikki, K. (2006). *The Fundamental Principles for the Re-organisation of Japan*. In: *Kita Ikki, and the making of Japan: A vision of an Empire*. Kent: Global Oriental.

Ivins, Jr., W. M. (1973). *On the Rationalization of Sight*. New York: De Capo Press.

Jackson Knight, W. F. (1949). *St. Augustine's De musica: A Synopsis*. Westport, Connecticut: Hyperion Press, p. 85.

Jacques Lacan, (1991). *The Ego in Freud's Theory and in the Technique of Psychoanalysis*. J. -A Miller (Ed.), Sylvana Tomaselli (Trans.). New York, London: W W Norton & Company.

Jeannery, J. -N. (2006). Seeing is everything. In: *Henri Cartier-Bresson: The Man, the Image and the World: A Retrospective*. London: Thames and Hudson, p. 15.

Johnston, W. (2005) *Geisha, Harlot, Strangler, Star: A Woman, Sex and Morality in Modern Japan. Asia Perspectives: History, Society and Culture* (1955). New York: Columbia University Press.

Jones, E. (1964). The legend of the Madonna's conception through the ear. In: *Essays in applied psychoanalysis*, pp. 268–269, quoting Langlois *Essai sur la Peinture sur Verre* (1832), p. 157.

Jones, E. (1922). A psychoanalytic study of the Holy Ghost concept, (read in the Seventh International Psycho-Analytical Congress, el 27 de September de 1922). *Essays in Applied Psycho-Analysis, vol. II: Essays in Folklore, Anthropology and Religion* (1951). London: The Hogarth Press and The Institute of Psycho-Analysis, p. 362.

Joyce, J. (1992). *Finnegans Wake*. London: Penguin.

Kean, J. (2011a). Tim Leura Tjapaltjarri. In: Ryan, J. & Batty, P. (Eds.) *Origins of Western Desert Art: Tjukurrtjanu*. Melbourne: National Gallery of Victoria, p. 182.

Kean, J. (2011b). Catch a fire. In: Ryan, J. & Batty, P. (Eds.) *Origins of Western Desert Art: Tjukurrtjanu*. Melbourne: National Gallery of Victoria, p. 51.

Kristeva, Julia. (1982). *Powers of Horror: An Essay on Abjection*. Leon S. Roudiez (Trans.). New York: Columbia University Press, p. 4.

Lacan, J. (1956–1957). *The Seminar, Book IV, The Object Relation*. L. V. A. Roche (Trans.). Unpublished.

Lacan, J. (1958–1959). *Desire and its interpretation*. Cormac Gallagher (Trans.). Unpublished.

Lacan, J. (1960–1961). *The Seminar of Jacques Lacan, XIV*. C. Gallagher (Trans.). Unpublished.

Lacan, J. (1961–1962). *The Seminar of Jacques Lacan. Book IX. Identification*. Cormac Gallagher (Trans.). Unpublished.

Lacan, J. (1962–1963). *The Seminar of Jacques Lacan, Anxiety, 1962–1963, Book X*. Cormac Gallagher (Trans.). Unpublished.

Lacan, J. (1964–1965). *The Seminar of Jacques Lacan: Crucial Problems for Psychoanalysis, 1964–1965*. C. Callagher (Trans.). Unpublished.

Lacan, J. (1966). Le Seminaire sur "La Lettre volée". *Ecrits*. Paris: aux editions du Seuil, p. 21.

Lacan, J. (1968–1969). *D'un Autre à L'autre* [From an Other to the other]. Paris: Éditions de l'Association Lacanienne Internationale, 2002.

Lacan, J. (1969–1970). *The Seminar of Jacques Lacan. Book XVII. The reverse side of psychoanalysis. 1969–1970*. C. Gallagher (Trans.). Unpublished.

Lacan, J. (1970). Of Structure as an inmixing of an otherness prerequisite to any subject whatever. In: *The Languages of Criticism and the Sciences of Man*. Richard Macksey & Eugenio Donato (Eds.). Baltimore and London: Johns Hopkins Press.

Lacan, J. (1971). *D'un discours qui ne serait pas du semblant* [Of a discourse that would not be of the semblant]. Paris: Éditions de l'Association Lacanienne Internationale, 2001.

Lacan, J. (1971–1972). *The Seminar of Jacques Lacan. Book XIX. … Ou pire* [… Or worse]. Cormac Gallagher (Trans.). Unpublished.

Lacan, J. (1972–1973). *Encore*. Paris: Éditions de l'Association Lacanienne Internationale.

Lacan, J. (1973–1974). *Les non-dupes errent*. Available at: www.ecole-lacanienne.net/seminaireXXI.php.

Lacan, J. (1973). L'Étourdit. In: *Scilicet, 4*. Paris, Editions du Seuil, p. 16.

Lacan, J. (1974–1975). *The Third*. Ellie Ragland (Trans.). Unpublished.

Lacan, J. (1975). *The Seminar, Book XXII: RSI*. C. Gallagher (Trans.). Unpublished.

Lacan, J. (1975–1976a). *Seminar XXIII, Joyce and the Sinthome*, Cormac Gallagher (Trans.). Unpublished.

Lacan, J. (1975–1976b). *Le Sintome*. Paris: Éditions de l'Association Lacanienne Internationale, 2001.

Lacan, J. (1976–1977) L'insu que sait de l'une-bévue s'aile à mourre. *Ornicar?* *N° 12–17*: 4.

Lacan, J. (1977a). The function and field of speech and language in psychoanalysis. In: *Écrits, A Selection*. Alan Sheridan (Trans.). London, Routledge, pp. 30–113.

Lacan, J. (1977b). The signification of the phallus. In: *Écrits, A Selection*. Alan Sheridan (Trans.). London: Routledge, pp. 281–291.

Lacan J. (1977–1978). *The Moment to Conclude*. C. Gallagher (Trans.). Unpublished.

Lacan, J. (1979 [1964]). *The Four Fundamental Concepts of Psychoanalysis*. J.-A. Miller (Ed.), A. Sheridan (Trans.). UK: Penguin.

Lacan, J. (1979). The neurotic's individual myth. *The Psychoanalytic Quarterly* *48 (1979)*: 405–425.

Lacan, J. (1980). Caracas seminar, July 12 de 1980. Oscar Zentner and María—Inés Rotmiler de Zentner (Trans.). *Papers of The Freudian School of Melbourne, volume II*, Melbourne.

Lacan, J. (1992). *The Ethics of Psychoanalysis 1959–1960: The Seminar of Jacques Lacan*. J.-A. Miller (Ed.), D. Potter (Trans.). UK: Tavistock-Routledge.

Lacan, J. (1993). *The Seminar of Jacques Lacan, The Psychoses*. Jacques-Alain Miller (Ed.). Russell Grigg (Trans.). New York, London: W. W. Norton.

Lacan, J. (1994). *Le Seminaire livre IV, La relation d'objet*. Paris: Édition Du Seuil, translated for this edition.

Lacan, J. (1998). *On Feminine Sexuality: The Limits of Love and Knowledge 1972–1973. Encore The Seminar of Jacques Lacan Book XX*. J.-A. Miller (Ed.), B. Fink (Trans.). New York & London: W. W. Norton & Company.

Lacan, J. (2002). *Logic of the Phantasm*. C. Gallagher (Trans.). Unpublished.

Lacan, J. (2007a). *Ecrits*. B. Fink (Trans.). NY & London: W. W. Norton & Co.

Lacan, J. (2007b). *The Seminar of Jacques Lacan Book XVII: The Other Side of Psychoanalysis*. R. Grigg (Trans.). New York & London: W. W. Norton & Company.

Lacan, J. (2008a). The place, origin and end of my teaching. Lecture of October 1967, Lyon. In: *My Teaching*. D. Macey (Trans.). London: Verso.

Lacan, J. (2008b). *Le savoir du psychanalyste* [The knowledge of the psychoanalyst]. Paris: Éditions de l'Association Lacanienne Internationale, 2008.

Lacan, J. (2013 [2005]). *The Triumph of Religion*. Includes: *Discourse to the Catholics*, Brussels 1960, and the *Triumph of Religion*, Press Conference, Rome, 1974. Cambridge: Polity Press.

Lawrence, D. H. (2005). Psychoanalysis and the unconscious. In: *Psychoanalysis and the Unconscious & Fantasia of the Unconscious*. New York: Dover publications.

Lawrence, D. H. (2006). Fantasia of the unconscious. In: *Psychoanalysis and the Unconscious & Fantasia of the Unconscious*. New York: Dover.

Leech-Wilkinson, D. (2002). *The Modern Invention of Medieval Music: Scholarship, Ideology, Performance*. Cambridge: Cambridge University Press.

Le Gaufey, G. (1997). *Le lasso spéculaire*, Paris: Epel, pp. 92–105.

Le Grand Robert (2001). *Dictionnaires le Robert, Vol. VI*, Paris, p. 820. cf. *The Shorter Oxford English Dictionary* (Third Edition), Oxford, OUP, (1933) 1964, Vol. II, p. 2058 (III, 3, c.).

Lévi-Strauss, C. (1969). *The Elementary Structures of Kinship*. Boston: Beacon.

Lévi-Strauss, C. (1963). The Effectiveness of Symbols. In: Lévi-Strauss, C. (1963) Structural Anthropology. C. Jacobsen & B. Grundfest Schoepf, (Trans). New York: Basic Books.

Lévi-Strauss, C. (1955). The Structural Study of Myth. *The Journal of American Folklore. Vol. 68. No 270. American Folklore Society, 1955*. Available at www.jstor.org/stable/536768: 428–444. p. 430.

Li-Young, L. (2001). Little Father. In: Li-Young, L. (2001). *Book of Nights*. New York: BOA Editions Ltd.

Loeb Schloss, C. (2003). *Lucia Joyce: To Dance in the Wake*. London: Farrar, Strauss, and Giroux.

MacLean, G. & Rappen, U. (1991). *Hermine Hug-Hellmuth: Her Life and Work*. New York: Routledge.

Markel, H. (2012). *The Anatomy of Addiction: Sigmund Freud, William Halstead and the Miracle Drug Cocaine*. New York: Vintage, p. 6.

McCord, D. (Ed.) (1955). *What Cheer: An Anthology of American and British Humorous and Witty Verse*. New York: The Modern Library.

Mauss, M. (1990). *The Gift: the Form and Reason for Exchange in Archaic Societies*. W. D. Halls (Trans.). New York: Norton.

Merleau-Ponty, M. (1964). Eye and mind. In: *The Primacy of Perception*, Northwestern University Press.

Millot, C. (1996). *Gide, Genet, Mishima: Intelligence de la perversion*. Paris: Gallimard.

Mountford, C. (1976). *Nomads of the Australian Desert*. Adelaide: Rigby.

Murray, P. (2011). *The NGV Story*. Melbourne: National Gallery of Victoria.

Myers, F. (2011). Intrigue of the archive, enigma of the object. In: *Origins of Western Desert Art: Tjukurrtjanu*. J. Ryan & P. Batty (Eds.). Melbourne: National Gallery of Victoria.

Nietzsche, F. (1968). *The Will to Power*. W. Kaufmann and R. J. Hollingdale (Trans.). Walter Kaufmann (Ed.). New York: Vintage Books, p. 434.

Nietzsche, F. (1998). *Twilight of the Idols*, Duncan Large (Trans.). Oxford: Oxford University Press, p. 48.

Page, C. (1993). The English *a cappella* Renaissance. *Early Music 21*: 459.

Panofsky, E. (1997). *Perspective as Symbolic Form*, Zone Books: New York.

Pereira, D. (1999). The infans and the (k)not of history. In: *Papers of the Freudian School of Melbourne 1999, Volume 20*. Melbourne: The Freudian School of Melbourne.

Pereira, D. (2004). Real, symbolic and imaginary: the times that bind, In; *Papers of the Freudian School of Melbourne, Anguish & Erotics, Volume 22, 2004*. Melbourne: The Freudian School of Melbourne.

Plato (1991). *The Republic. The Complete and Unabridged Jowett Translation*. B. Jowett (Trans.). New York: Vintage Classics Edition.

Porge, E. (2005). *Transmettre la Clinique Psychanalytique: Freud, Lacan, Aujourd'hui*. Ramonville Saint-Agne: Érès.

Porge, E. (2012). Some cases of "name of the father subject supposed of knowledge". In: *Intervention in the Real: Papers of the Freudian School of Melbourne 2012, Volume 24*. Melbourne: The Freudian School of Melbourne.

Porge, E. (1996). *Freud-Fließ: Mythe et chimère de l'auto-analyse*. Paris: Anthropos, p. 67.

Roudisnesco, E (1990). *A History of Psychoanalysis in France, 1925–1985*. Chicago: University of Chicago Press.

Ryan, J. & Batty, P. (Eds.) (2011). *Origins of Western Desert Art: Tjukurrtjanu*. Melbourne: National Gallery of Victoria, 2011, p. 191.

Ryan, J. & Batty, P. (2011). Introduction. In: *Origins of Western Desert Art: Tjukurrtjanu*. Melbourne: National Gallery of Victoria.

Sándor Márai. M. G. (2012). *A History of Books*. Sydney: Giramondo, 117, 119.

Sartre, J. -P. (1966). *Being and Nothingness: An Essay on Phenomenological Ontology*. New York: Pocket Books, p. 347.

Secundus, C. P. (1847). *Natural History, Book. X*. P. Holland (Trans.). London: Wernerian Club.

Shillony, B. -A. (1973). *Revolt in Japan, The Young Officers and the February 26, 1936 Incident*. Princeton, N. J.: Princeton University Press.

Sisman, E.R. (Ed.) (1997). *Haydn and his World*.Princeton: Princeton University Press, p. 1.

Snyder, Joel (1980). Picturing vision. *Critical Inquiry. Vol. 6, No. 3.*

Strachey, J. (1895d). Editor's introduction. In: Freud, S. (1895d) *Studies on Hysteria. S.E., 2.* London: Hogarth, p. xvii.

Tanizaki, J. (1977). *In Praise of Shadows.* New York: Leete's Island Books.

Weiss, E. (1970). *Sigmund Freud as a consultant.* New York: Intercontinental Medical Book Corporation, p. 81.

Wilcken, P. (2010). *Claude Lévi-Strauss: The poet in the laboratory.* New York: Penguin, p. 282.

Wittgenstein, L. (1992). *Tractatus Logico-Philosophicus.* C. K. Odgen (Trans.). London: Routledge. p. 189.

Zentner, O. (2007). From the Lacan ◊ Joyce Correspondence. In: *Papers of the Freudian School of Melbourne.* Linda Clifton (Ed.). Melbourne: The Freudian School of Melbourne.

Zentner, O. From Nietzsche's *Thus spoke Zarathustra*, quoted in *Fucking with death—preceded by cure or life,* unpublished.

Zentner, O. (1982). La psychanalyse en Australie. *La historia Universal de la infamia,* Jorge Luis Borges, *Ornicar? N° 25:* 188.

Zentner, O. (1979). Aphanisis. In: *Papers of the Freudian School of Melbourne, Volume, I, 1979.* Melbourne: The Freudian School of Melbourne.

Zentner, O. (2003). An Architecture of death from Tanizaki to Mishima. Conference given in the Sydney Society for psychoanalysis and culture, Macquarie University, NSW, June 2003. In: *Invention in the real, Papers of The Freudian School of Melbourne.* Linda Clifton (Ed.). London: Karnac, 2012.

Zentner, O. (2004). The exile of James Joyce—après le mot le deluge. In: *Papers of the Freudian School of Melbourne, Volume 22, Anguish & Erotics.* Melbourne: The Freudian School of Melbourne, p. 328.

For Product Safety Concerns and Information please contact our EU
representative GPSR@taylorandfrancis.com
Taylor & Francis Verlag GmbH, Kaufingerstraße 24, 80331 München, Germany

www.ingramcontent.com/pod-product-compliance
Lightning Source LLC
Chambersburg PA
CBHW050339270326
41926CB00016B/3526